TRAVELLERS TO THE EAST SURVIVAL KIT

TRAVELLERS
TO THE EAST
SURVIVAL KIT

by
SUSAN GRIFFITH

Published by Vacation Work, 9 Park End Street, Oxford

First edition
published by Vacation-Work in 1979
Second edition 1982
Third edition 1986

ISBN 0 907638 60 0 (hardback)
ISBN 0 907638 59 7 (softback)

Cover cartoon by Mel Calman
Cover design by Miller, Craig & Cocking Design Partnership

Chapter headings, section headings and maps by William Swan

Distributed in the U.S.A. and Canada by
Bradt Enterprises, 95 Harvey Street, Cambridge, Mass. 02140

Printed by **Gibbons Barford Print,** Wolverhampton, England

Contents

Maps and Charts

Preface

The East is an evocative term which rather awkwardly bundles together Tibetan refugee settlements in the Himalayas and elegant Istanbul suburbs, the jungles of Thailand and the slums of Calcutta. Yet it is a term whose attractions are hard to resist. Once the overland trip to India was the domain of the hippy who was disillusioned with the values of the West and who went in search of truth and enlightenment. But now the mentality has changed, the hair is shorter, the curiosity about Eastern cultures more detached. A broader spectrum of traveller is choosing Asia as a holiday destination, realizing that the £300 return flight to Delhi or Bangkok is not difficult to afford. No longer is there a mass migration to the old hippy pilgrimage places of Goa, Freak Street in Kathmandu and the Pudding Shop in Istanbul. Instead, travellers are now more likely to be seen exploring groups of temples on a bicycle, trekking in the mountains or stalking crocodiles in a wildlife sanctuary. These days there is more hiking than hepatitis, more museums and mosques than marijuana. People are beginning to realize what a wealth of interest is contained in the landscapes and cultures east of Istanbul.

The reasons which people have for finally going on an expedition are many and various, but the idea of the exotic and the unknown appeals to all of them. Even familiar institutions like banks and youth hostels are transformed. Without seeking them out, bizarre and amusing situations arise. In my own case, I have had my ears cleaned (by a trained professional) in Delhi's Connaught Circus, eaten a sheep's head in Turkey, temporarily joined a motorcycle gang in Bali, witnessed a supposed case of demon possession in the Hunza Valley, shared a youth hostel dorm with a distinguished gentleman from Lucknow who had travelled 2,000 miles to study yoga, been engaged in conversation with someone whose knowledge of English extended no further than "What is your shoe size?", been asked to play a minor role in a Pakistani film, etc, etc.

The pace of life in the East is slow, which is one of its glories. Although this is often cause for frustration, especially when dealing with officialdom, it is possible to enjoy the nonchalance and to be amused by the absurd amount of paperwork. There is something to be learned from experiencing attitudes and customs so unfamiliar to our ultra-efficient Western ways.

The aim of this book is to provide a skeleton of practical information to help those — especially those on a limited budget — to make their own travel arrangements. Visa, currency and health requirements have been listed as well as a little of the history and places of interest to visit. All guide books run the risk of including out-of-date information but the dangers multiply when describing conditions in the countries of Western Asia. However, the material included in this book will give the reader some idea of what to expect and how to prepare, and I hope will convey some of the enthusiasm which the author feels for travelling in distant lands and by unconventional means.

Susan Griffith
January 1986

Acknowledgments

I would like to express my gratitude to the many people who have not only provided information and hospitality but have enlivened my journeys, among them Ibrahim Baig in Hunza, Krystyna Cech, Daniel Petitmermet of the Red Cross Delegation in Quetta, the Pleasance Family in Kodaikanal, Bob Porter of Jaffna, Mr. & Mrs. Sikander in Dambulla, Felix Ansell, Annie Williams and Richard Speir on his yacht *Gaia Quest*. Finally many thanks to my family, friends and colleagues who made such liberal use of my list of poste restante addresses, especially Philip who used it 24 times in a period of two months.

NOTE: While every effort has been made to ensure that the information contained in this book was correct at the time of going to press, political and economic changes are bound to create some inaccuracies. Prices and exchange rates are intended merely as a guide. If in the course of your travels you encounter errors or omissions, or would like to suggest other material for inclusion, please write to Susan Griffith at Vacation-Work, 9 Park End Street, Oxford OX1 1HJ. Those whose contributions are used will be sent a free copy of the next edition.

BEFORE YOU GO

GETTING THERE

Air

Unless you are lucky enough to have months at your disposal to make an overland journey, a longhaul flight will be necessary. The cheapest destination available from bucket shops is Karachi which (as of early 1986) is advertised for as low as £255 return (twice a week with THY Turkish Airlines). The best places to look for bucket shop prices and phone numbers are in the classified sections of *LAM* and *TNT* (free magazines in London), *Time Out* and *The Times* (especially the Saturday edition). Ring about half a dozen of these and you will soon discover which airline offers the cheapest service (usually one like Syrian Arab or Aeroflot). Fares on the same airline can differ by as much as £25 depending on the bucket shop's mark-up.

If you don't want to hunt through advertisements in the press, you can ring the Air Travel Advisory Bureau on 01-636 5000 which will give you the phone numbers of discount travel agents who specialize in your chosen destination. But because not all bucket shops are registered with them, this does not guarantee the best fare.

If airlines such as Ariana Afghan or Bangladesh Biman frighten you, you might want to go with more reputable and more expensive airlines. Contact Trailfinders Travel Bureau (46 Earl's Court Road, London W8; tel: 01-937 9631) for their quotations. One bucket shop worth trying is called North South Travel (01-624 4416) which invests its profits in third world development projects.

An even cheaper way of getting to Asia by air is to act as an air courier on scheduled flights to Bombay. You will be restricted to taking only hand luggage and to staying only two or three weeks, but a return fare of £229 cannot be outdone. Contact Fleet Street Flights in Weybridge (0932 57455).

If you want to visit several countries by air, it is very difficult to know whether it is cheaper to buy a multi-sector ticket at home or once you are abroad. Although there are places in Asia where it is possible to buy cheap tickets (principally Bangkok, Penang, Hong Kong and to some extent Colombo) many travellers prefer the security of setting off with a return ticket. If you are worried about losing your plane ticket you can arrange to leave it in the safekeeping of the airline office, while you trek round the country. If you want to visit Sri Lanka and South India, for example, it is probably better to buy a return to Colombo (£375) and then buy a ticket Colombo-Trivandrum-Colombo (Rs1880 or £50 from George Travel, 68 Bristol Street, Colombo who offers competitive prices), than to buy three one-way tickets along a triangular route. One solution is to buy a return to your furthest destination on an airline which allows stop-overs at intermediate airports. For example, Pakistan International fly from London to Singapore via Karachi, Colombo and Kuala Lumpur and for a fee (which varies among agents) you can book lengthy stop-overs.

A further option is to buy a round-the-world fare valid for a year. The airline combinations and routings are complex and so it's probably best to consult a good travel agent. It is also possible to put together your own RTW fare. For example you could get a one-way ticket to Delhi (£200), overland to Kathmandu (£10), Kathmandu-Calcutta-Rangoon-Bangkok (about £175), overland to Penang, Penang-Hong Kong (£170), Hong Kong-San Francisco (£200), overland to New York (Greyhound bus pass £50) and then back to London on People Express (£150), which totals about £950 and undercuts the official RTW fares to these destinations substantially. Another example: one-way to Colombo (£200 on Aeroflot), Colombo to Los Angeles via Bangkok, Hong Kong, Tokyo and Honolulu ($505 from George Travel mentioned above) and San Francisco-London on People Express (£257), which comes to under £800.

THE OVERLAND ROUTE

For a while it looked as though the overland route was finished. The famous Asian Highway which connected Istanbul, Tehran, Mashhad, Herat, Kabul and Peshawar via the Khyber Pass closed with the Soviet invasion of Afghanistan. Then it became almost impossible for individuals to obtain visas to Iran, and so the southern route which bypasses Afghanistan also became impossible. But Iran is now relaxing its restrictions somewhat, visas are not that difficult to get and it is now possible to travel by public transport from Istanbul to Delhi (assuming the Indo-Pakistan border is open). The reported cost of this journey by public transport was £55 not long before this book went to press, with additional living expenses of about £3 per day. Travelling non-stop would take 11 days, though the journey is already sufficiently gruelling that you wouldn't want to do it without some rests.

Not everyone relishes the thought of venturing into such an unknown, though the following chapters attempt to demystify the route. An alternative preferred

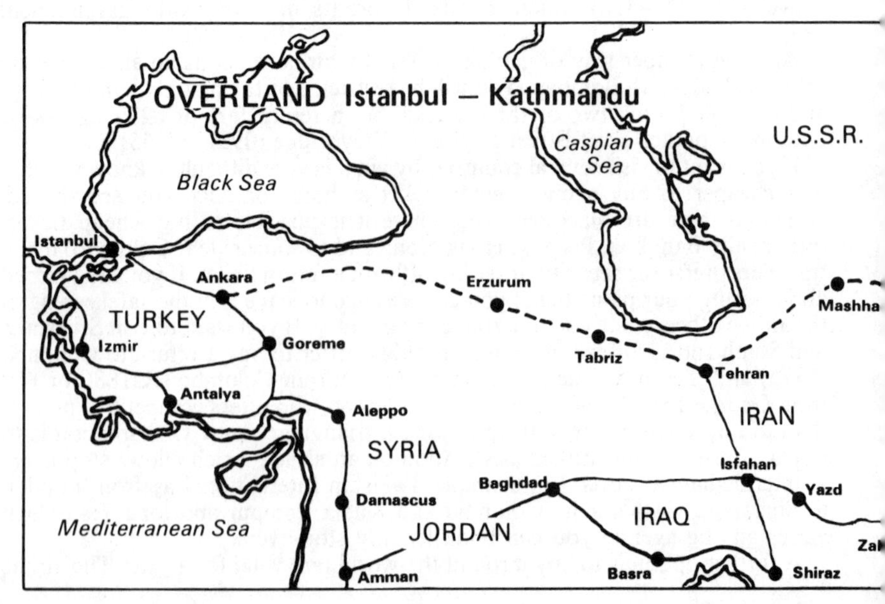

by many is to make the journey with an established overland company such as Exodus Expeditions (All Saints Passage, 100 Wandsworth High Street, London SW18; tel: 01-870 0151), Hann Overland (85 Streatham High Road, Streatham, London SW16; tel: 01-769 6659) or Encounter Overland (267 Old Brompton Road, London SW5; tel: 01-370 6845). A good source of information about the overland companies is Trailfinders (address above). Including the food kitty, an overland expedition will cost (very roughly) £100 a week. Most of the advantages (leaving the worrying to someone else) and disadvantages (being expected to join in watermelon eating contests with people you don't particularly like) of joining such a trip are obvious. One important advantage is that otherwise impossible visas can sometimes be obtained by an approved agent, e.g. Hann Overland is the only agent in Britain who can take you to Iraq, an otherwise closed country.

Whether you are planning to drive, hitch-hike or travel by public transport you will be interested in the basic overland route.

Overland to Istanbul

The shortest route from London to Istanbul is through Belgium and West Germany to Munich, through Austria via Salzburg and Klagenfurt, then into Yugoslavia. (Americans require a transit visa for Yugoslavia, available at the border. No visa is required for U.K. citizens). The road passes through Ljubljana, Belgrade and Nis, where it divides. Turn left and go via Bulgaria (transit visa needed — £6 one way, £10 return) if you wish to take the shortest route. Alternatively, turn right to Skopje and then through northern Greece: this route is 280 miles longer.

Istanbul to Tehran

Turkey	*Iran*
Istanbul	Bazargan

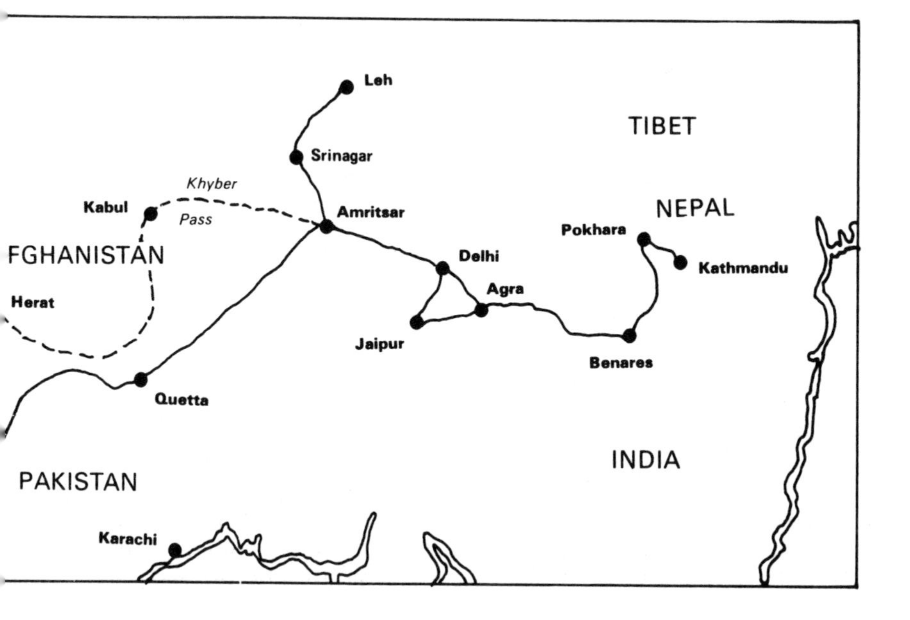

Adapazari
Ankara
Sivas
Erzincan
Erzurum
Ağri
Doğubayazit

Marand
Tabriz
Mianeh
Zanjan
Qazvin
Karaj
Tehran

Tehran to Amritsar

Iran
Tehran
Delijan
Isfahan
Yazd
Kerman
Bam
Zahedan
Mirjaveh

Pakistan
Nok Kundi
Quetta
Jacobabad
Sukkur
Multan
Lahore

India
Amritsar

There are of course variations on the above route. A recommended alternative through Turkey, for example, is to drive along the Black Sea coast to Kars (an old Armenian capital) and on to the Iranian border. All travellers are encouraged to use their imaginations and to stray from the primary tourist routes at least in those countries where it is safe to do so.

Beyond India
It is not possible to continue overland from India or Bangladesh to Burma. All land frontiers are closed. There used to be a service from Madras to Penang or Singapore provided by the Shipping Corporation of India, however since a fire ravaged the ship in 1984, the government suspended the service, with no likelihood of renewal.

Sea
Sailing from the Middle East to India would be an attractive option if it were not so difficult to arrange. The Pan-Islamic Steamship Company has monthly sailings between Jeddah and Karachi/Bombay, though they don't appear to carry passengers between Karachi and Bombay. The addresses are as follows:

P.O. Box 4855,
Writer's Chambers,
Dunolly Road,
1.1 Chundrigar Road,
Karachi 2, Pakistan
Tel: 237069

P.O. Box 1691
8 King Khalida Street,
Jeddah,
Saudi Arabia

You can get to Jeddah by the Misr-Edco ferry either from Suez or from Aqaba in Jordan. The deck class fare for the seven day crossing Jeddah to Karachi is Rs4,600 (just over £200) second class Rs5,600 and first class Rs6,100. If you are taking a large freight object such as a motorcycle, you will have to haggle over the cost. Getting a transit visa for Saudi Arabia in Cairo or Amman can be a lengthy procedure and impossible for unmarried women. On the other hand, the experience will undoubtedly be an interesting one, and you will be befriended by the other passengers, most of whom will be pilgrims to Mecca.

WHAT TO TAKE

Luggage

A small comfortable rucksack is ideal. Even a 32 litre pack can be taken onto airplanes as hand luggage if not overstuffed. Large rucksacks, especially ones with outside frames, can be very awkward on crowded buses. Some people maintain that border and customs officials equate rucksacks with hippydom but this attitude is disappearing as quickly as the number of hippies. You may prefer a soft hold-all or shoulder bag, which serves the purpose well until you find yourself in a situation in which it would be pleasant to walk between villages or in the hills. The key is that your bag be small and light. It is perfectly possible to travel comfortably for a month in hot countries with just 8-10 pounds, assuming you have no specialist interest like trekking, surfing or painting.

It is also a good idea to take a lightweight day-pack; the cheap nylon ones from the Army Surplus (£3) will do for carrying your camera, a book and a snack on day outings or for keeping your essentials near you when your pack goes on a luggage rack. It is inevitable that you will end up buying a few gifts and souvenir handicrafts. The small pack increases your luggage capacity for the return journey, when you may check your larger bag and carry the small one onto the plane.

Some travellers prefer more conventional luggage to rucksacks since zipped bags can be locked. Unless you are planning to stock up on valuable electronic gadgets in Singapore there doesn't seem much point in bothering with a lock.

Inside your luggage, it is a good idea to have several cloth bags for organizing your belongings, e.g. one for clean underwear, another for miscellaneous cosmetic objects. These drawstring bags should preferably be made of easily distinguishable fabrics (e.g. one of corduroy, the other of cotton) for identification in the dark.

Money Belts

The form in which you carry your money is discussed below. But you should give careful thought to the question of where to carry your travellers' cheques and cash. Do not keep all your wealth in one place, but on the other hand don't distribute it in so many places that you can't keep track of it. Although theft is not as rife as your doom-ridden friends and relations will tell you (it's far worse in South American cities or even in Naples) a money belt worn inside your clothing is good for the peace of mind it bestows.

If you have access to a sewing machine, money belts can easily be manufactured from a left-over length of cotton or silk (preferable to manmade fibres). Just cut a strip of cloth several inches longer than your waist with a six inch bulge in the middle large enough to accommodate notes and cheques folded once lengthwise. Use Velcro to close the flap over your money and also to fasten it round your waist. You can buy commercial moneybelts, though the comfortable and discreet ones tend to be expensive. It is a good idea to wear your belt for a few days before departure to make sure that it is comfortable and to prove to yourself that it won't fall off.

Keep only one or two large denomination travellers' cheques and any hard currency cash there plus a large note of the local currency. Then, if your wallet is stolen, you will not have to wait for the banks to open in order to get some local currency.

Leather money belts should be avoided if possible since leather garments must sometimes be removed before entering Hindu or Jain temples. If you plan to travel through the monsoon season, you should keep the cheques and notes inside a plastic bag.

Maps and Guides

Although it is possible to rely on tourist office hand-outs, great pleasure can be derived from poring over a good map both before you set off and while you are travelling. For a good overview of the sub-continent get John Bartholomew's map of India, Pakistan, Bangladesh and Sri Lanka which shows a wealth of detail for the scale (1:4,000,000). It was last revised in 1984 and costs £2.50.

If you are able to shop in London, then visit Edward Stanford Ltd. near the Covent Garden tube stop (12-14 Long Acre, London WC2; tel: 01-836 1321). In addition to a complete collection of the standard series (Geographia, Kummerly & Frey, etc.) they also have drawers full of detailed maps. So if you know you want to do a certain trek in Nepal or India, or you want to spend some time in a certain region of Turkey, be sure to enquire.

If it is not convenient to visit Stanford's, then write to A. T. Atkinson & Partner (The Map Shop, 15 High Street, Upton-on-Severn, Worcestershire WR8 0HJ; tel: 068 46 3146) and ask for a catalogue. They do most of their business by mail order, and will send you any maps which they have in stock with an invoice.

You can usually buy maps after you arrive in a country, and the addresses of Government Survey offices and other map purveyors can be obtained from tourist offices.

You may also want to find more detailed or specific travel guides and related literature. Roger Lascelles (47 York Road, Brentford, Middlesex TW8 0QP; tel: 01-847 0935) specializes in travel literature and will send a catalogue upon request. Lascelles is the UK distributor for the series of guides published by Lonely Planet in Australia; individual titles are mentioned in the brief bibliographies which follow the country chapters. Another comprehensive source of books is the Travel Bookshop (13 Blenheim Crescent, London W11; tel: 01-229 5260) which stocks travel reminiscences as well as guide books. In the USA, contact Nomadic Books, P.O. Box 454, Athens, Georgia 30603.

Clothing

Unless you are planning to attend a Hindu wedding or to visit the Hindu Kush in mid-winter, take the minimum of comfortable old clothes which you don't mind sacrificing to the rigours of travel. (The dye used in the water bombs thrown during the spring Holi Festival in India and Nepal doesn't wash out). For an extended trip, here is a suggested list:

Men	*Women*
2 lightweight trousers	1 cotton skirt
1 pair shorts	1 cotton dress
2 short-sleeved shirts or T-shirts	1 pair loose-fitting trousers
1 pair swimming trunks	2 short-sleeved blouses
	1 swim suit

Both

1 lightweight jumper (for high elevations)
1 long-sleeved shirt (to avoid mosquito bites, sunburn and offending in temples)
several handkerchiefs (for mopping your brow, and

doubling as face cloths)
4 pairs of underwear
1 pair broken-in rubber flip flops (good for unhygienic showers as well as street and beach wear)
1 pair plimsolls
1 pair socks
1 sunhat (headscarf good for women for windy bus journeys and visiting mosques, and for use as eye shades when trying to sleep on brightly-lit trains)

This may seem too skimpy. But when travelling in hot countries it is very easy to wash a set of clothing each night which will dry in the wind of your hotel fan. If you lose or ruin one item, just visit the bazaar and buy a replacement, or ask a tailor to make one to your specifications.

Sundries

Unless you intend to go trekking, a sleeping bag is unnecessary. However a youth hostel style sheet sleeping bag or simply a cotton sheet is a welcome luxury in hotels which provide little bedding or bedding of dubious provenance.

In addition to a basic wardrobe, it is advisable to set off with a towel, soap, shampoo, toothbrush, comb, sewing kit, nail scissors and toilet paper. A box of the waxed sheets is compact and should last (Vishnu willing) about a month. A water bottle and a knife are essential; a plastic or aluminium cup is handy. The contents of your first aid kit including water purifying techniques are discussed in the section on *Health,* and necessary documents under *Red Tape* below.

You are unlikely to forget your camera, but be sure to take more film than you think you'll need. Since a roll of film can cost about £12 in India, you will have no trouble selling any excess, and at a profit. It would be fun to have a Polaroid camera so you could give away photos of locals who befriend you, but the film cassettes are too bulky (and too expensive) to be very appealing. Also remember a supply of spare photobooth photos; even if you have obtained all your visas beforehand, you may need extra photos for a trekking permit in Nepal for example. Women travellers may want to carry a photo of their "husband and children" to corroborate their "wedding ring".

Sun glasses are useful, though can be bought locally at little cost. A supply of plastic bags (for partially eaten watermelons) and rubber bands and string (for improvised repairs) always comes in handy. You must compromise about the number of books you would like to take and the number you are willing to lug around. You can usually find a fellow traveller with compatible tastes with whom to swap books. There are English language bookshops in all big cities but imported books are expensive. Phrase books often provide entertainment but they are not much good in a crisis. Take a notebook, stationery, a list of addresses for postcard writing and a substantial number of biros. The biros in India, for example, are seldom functional. The life of the batteries in your torch can be lengthened by carrying two small candles (easily replaceable) for dealing with electricity shortages.

A supply of old stamps from your country or a cheap European biro can be a good way to repay the friendliness of the locals. You can probably manage without a travel alarm, but you may want to have something to rely on in addition to hotel staff when it comes time to catch your dawn bus. Further luxuries would include a "universal plug", a sucker-like object which fits all sinks, and a pair of ear plugs for long journeys on coaches equipped with videos. Boots has a product called "Travelwash" which comes in a tube and lathers up in cold water or even salt water; however ordinary hand soap can suffice for washing yourself and your clothes. If you're nervous about thieves or nocturnal visitors, take a small padlock and chain for securing hotel doors or for tying your camera to your belt while jostling through crowds.

Passports

Allow up to ten weeks for the processing of a passport application, as delays, especially in summer, are quite long. Passport application forms are available from any post office. You need a full 30-page, 10 year passport for travel to Asia, which should not be too close to expiry. With family passports only the bearer may travel alone. The passport application form should be sent to the regional office mentioned on the form, together with two photographs, birth certificate and a fee of £15.

Arab countries frown on an Israeli stamp in your passport. However none of the countries in this book prohibits visits from travellers who have been to Israel, so there is no need to get a second full passport.

One of the worst things that can happen to you abroad is to lose your passport. It is both tiresome and expensive to get another one. Replacement will be easier if you have a record of its number and issue date, preferably a photocopy of the first few pages, a copy of your birth certificate, some spare photos and the necessary fee. Keep this record separate from your passport and money, ideally in a safe place along with the list of your travellers' cheque numbers and a small amount of emergency cash (about £20). Report the loss of your passport to the police and then to your nearest Embassy, Consulate or High Commission without delay.

Visas

Visas are required for some countries and can be obtained from their embassies abroad. It is generally a good idea to get as many visas as you can before leaving home since there can be delays and hassles if you're applying outside your country of residence.

The first step is to write to the Embassy/Consulate and request a visa form (addresses on page 39). For travellers who cannot get into London to get their visas personally and who don't wish to trust their passport to the post, Thomas Cook and Trailfinders offer a visa service which costs £10 per visa in addition to the visa fee. (Trailfinders offer this service only to clients). Alternatively you can contact an independent firm called Travcour (Tempo House, 15 Falcon Road, London SW11; tel: 01-223 4772) who process visas for £6 + VAT. Write mentioning the countries you want to visit, with £1 per visa, and they will send you the forms. Then the £1 is deducted from the charge. Visas cannot usually be obtained at frontier posts, and applications may sometimes take several days or weeks to process.

The table below shows the visa requirements and cost in the case of British nationals. There may be a time restriction which must be checked with the Embassy (e.g. 7 days maximum in Burma).

Visas

	UK	*Eire*	*Australia*	*Canada*	*N.Z.*	*U.S.A.*
Bangladesh	Yes—£10	No	**Yes	No	Yes	**Yes
Bhutan	Yes	Yes	Yes	Yes	Yes	Yes
Burma	Yes—£3	Yes	Yes	Yes	Yes	Yes
India	Yes—£10	Yes	Yes	Yes	Yes	Yes
Indonesia	No	No	No	No	No	No
Iran	Yes—£8	Yes	Yes	Yes	Yes	Yes
Malaysia	No	No	No	No	No	No
Nepal	Yes—£10	Yes	Yes	Yes	Yes	Yes
Pakistan	No	No	No	No	No	No (with restrictions)
Singapore	No	No	No	No	No	No
Sri Lanka	No	No	No	No	No	No
Thailand	*No	*No	*No	*No	*No	*No
Turkey	No	No	No	No	No	No

**unless staying less than 7 days with confirmed onward ticket
*for maximum stay of 15 days. Two-month visas available at a cost of £5

Customs

Customs regulations are mentioned briefly under each country, although the tobacco and alcohol allowances are fairly standard and are set out in the table below. If you intend to travel to certain Moslem countries, no alcohol at all is permitted.

Duty Free Limits

	Cigs.	*Cigars*	*Tobacco*	*Wine*	*Spirits*
Bangladesh	200 or	50 or	½lb	2 bottles of ⅓ gallon each	
Burma	200 or	50 or	250g	1 quart of alcohol total	
India	200 or	50 or	250g	1 bottle (not over .95 litre)	
Indonesia	600* or	150 or	300g	2 litres of alcohol	
Iran	200 or	50 or	250g	—	—
Malaysia	200 or	50 or	225g	1 litre	*or* 1 litre
Nepal	200 or	50 or	250g	1 bottle	*or* 1 bottle
Pakistan	200 or	50 or	½lb	—	—
Singapore	200 or	50 or	250g	1 litre	1 litre
Sri Lanka	200 or	50 or	12oz	2 bottles	1½ litres
Thailand	200 or	250 or	250g	1 litre of alcohol total	
Turkey	400 or	50 or	200g	5 litres of alcohol total	

*For stays of over a fortnight

Details of foreign customs regulations are obtainable from the British Overseas Trade Board, Dept. of Trade & Industry, 1-19 Victoria Street, London SW1 (tel: 01-215 7877).

Health Certificates

Even experienced travellers mistakenly assume that vaccination certificates are a requirement of entry to many countries. In fact there are very few legal health requirements for travellers nowadays. This is not an easy area in which to be dogmatic as with some countries what may be demanded at the point of immigration may not accord with the regulations as laid down by the respective governments and published in good faith by the World Health Organization.

For example the World Health Organization has recommended that the requirement for a cholera certificate should be abolished (since its benefits are so limited), however Pakistan's official regulations still list this as a requirement. (In practice there is no health check at Karachi Airport). No country requires evidence of typhoid immunization, though Nepal has been known to ask travellers to show a certificate. Smallpox has been completely eradicated, despite the claims made in a few outdated sources (including some embassy literature).

The only certificate for which there is a legitimate requirement is for yellow fever. Yellow fever inoculations are required if you are coming from or have recently visited a yellow fever risk area (i.e. most of central Africa and the northern part of South America including Panama) but are not needed for Asia if you are travelling from Britain or North America. The yellow fever certificate is not valid until ten days after the inoculation and will last for ten years.

This of course does not mean that you shouldn't get your shots before departure. For advice on how to stay healthy, and the amount of protection available from the inoculations, see the section on *Health* below.

Insurance

Medical treatment is free in many countries of the East, but public health services may not always be of the highest standard. Travellers are therefore recommended to use private hospitals and clinics if they think they are suffering from something serious. The cost may be prohibitive unless you are covered by insurance.

In Britain one of the most economical policies is available from Endsleigh Insurance Services Ltd., who run the ISIS worldwide insurance scheme. This is one of the few policies which is available at a low cost for periods of up to 18 months. They have offices throughout the UK, or you can contact their head office at Endsleigh House, Ambrose Street, Cheltenham, Glos. GL50 3NR; tel: 0242 36151. A sample premium for 6 months (medical coverage of £100,000 and baggage cover of £600) is £68.75. WEXAS (45 Brompton Road, London SW3 1DE; tel: 01-589 0500) offer thorough cover for £92 for 6 months but this is open only to people who have paid the £17.28 membership fee. Trailfinders cooperate with Campbell Irvine (48 Earls Court Road, London W8; tel: 01-937 6981) and offer a special policy for overland and adventure holidays; however, this will cost £167.50 for 6 months. All of these policies cover repatriation by air.

If you claim for medical expenses you must have the doctor sign the original of your policy. If you claim for theft of baggage, you will need a policy report and documentary evidence of the cost of the lost items. The best insurance against luggage loss is to take sensible precautions while travelling, e.g. not to leave your cash on display in your hotel room and not to leave an expensive camera on the beach while you go swimming. Keep a separate record of your insurance policy number at home in case your form is lost or stolen.

Motoring Documents

An International Driving Permit (IDP) is required for most countries if you are taking your own vehicle abroad or intend to drive whilst abroad. The IDP is valid for one year and is available from the R.A.C. or A.A. on production of a current British driving licence, passport photo and £2.50 fee. One complicating factor is that there are two conventions which govern IDP's: the 1926 Convention is required in Pakistan whereas the 1949 IDP is valid in the other countries dealt with in this book. These must be applied for separately. While travelling, you should also carry your British licence.

You will also require third party insurance, which can be bought at the borders of Turkey, Iran, Pakistan and India, though the cover may not be as high as you would like. An International Motor Insurance Certificate or Green Card is not really international at all since it doesn't cover countries beyond Iran. If you are planning to drive in Turkey or Iran you should obtain a Green Card through the A.A.'s Insurance Services (P.O. Box 2AA, Newcastle-upon-Tyne NE99 2AA) or from the R.A.C.

A *carnet de passages en douanes* is a customs document which guarantees the full payment of customs duty on a temporarily imported vehicle should it be sold (or destroyed). *Carnets* are issued only by motoring organizations to their members, who will be required to arrange an indemnity against any possible claim, either as a lump sum deposit, as an insurance guarantee or as a bank guarantee at a fee of £25 (usually the latter). The amount is calculated according to the duty rates for the countries being visited and is usually about twice the value of the car except in the case of India when it is between 3 and 4 times the car's value. Unfortunately, certain countries (e.g. India, Pakistan and Bangladesh) may be excluded from the *carnet* if the politics are deemed unstable. A *carnet* also becomes invalid if you are not accompanying the vehicle. If you freight your vehicle back unaccompanied you need Customs and Excise form C179B.

The cost of a *carnet* (maximum validity one year) from the R.A.C. is £15 for an 11-page document and £20 for 25 pages. The A.A.'s charges are slightly higher plus they charge a returnable deposit of £100. To find out more on this subject contact either the Automobile Association (Fanum House, Basingstoke, Hants. RG21 2EA; tel: 0256 20123) or the Royal Automobile Club (Touring Information Department, P.O. Box 100, Lansdowne Road, Croydon CR9 2JA; tel: 01-686 2525).

The A.A. in conjunction with Campbell Irvine Ltd. (48 Earls Court Road, London W8; tel: 01-937 6981) and the R.A.C. in conjunction with R. L. Davison & Co. (5 Stone House Court, London EC3A 7AX; tel: 01-377 9876) operate insurance schemes for *carnet* indemnity insurance.

There is also a document called an International Certificate for Motor Vehicles (ICMV) which is the equivalent of a registration book. This document costs £2.50 and is issued by both motoring organizations. It is seldom required but is recommended for most countries outside Europe.

The table below indicates the documentary requirements as well as the side of the road on which people drive.

Motoring Document Requirements

	Carnet de Passages	*IDP*	*Insurance 3rd Party*	*Traffic Circulation*
Turkey	No	Recommended	Yes	Right
Iran	Yes	Recommended	Yes	Right
Pakistan	Yes	Yes	Yes	Left
India	Yes	Yes	Yes	Left
Nepal	Yes	Yes	Yes	Left
Bangladesh	Yes	No	Yes	Left
Sri Lanka	Yes	Recommended	Yes	Left

*At the time of writing, *carnets* for Iran, India, Pakistan, Bangladesh and Sri Lanka are not always available.

International Student Identity Card
With a student card (ISIC) it is possible to obtain discounts on charges to museums and galleries, reduced fares on trains, planes and buses (25% reduction on flights in India, boats in Turkey, etc).

To obtain a card you will need proof of full time student status, a passport size photo and a £3.50 fee. Take these to a local student travel office or send them to ISIC, P.O. Box 190, London WC1 with the documents and an s.a.e.

If you are not eligible, there are many places where you can get a "student card" from Athens to Bangkok. Be sure to know what the authentic card looks like, so as to avoid forgeries, though genuine ISIC cards are widely available.

Youth Hostel Card
Membership of the International Youth Hostels Federation is not as useful in Asia as in Europe. Although there is a scattering of hostels (especially in India), most of them are not conveniently located and won't insist on seeing a membership card. Nevertheless it is worth spending £5.50 (if you're over 21) to get a card (available from any youth hostel or from the Association headquarters at 14 Southampton Street, London WC2; tel: 01-240 3158). In remote places you can often pass a youth hostel card off as a student card and get the relevant discounts.

Drugs
Sooner or later when travelling in Asia, someone will approach you and offer you one substance or another. Drugs in all countries now carry severe penalties. Often, drug sales are also deals between informers and police, either for financial gain or to boost arrest statistics or both, and possession of only a small amount can lead to ridiculous prison sentences or, if you are very lucky, a huge fine. Exporting any quantity of heroin at all from Thailand carries a mandatory 19 years, and countries hitherto known to be lenient are tightening up very fast.

Customs at borders, especially on return journeys, are very tight and although prices are cheap in the producing countries, the worry, sweat and risk is simply never worth it as the many Western travellers stranded in Asian prisons will testify. If you are taking your own vehicle be careful of carrying any parcels or luggage belonging to anyone else who is not travelling with you. You may be acting as an unwitting courier, and ignorance is impossible to prove in court.

With a little organization it is often possible to visit Western prisoners on your journey. There are many serving over 20 years. Food, clothes, medicines and books are especially welcome. Visits are very much appreciated and may make all the difference between sanity and despair. For information please contact The National Council for the Welfare of Prisoners Abroad (NCWPA), 347A Upper Street, London N1; tel: 01-226 1668.

The cost of a trip varies tremendously, depending on your mode of transport, your willingness to sleep in flophouses, eat modestly, bargain for goods, deny yourself souvenirs, etc. It is wise to set out a budget before leaving, allowing so much money per day, and then stick to it as much as possible. It is possible to live humbly but comfortably for about £35 a week in most of the countries in this book. Singapore is more expensive, of course, as is Western Turkey. If your trip includes an extended trek in Nepal, you will spend less than £35. A 2-month budget for India, Sri Lanka and Pakistan in 1985 worked out as follows:

Accommodation £48.57
Food £78.32
Alcohol £16.77
Buses and Trains £58.31
Entertainment (museums, etc.) £10.84
Postage (higher than most) £34.45
Miscellaneous (newspapers, candles, departure taxes, etc.) £30.24

The total spent in 59 days of travelling was £277.50 which works out to be £4.70 per day.

An emergency fund is a good idea though its size will depend on your finances and your cautiousness.

Despite the sometimes wild fluctuations in currency and high rates of inflation, we have included the exchange rates against the pound sterling and the American dollar at the time of writing. For current exchange rates check any Tuesday edition of the *Financial Times* which lists the value of the pound against all the currencies of the world.

As you enter each new country, you would be well advised to change no more money than you are likely to need. If you try to reconvert any of it just before leaving, you are bound to lose on the transaction. Don't assume you can spend it in the airport duty-free shop, since many accept hard currencies only. On the other hand, you do not want to spend 2 or 3 hours in a bank every other day, so change enough to keep you going for a week or so. If your fund of cash is depleted, make sure that the weekend is not coming up, and that there are exchange facilities in the next place on your itinerary. Do not take for granted that a reasonably sized town will have such facilities. Even banks which are visited by tourists may still be in the process of applying for permission to cash travellers' cheques, so you shouldn't allow your store of cash to dip too low. If you are leaving by air, confirm in advance what the departure tax is, and check the figure with more than one source.

Travellers' Cheques

Travellers' cheques are the safest way to carry money, as they need your counter-signature and passport before they can be cashed. In theory, lost or stolen cheques can be cancelled and a new set re-issued. Always report a theft of travellers' cheques as soon as possible, as any that are cashed prior to notification are your loss. It also helps to have a separate list of the cheque numbers to speed up repayment.

Until recently American Express travellers' cheques presented the fewest difficulties worldwide. They were almost universally recognized (except in Iran where they are banned) and the company was generally prompt to replace lost or stolen cheques. Unfortunately there have been so many claims (many of them from travellers who have sold their original set on the black market) that American Express have stopped reimbursing Indian banks for cashed cheques which turn out to be stolen, which means that Indian banks are now reluctant to cash any AmEx travellers' cheques. If possible use the banking services at an American Express office (addresses in country chapters) where you can also collect poste restante mail if you are carrying AmEx cheques. You can get commission-free American Express travellers' cheques if you have an account at the Leeds Permanent Building Society.

Because of the potential difficulty in cashing any one kind of travellers' cheque, it is a good idea to carry more than one brand. You should have a minimum of difficulty cashing Thomas Cook and First City National Bank cheques; Barclay (Visa) are not so internationally known.

You usually get a better rate for travellers' cheques than for cash, and are charged a smaller rate of commission at banks than at hotels or private *bureaux de change*.

Although the American dollar is the most widely recognized currency, you should have no difficulty exchanging sterling. If you think in pounds rather than dollars, it is more satisfactory to carry sterling, plus you don't have to pay an exchange commission twice.

Personal Cheques and Credit Cards

If you have a British current account, it might be worth taking your cheque book and banker's card, as the Eurocheque system is not totally unknown in Asia. You will find occasional banks that display the "EC" symbol. Other banks, particularly in India, have been known to cash cheques (albeit in local currency), although you may need a long chat with the bank manager first. In an emergency the British Consulate can (for a fee) cash a sterling cheque for £50 if supported by a banker's card.

In some surplus currency countries (such as India), American citizens are permitted to cash up to $200 in personal cheques at the American Embassy.

Very few hotels and restaurants which the traveller on a budget is likely to frequent will accept Access or Visa. However a credit card can be useful in an emergency for, say, buying an air ticket. If you do buy a meal in Kathmandu or Kandy on your credit card, there is a fair chance that the bill will never reach your home address.

Cash

It is always advisable to have a small amount of sterling or dollars in reserve, as it is often difficult to cash travellers' cheques. This should be kept in a safe place such as an inside pocket or a waterproof money belt. Your foreign currency might qualify you for price reductions (e.g. 25% on domestic flights in India and in some hotels).

If the country you are staying in has a black market, then you may choose to sell your cash to individuals rather than banks; but make sure you are already aware of the exchange rate in the banks, as some of the dealers will offer less than the official rate and rely on the gullible traveller for profit. You always get a better rate for larger denomination bills. Beware of handing over your money first or showing where you keep it. It is better to be cautious and untrusting than to lose it all.

There is a shortage of change in some Asian countries, so get into the local habit of hording change. It is better not to keep all your local currency in the wallet which is in constant use. Japanese paper wallets are handy for storing excess cash.

Some further advice: just because a professional money dealer has given you a favourable street rate, do not insult an honest merchant by insisting he give you more than the bank rate for your cash. He is likely to reply with dignity that he does business with a bank, not on the black market.

Emergency Cash

The best way is to arrange for the money to be transferred by telex through an international bank, e.g. Thomas Cook, American Express, Grindlays or alternatively from your own bank to a nominated branch of a local Asian bank. Ask the sender to get written confirmation from your bank that the remittance has been made and to send you a copy. It is best to have money sent to one of the major city branches. The main drawback with having money sent by banker's transfer is that unless your sender insists that the money remain in a hard currency the cash will most likely be given in local currency at the official exchange rate. An urgent transfer from a Thomas Cook branch in Britain to one in Asia usually takes less than 48 hours and costs about £15.

In emergencies, your Embassy may be able to advise and assist. For instance, both British and American representatives abroad will help you to contact a possible source of borrowed money and arrange for its transfer. Upon receipt of an official cable, American consuls can issue a cheque in local currency within twenty-four hours and a dollar cheque within ten days.

Selling anything is very difficult and a slow process as Easterners are probably much better at the game than you are. Try not to show you are desperate for the money or you will receive the lowest price. Be firm over the price. Articles such as whisky, cassettes, watches, cameras, quality film and calculators are all fairly easy to sell, but you may have to search around for a good price and you should be wary of disapproving authorities. In some countries valuable items such as cameras, tape-recorders and vehicles are marked on the passport to prevent their sale. If you have any articles for sale, try putting a notice on the hostel boards.

Finding paid employment is virtually impossible. For information about voluntary opportunities see the chapter on Asia in *Work Your Way Around the World.*

Repatriation

For those who are desperate or ill, there may be no alternative but to fly home. Go to your nearest Embassy or High Commission and they will arrange a flight on the first available plane. This is a serious and costly procedure, and will result in the withdrawal of your passport on arrival back in the U.K. until all debts have been repaid.

Bargaining

Bargaining is an art which comes hard to Westerners who are used to fixed prices. In the East you have to bargain for many things: rickshaws, taxis, clothes, souvenirs and food (though not usually in restaurants). It is not always obvious when and when not to haggle. Many items have fixed prices. Always settle the price of a taxi fare before embarking; otherwise you will be charged over the odds because there is seldom a working meter.

The hardest part of course is not to pay the first price asked, because in many cases it will seem absurdly cheap to you. If you discover later that you have paid far too much for that first bunch of bananas you bought, console yourself with the thought that the man in the market probably had a greater need for the money than you. It is surprising how quickly you get to know what the local price for goods and services is.

As a rough guide to bargaining cut the price first quoted by half, then start haggling. Never lose your temper: be firm and definite over the amount you are prepared to pay. You may even have to walk away and thereby run the risk of not being implored to come back. Local bargainers spin elaborate yarns about why they can afford only 20 rupees or 30 baht for the item in question as much to amuse and entertain the merchant as anything else. On the other hand, don't enter into lengthy and serious negotiations unless you're serious about buying the object.

Beggars

In all Asian countries, particularly India, you will be confronted with poverty such as is not known in the western world. Beggars are the most obvious outward sign of this poverty, and it is difficult to pass them by without feeling pity. They are often severely disabled, blind or limbless with leprosy, and as a result have no other way of making a living. Whether you give them money is obviously a personal choice. Your decision will depend on your own financial position, the degree of pity you feel, your conscience and how strongly you object to professional begging. At one end of the scale there is a very thin dividing line between beggars and confidence tricksters, as is explained in the following paragraphs.

Thieves and Con Men

Many a traveller returns penniless from the East after falling foul of some unscrupulous character who, one way or another, has taken possession of all his money and valuables. It is a wise precaution to register with your Embassy (leaving copies of your documents, etc.) as soon as you arrive in case you are robbed. The most straightforward method of losing your money is to a thief or pickpocket. We have already discussed ways of outwitting thieves by using a money belt, etc. If possible never show where the main bulk of your money is kept: to a thief, knowing where the money is kept means half the battle won. Beware of someone asking you for change, then grabbing your wallet and fleeing. Be especially careful on trains, especially just before departure when someone may set up a diversion and then throw your luggage out the window to a partner.

Less straightforward are the confidence tricksters, who will appear in a wide variety of guises and use an enormous range of tricks to get your money. It would be impossible to list all the ploys and ruses that have been successful in the past, but they range from light deception (like beggars pretending to be blind) to blatant blackmail (like planting drugs on you, locking you up and threatening to call the police). Between these two extremes there is a lot of scope for ingenuity. Even the most obvious methods (phoney tales of relatives' illnesses, promises to repay money, trading in fake gems) are made so convincing that cautious travellers have been caught out by them.

Hotel managers are often reported to be running rackets, so beware when you retire to sleep or take a shower. Even if your room has a lock, it is unlikely to be working as effectively as it appears to be. When all your money has been stolen from under your pillow and you mention this fact to the hotel manager, you will find him most apologetic, and, "in order to protect his reputation", he might pay you back half of what you lost. His story, too, will be so well rehearsed that you may be hundreds of miles away before you even begin to suspect.

Lahore is notorious for this. Advice for staying in a hotel which gives off bad vibes includes not accepting a room with a balcony, not trusting their locks, not allowing strangers into your room and not telling the truth about when you're leaving since they prefer to rob you just as you are about to leave. If you do feel threatened, for example by someone following you, don't hesitate to bring it to the attention of a local policeman who will generally be on your side.

After saying all that, few places are at all like Lahore and there is no need to mistrust everyone you meet. For every thief and swindler, you will meet dozens of friendly, concerned locals who will warn you of lurking evil, keep an eye on your luggage in your absence, etc.

Motoring

The complex and expensive documentation has already been discussed. If you are convinced that you want to take your own vehicle off the beaten track, it is worth checking accessibility with the local motoring organizations (addresses provided in individual chapters) prior to departure.

When choosing what vehicle to take, it must be said that every type of vehicle on earth has been driven or ridden to the East from 1929 Chryslers to tandem bicycles. The most commonly seen is the Volkswagen camper. The primary considerations are whether you will be allowed to take your vehicle into a given country, whether the vehicle will make it and whether spare parts are easily obtainable. Volkswagens seem to be the best bet as parts are easy to obtain, they are economical on fuel and there is a secondhand market for them, though it will probably be impossible to get round the customs regulations.

The serious motorist might like to consult *Overland and Beyond* (from Roger Lascelles, 1981) or *The Asian Highway* (1979) by Jack Jackson and Ellen Crampton. It is also possible to have a consultation with one of the overland companies who can provide the latest information on routes, borders, fuel supplies, etc. Encounter Overland charge £60 for a 3-hour session and Hann Overland charge £20 for one or two hours (addresses above).

List of Essential Spares

Fan belt, sparking plugs, distributor contact set, condenser, light bulbs, spare tyres, spare wheels, petrol pump, oil filter, radiator hose, rotor arm, jump leads, fuses, starter brushes, dynamo brushes, distributor cap, lockable petrol cap, ignition coil, tool kit (jack, wheel brace, tyre pump, puncture outfit, tyre levers, wire, adhesive tape, tow rope, torch, warning triangle). You should also take a fully illustrated car manual.

Motorcycling
A fuel tank of minimum 25 litres is recommended; a reliable supplier of good alloy tanks is Bartels Ltd. of Walthamstow (01-521 7161). A full bike cover will deter most fiddlers. The most powerful horn which your electrics will cope with is an essential piece of equipment. On most Asian roads, might is right, so don't fall into arguments.

Public Transport
A combination of bus, train and hitching constitutes the best way of moving around the East. For reasons of economy, hitching is best in Europe, where traffic conditions are also favourable. Beyond Istanbul, the buses and trains are so cheap and traffic so sparse, that hitching becomes less worthwhile.

The choice between bus and train depends on several factors such as time and cost. In Turkey, for instance, the trains are cheaper than the buses but also much slower. On Indian trains and Sri Lankan buses, discounts are given for booking long journeys: it is therefore cheaper to book a long journey in a single stage than in several short stages. Often there are several competing transport companies and price differences reflect the different standards of luxury that you can expect.

In addition to ordinary buses and trains, Asian countries employ an impressive and ingenious range of vehicles to transport people cheaply. The shared taxi takes many forms from the *dolmuş* of Turkey to the Suzuki of northern Pakistan to the *bemo* of Indonesia. In the course of one Asian holiday you are quite likely to travel on a bullock-drawn cart, a horse-drawn tonga, a tractor, a truck and a motorcycle, as well as buses and trains.

Post
Poste restante services in Asian countries can be a haphazard affair and in rural locations non-existent. Try to use only the central post offices in major cities. Letters sent to Poste Restante, Main Post Office, should be addressed in block capitals and written as clearly as possible. To avoid confusion ask your correspondents to place your underlined surname first and to omit Mr. or Ms. or your Christian name. When collecting mail, take your passport as a means of identification, though you won't always be asked for it.

You need not rely solely on post offices to hold mail for you. Many of the more popular hotels or hostels will hold mail, and if you have a clear idea of where you will be staying, you can use their services. If you are using American Express travellers' cheques, you are entitled to use their offices for poste restante. As a rule they hold travellers' mail for one month and do not charge customers for the service. They do, however, charge about US$3 for forwarding mail.

When sending mail from Asia, private aerogrammes are safest and most economical. Potential thieves can see that there are no enclosures and it is impossible to steam off the stamps, which occasionally happens to stamped envelopes. If you send a postcard or letter, you might like to put your mind at rest by seeing the stamp franked. Sending cash through the post is never a safe policy.

Telephone and Telegrams

Phoning home from a large and crowded Asian post office can be a daunting experience. In an emergency you might do well to enlist the help of a hotel experienced in such matters or to use a private telephone office (such as are common in Colombo). These will be expensive but will save you hours of waiting or, worse, waiting in vain.

If you want to convey to your loved ones the simple message that you are alive and well, send a telegram. If your message is short, this will be much cheaper than phoning, but then of course you have no guarantee that it has reached its destination. Wordage rates vary from 3 or 4 pence in Bangladesh to 27 pence in Singapore. Some wily travellers combine words to reduce the cost, especially in countries where English is little spoken and the message will have to be spelled out in any case. If the telegraphist doesn't decode the message, your mum will.

Broadcasting and Newspapers

The BBC World Service broadcasts over the short-wave band around the world. The wavebands are as follows (except Turkey's which are listed in that chapter):

49m	6.195kHz	16m	17.770kHz
31m	9.740kHz	13m	21.550kHz
25m	11.750kHz	11m	25.650kHz
19m	15.310kHz		

For more detailed information contact BBC External Services, Bush House, London WC2B 4PH.

All of the countries treated in this book publish English language newspapers which make interesting reading, if not for the unbiassed coverage of world events then for the misprints (e.g. the *Pakistan Times* evoked a wonderful picture of some corrupt politicians with the word "psychophants" and the Sri Lankan *Daily News* aptly described the Gujarat police force as an "uninformed service" instead of "uniformed"). *The International Herald Tribune* and *Time* magazine are easier to find in large cities than *The Times* or *The Guardian*. They will be expensive. Slightly out-of-date British and American newspapers can usually be read at their Embassies or cultural centres such as the British Council (office and library addresses listed in individual chapters).

The hygiene practised in most of Asia results in the risk of many serious food and water-borne diseases such as cholera, typhoid, hepatitis and dysentery. You should take as many precautions as are reasonable, which means getting jabs before you go, taking your malaria pills religiously and being careful about the water.

Inoculations

The first step is to consult your physician about recommended inoculations, including cholera and typhoid, polio and tetanus and gamma globulin for hepatitis. There is now also a rabies vaccine. If your local doctor does not seem clued up (and many aren't) it is worth ringing an expert, for example the Hospital of Tropical Diseases (4 St. Pancras Way, London NW1; tel: 01-387 4411), the Liverpool School of Tropical Medicine (Pembroke Place, Liverpool L3 5QA; tel: 051-708 9393), the Trailfinders Immunization Centre (46 Earl's Court Road, London W8; tel: 01-937 9631) or the Thomas Cook Vaccination Centre (45 Berkeley Street, London W1; tel: 01-499 4000/01-408 4158).

It is also worth consulting a specialist book such as *The Tropical Traveller* (details under Sources of Information), *The Traveller's Health Guide* revised in 1985 by Dr. Anthony Turner (available from Roger Lascelles, 47 York Road, Brentford, Middlesex; tel: 01-847 0935 @ £4.95 plus 50p postage) or *Preservation of Personal Health in Warm Climates* (from the Ross Institute of Tropical Hygiene, Keppel Street, London WC1; tel: 01-636 8636 at a cost of £2.50).

It is a good idea to join the International Association for Medical Assistance to Travellers (IAMAT) whose headquarters are at 123 Edward Street, Suite 725, Toronto, Ontario M5G 1E2, Canada. This organization co-ordinates doctors and clinics around the world who maintain high medical standards at fixed costs, e.g. $25 per consultation. Addresses are given in the country chapters. There is no set fee for joining the association, but if you make a reasonable donation they will send you country by country climate and hygiene charts, and very detailed leaflets about malaria and other tropical diseases. Unfortunately they can't be relied on to answer correspondence.

There are some profit-making medical advisory services which act as consultants to businesses and other organizations which send people abroad. It is unlikely that the independent traveller will want to avail himself of such a scheme; for example MASTA (Medical Advisory Services for Travellers Abroad), Keppel Street, London WC1, charge £4.75 for basic advice (which is free from your doctor) and £25 for their Executive Package.

The cholera and typhoid vaccines are usually combined and are given 3 weeks apart. It must be emphasized that a cholera shot does not give complete protection, in fact some estimates are as low as 25% for the reduction of risk during the months of its validity. In 1985 there were rumours from Adelaide of an oral cholera vaccine which would protect a person for life, but this is not yet in use. The dosage of your hepatitis shot (which really is quite effective) varies according to the length of time you intend to travel. Both can cause soreness in the injected part, so it is best to have them well in advance of a long plane ride. The rabies vaccine is also administered in two doses, and is given to people who intend either to reside abroad or to travel through really wild areas. It is a personal choice whether you pay the high fee to protect yourself against a very small risk.

Fees vary from clinic to clinic, for example the London vaccination centres charge £15 for a large dose of gamma globulin whereas the Liverpool School charges £2. Some G.P.s don't charge at all for inoculations; others simply issue prescriptions for the vaccine which can be filled on the National Health. Here is the table of charges from both the Trailfinders and Thomas Cook Vaccination Centres:

Cholera	: 2 shots @ £3.50 each
Typhoid	: 2 shots @ £3.50 each
Hepatitis	: 2-3 months protection @ £7.50
	: 5-6 months protection @ £15.00
Tetanus	: £3.50
Rabies	: 2 shots @ £10 each (available only at certain times)
Polio	: £3

Malaria

Malaria is continuing to make a serious comeback in many parts of the world due to the resistance of certain strains of mosquito to the pesticides and medications used so heavily in the past. Chloroquine was once considered the be-all and end-all of malaria prophylactics, but now many countries report resistance to the drug, namely Bangladesh, Burma, India, Indonesia, Nepal and Thailand. More detailed malaria information is given in the country chapters. If you are intending to visit any of these countries you should take both chloroquine and proguanil (brand name: paludrine). At the time of going to press the Ross Institute of Tropical Hygiene in London (01-636 8636) was recommending 30mg of choloroquine once a week plus 200mg of paludrine daily. If your local physician is not aware of the various kinds of malaria pills, phone one of the specialists listed above.

You must take the pills for 6 weeks after leaving a malarious area. If you develop a fever either during your travels or after your return, see a doctor. If you're back home be sure to tell your doctor where you've been and if he diagnoses 24 hour flu more than once, insist on being referred to a tropical specialist.

Unfortunately these prophylactic medications are not foolproof. Resistance to both groups of drug have been found in India and Thailand. It is therefore wise to take mechanical precautions against mosquitoes. Sleeping under a mosquito net or in a room with screened windows is not always possible in budget hotels where the windows are entirely open (to mosquitoes, birds, etc.) At nightfall cover your limbs with light coloured garments, apply insect repellant to exposed parts (these can be bought locally, e.g. "Odomos" in India, "Flypel" in Sri Lanka) and sleep with a fan on. Mosquito coils are partially effective, but are difficult to transport intact.

First Aid Kit

The essential component of your first aid kit is water purification tablets. The tap water throughout Asia is unsafe for travellers to drink. It is likely to contain disease organisms to which the Westerner has had no chance to develop immunities. Do not assume that you can get by with substitute beverages such as coke or tea or even bottled soda water. In hot climates, it is imperative to drink large quantities of water to avoid dehydration, possibly as much as 6 pints a day. The most effective method of purification is boiling for at least 5 minutes. However this is seldom convenient and in hot weather the water never gets cooler than lukewarm.

A more manageable method of water sterilization is to use chemical purifiers. It is possible to find an appropriate chlorine solution in some Asian chemist shops. However it is simplest before you set off to buy Sterotabs from Boots or Puritabs from other chemists. The latter are preferable because they are effervescent and take effect in only 10 rather than 30 minutes. You should take a supply of the one-litre pills as well as the single glass dose: the former can be used in you water bottle, the latter in water served at restaurants. You will soon get used to the slight swimming pool taste. Some people claim that the taste of tincture of iodine is less offensive, but regulating 3 drops into a litre is more fiddly than dropping in a tablet. You might want to experiment at home first.

In addition to chlorine and malaria pills, you should take antiseptic cream and plasters. Sores heal much more slowly in the tropics and are likely to become infected if not covered.

Although a mild case of diarrhoea is virtually inevitable, it is not necessary to take drugs to treat it. (Dietary treatment is discussed below under Ailments). However some travellers prefer to take something to deal with the symptoms. Lomotil is a popular remedy which simply slows down the digestion and thereby relieves cramps and stops you from having to rush to the toilet so frequently. (Some people experience dizziness as a side effect). Codeine-phosphate or simple codeine achieves the same ends, and is preferred by many doctors. Imodium tablets are safe and can be bought without a prescription.

The remedy for dysentery or giardiasis (an intestinal parasite which results in persistent diarrhoea) — both diseases are rampant among travellers especially in Northern India and Nepal — is metronidazole (UK brand name: flagyl) which you may want to take with you as a precaution.

Salt tablets were once a standard part of the tropical traveller's baggage. If you do feel some uncharacteristic twinges in your muscles this is probably due to excessive salt loss through sweat. You can usually solve the problem by putting extra salt on your food rather than taking tablets (which make some people ill). Remember that you sweat just as much in dry as in humid climates; you just don't notice it as much.

Food

Deciding what food is safe to eat is not always easy. Many people are nervous to eat in streetside stalls and bazaar restaurants and stick to the more hygienic (and boring) menus in upmarket restaurants. On the whole food in humble establishments is safe provided that it has been thoroughly cooked and does not look as though it has been hanging around in a fly-invested environment. Hot food is therefore preferable to cold. A vegetarian diet is less likely to give trouble than meat or fish. Fresh fruit and vegetables bought in the market should either be cooked, peeled or (in the case of grapes) washed thoroughly in purified water. This means that you should avoid eating the garnishes of tomatoes and lettuce served with many meals.

Tropical Heat

The heat of the tropics must be adjusted to gradually. When you step off your airplane into a wall of heat in Bombay or Bali, you may find yourself wishing that you had chosen to go to Lappland after all. When first arriving in a hot climate go straight to a comfortable hotel with a fan and lie under it. Drink plenty of water (even if at first you don't feel thirsty). After your first relaxing day, gear the day's activities around morning and evening.

If you are finding the heat really oppressive, head for the hills. A temporary despondency (from heat or any other cause) can often be treated by a morning in your air-conditioned Embassy lounge or by a leisurely pot of tea in the local equivalent of the Ritz Hotel; even if you have to pay the equivalent of 3 dinners for the pot of tea, the air-conditioning may make it worthwhile. Many posh hotels will let you use the swimming pool for a fee.

If you have pale skin or are not used to the sun, try not to expose yourself to sun too quickly. Excessive exposure will not produce a tan, but only a lobster red colour, which is also extremely painful especially if it blisters. Lightweight cotton shirts with long sleeves and a hat with a brim are essential. If you are unfortunate enough to be sunburnt, apply calamine lotion (brand name in India caladryl) or cold cream liberally, or soak a towel in cold water and place this over the most tender areas. Yoghurt is an easily accessible substitute for cold cream and is very effective. Don't believe anyone who tells you that crushed tomatoes achieve the same end.

If you experience headache, giddiness or cramps after exerting yourself in the heat of the day (which may include anything as unstrenuous as walking to the bank), you probably have a mild case of heat exhaustion caused by a water and salt deficiency. Do not ignore the symptoms. Simply drink some water and sit in the shade for at least 20 minutes until the throbbing in your head subsides.

A more serious condition is heat stroke in which the body temperature rises in addition to a host of unpleasant symptoms. The victim should be kept cool while medical attention is sought.

AILMENTS

There are many tales in general circulation about travellers picking up rare and exotic diseases and gradually wasting away. In fact most travellers suffer from nothing worse than diarrhoea which, although inconvenient, is not deadly. We have already seen what steps can be taken to avoid the most serious diseases (i.e. cholera, typhoid, hepatitis and malaria). It is worth bearing in mind that chemists in foreign countries are a free source of medical information about simple ailments, and can recommend local remedies.

Diarrhoea

Also known as the trots, the runs, runny tummy, gippy tummy, Spanish gut, Delhi belly, Bali belly, squitters or Montezuma's revenge. Whatever you call it, this is the most common complaint of all. As precautions against it, avoid drinking untreated water or eating any unpeeled or unwashed fruit or vegetables. Eat lots of yoghurt since the bacteria helps to combat the bugs in the stomach.

If left to its own devices, diarrhoea should clear up in 2 or 3 days, although in an extreme bout the fluid loss may leave you weak and tired. You should keep drinking to avoid dehydration. It will clear up more quickly if you can get a lot of rest and stop eating altogether. When you begin eating again, stick to yoghurt, boiled rice and tea without milk if possible. If the problem persists, try an appropriate medication such as kaolin and morphine or codeine phosphate.

Dysentery

If diarrhoea does not clear up after 48 hours and you begin to notice blood or pus in your excreta and start having stomach cramps, then it is possible you may have amoebic dysentery. If you also have a fever you might have bacillary dysentery. Both can and should be treated with drugs which are best administered by a doctor but can be taken on your own if necessary. For amoebic dysentery take flagyl. For the bacillary variety take an antibiotic such as tetracycline or a sulphonamide (e.g. septrin). Take things very gently while your digestion recovers.

Hepatitis

Hepatitis can be caught by eating or drinking anything which has been contaminated by saliva, mucus, urine or excrement from an infected person. A gamma globulin shot reduces the risk considerably but not completely. The symptoms, which appear 15 to 50 days (usually 25 days) after infection, are: fever, loss of appetite, nausea, loss of energy and pains in the abdomen. The skin turns yellow or orange (though this can be difficult to see if you have a suntan) as well as the white of the eye, the urine turns deep orange and the stools become white. If you think you have hepatitis, you must rest and seek medical advice immediately. Do not smoke or drink alcohol and try to keep to a fat free diet. Hepatitis can often take 6 months to clear up, so it might be better to think about going home or being repatriated on your medical insurance policy.

Insect Bites

There is only one variety of mite which afflicts man and causes scabies or "the itch". This can be transmitted by human contact, or by using the bedding or towels of an infected person. The resulting affliction takes the form of an itchy rash in the hairy parts of the body. Unless exterminated, the mites will spread over the body. The overnight cure is to cover your body in benzyl benzoate, available from any chemist.

There are three types of lice: head lice, body lice and crab lice. They all respond to Lorexane ointment or shampoo from chemists. Delousing may also be done by blowing a 10% D.D.T. powder into the clothing of the victim. It may be wise to discard all infested clothes and shave body hair.

Bed bugs are unpleasant companions but harmless.

Wear shoes out of doors since many worms and parasites are able to penetrate even unbroken skin. Also beware of rattan or cane chairs in which may live rattan bugs. If you see other people arranging newspapers on their seats, do not assume they are being unduly neurotic about hygiene.

Snake and Scorpion Bites

It is extremely unlikely that you will tangle with a snake and you would be very unlucky to be bitten by one. If you are, try not to panic. Try to remember a description of the snake, i.e. size, colours and markings. Do not try to suck the venom out as this only increases the blood circulation and will spread the venom more quickly. Seek medical advice as soon as possible. Although it is unlikely that the snake was poisonous, local hospitals keep supplies of serum for the most common venomous snakes.

Scorpions are fairly common and their bite is almost never fatal. If you are unlucky enough to find one in your hotel room you should tell the management who will probably be better prepared to do battle with it; a heavy saucepan is a suitable weapon whereas a rubber thong or paperback is not.

A good habit to develop is to shake out your shoes for lurking snakes or scorpions every morning.

Jellyfish
Jellyfish stings are rarely fatal, but are painful. If stung, remove any remaining tentacles with tweezers or a gloved hand (otherwise your fingers may get stung too). Bathe the area in methylated spirits or vinegar. If the rash persists, apply an antihistamine cream or take an antihistamine tablet.

Toothache
Holding whisky or oil of cloves in your mouth can relieve the pain. Dentist offices in Asia do not always inspire confidence, especially the ones which have on display a heap of recycled dentures. Have a dental check-up shortly before leaving home and hope for the best. If some serious problem does arise, it's probably best to head for a large city and ask an experienced expatriate or your Embassy to recommend a good dentist.

Customs and Etiquette
Once you move out of Europe you are entering a world that is based on different religious, social, moral and cultural values. While it is important to adjust as much as possible to the social climate of whichever country you are in and to show respect by conforming, you will not be expected to arrive with a complete knowledge of all the necessary formalities, customs, manners and etiquette. Your Western ways will often cause strange looks or laughter. But, if you are able to laugh with them and are prepared to risk slight humiliation by following local custom, you will be well on the way to learning how to interact successfully with the inscrutable East.

Many customs, social formalities and rituals will arouse your curiosity as to their origins, such as when Asians tip a little water on the ground before drinking. Some have a basis in practicality; others are overtly symbolic; many are now meaningless because their original significance has been forgotten and they continue solely through the strength of habit and tradition. Observing one's fellow men is one of life's great delights, and the inquisitive traveller will find much to ponder and learn in the general area of manners, social customs and religious observances. A few examples of common rituals are described below.

Knives, forks and spoons are not used much for eating, although they may be specially offered to Western travellers, so washing your hands both before and after meals is an extremely practical ritual. You will notice that only the right hand is used for eating and for handing things to you. If you enquire about this, you will be laughed at and told that the left hand is unclean. This is not pure superstition. In the East people use their left hands instead of toilet paper, so try to get into the habit of using your right hand. Pointing at a person is considered rude in the West, but it is more so in many parts of Asia. In India and Thailand don't show the soles of your feet or point them at any person or religious image.

Many customs are obviously religious in origin. If you are visiting mosques, temples or shrines, for instance, then you will have to remove your shoes or sandals before entering. This is usually done when entering a private home as well. At some temples, you may even have to wash your feet first. When entering

Sikh temples or Moslem mosques you should also cover your head. Bare arms and legs are frowned on in any place of worship. In some areas you will find the natives, especially women, reluctant to be photographed. It is unlikely that they believe the camera will take away a part of their soul, although this is an old wives' tale that circulates widely. Nevertheless the camera may be associated with bad luck and you should be sensitive to their culture and beliefs. If you wish to photograph anyone, seek their permission first and establish whether they want payment. If they are the types to want money, they will no doubt initiate the bargaining.

The common western handshake is now universal, but an attempt to learn local gestures is always appreciated. In India, for instance, you put your hands together when you say "Namaste". In the Moslem world it is common, after shaking hands, to put your hand on your heart or your lips. As in Europe and North America, people shake hands at every meeting, i.e. much more readily and frequently than in Britain. (Strict Moslems will not shake hands with women.)

The Natives

One of the most noticeable differences in attitude between the East and the West is the attitude to privacy. For example within 60 seconds of sitting down in a Delhi park to write a post card you are likely to be surrounded by a peanut salesman, a snake charmer, an ear cleaner (belonging to the official Delhi Massage Workers and Ear Cleaners Union) and umpteen children clamouring to see the picture on your post card. You will be asked a hundred times a day (or so it will seem) "Where are you coming from? how long in my country? what is your name?" The first few times you are delighted to engage in conversation but, sadly, the repetitions soon become boring and you realize that the questions are often just conventional greetings. If you reply that your name is Sappho and you come from Lesbos, you get the same polite reaction as when you tell the truth. Even if you find the constant questioning tiresome, it is churlish not to answer with a smile. In fact you will smile so much that you will begin to sympathize with the Queen after a Royal Progress.

The social structures are often impenetrably elaborate and are accompanied by a complex division of labour. There are often a dozen locals loitering around a hotel, all of whom are likely to have a clearly defined role (porter, cook, cleaner, maintenance man, and so on). Some tourists wrongly assume that they can expect service from any of these people, and will loudly demand to know when breakfast will be ready of the man who has come to change a fuse. When he looks blank, they become annoyed and conclude that it is no wonder that the Third World is in difficulties. You must expend time and effort finding the appropriate employee or official and then you will almost invariably find them obliging.

On the whole, couples should behave more circumspectly than they would at home. Holding hands in public is frowned upon by many of the older generation and considered vaguely pornographic by the younger. Obviously this is not true in cosmopolitan Istanbul or Singapore, but it is especially important in conservative or rural places.

It is the height of stupidity to apply the standards of one culture to those of another and to assume that this is a just basis for criticism. Of what possible use can it be to tell a harassed postal clerk that in your country stamps stick properly or to inform the youth hostel warden that the porridge (which has been made to please the bizarre tastes of Westerners) is disgusting and nothing like it is in Perthshire? It is surprising how discourteous travellers can be in an alien setting.

Women Travellers

It is a universally accepted dictum that women should not travel alone. It must be said, however, that the dangers and annoyances are probably worse in Italy than in India. In Hindu and Buddhist countries, the smiles of the men are almost always as innocent as the smiles of the women. It is not difficult to recognize the occasional suspect overture and to quash it immediately.

Travelling in Islamic countries presents special problems because women are simply not seen in public. Good Moslem men will treat you a little like a leper (won't include you in conversation, won't shake your hand). Bad Moslems may try to peep into your hotel room or grab at you in the street. When checking into a hotel, make sure that the door can be bolted (this is usually the norm in any case), and the windows or chinks blocked. If you receive a knock, just repeat "Go Away" in uncompromising tones. A stern "no" is understood and heeded throughout the world.

You are more likely to encounter problems in resorts which have been exposed to Western sex, drugs and rock and roll. Outside Europe dress with extreme modesty (no shorts or T-shirts). Loose fitting clothes are essential, and are cooler in any case. A full skirt is useful for covering your legs when sitting on the ground. You may want to wear a wedding ring (cheap imitations turn green within a week in the tropics) and to carry a photo of your husband preferably standing with your two sons. But for the most part you will not have to rely on these props to discourage unwelcome approaches but rather on your wholesome, confidently independent and (if necessary) aloof manner to strangers.

RELIGION

The dominant religion of each country is shown below along with the percentage of citizens who adhere to it:

Bangladesh:	Islam (86%)
Bhutan:	Buddhism (70%), Hindu (25%)
Burma:	Buddhism (85%)
India:	Hinduism (83% compared to 66% before Partition)
Indonesia:	Islam (90%)
Iran:	Islam (93% Shia)
Malaysia:	Islam (50%), Buddhism/Taoism (36%), Hindu (10%)
Nepal:	Hinduism/Buddhism (97%)
Pakistan:	Islam (97%)
Singapore:	Buddhism/Taoism (75%)
Sri Lanka:	Buddhism (69%), Hindu (15%)
Thailand:	Buddhism (95%)
Turkey:	Islam (98%)

Islam

The Moslem religion is based on the same historical facts as Christianity and Judaism. The main difference is that Moslems regard Jesus as a minor prophet and Mohammed as the greatest prophet of all. The Moslem embraces only one

God, Allah. The Koran is a code of life which affects the believer in all aspects of his life, not just worship. If it is obeyed, one can perfect all that is good in oneself.

Koranic law is harsh and the current swing towards fundamentalism in Iran, Pakistan and to some extent Bangladesh and Indonesia is worrying. One of the most obvious results has been a re-emergence of barbaric forms of punishment for comparatively trivial offences. Recently a Christian couple who were co-habiting in Pakistan were sentenced to 30 lashes, until a high court judge over-ruled the decision (after a public outcry). Travellers often find it difficult to adjust to the treatment of women in Moslem societies, since to say the society is male-dominated is an extreme understatement. There is a proverb (from the Pathans, conservative Moslems from Afghanistan/Pakistan): "For a woman either the house or the grave".

The two principal branches of Islam are Sunni (which means "orthodox") and Shia. The Shias broke away shortly after the founding of Islam, over who was the rightful successor to the Prophet; the Shias regard Ali, Mohammed's son-in-law, as the successor, while the Sunnis favour the Caliphs who did actually succeed as the legitimate heirs. Within modern Islam, Sunnis have a clear majority, though in Iran Shias outnumber Sunnis. This split contributes in some measure to the war between Iran and Iraq.

Ismaeli Moslems form a comparatively small but important group within Islam. They follow the Aga Khan (an urbane gentleman who lives in Paris) and are more liberal than most (some alcohol, less purdah). For example they don't necessarily fast for Ramadan. Although the largest membership is thought to be in western China and the U.S.S.R., Ismaelis predominate in northern Pakistan and in some areas of Iran.

If you are planning to travel in an Islamic country, you should take note of the festivals and holy days. The Islamic year is approximately 11 days shorter than the Christian year, so that holidays are about 11 days earlier each year. This cannot be determined definitely since it depends on sightings of the new moon from the Naval Observatory in Cairo.

The main festivals are Ramadan (the month of fasting), Eid-ul-Fitr (which marks the end of Ramadan), Eid-ul-Azha (the Feast of the Sacrifice), Mawlid-un-Nabi (the Prophet's birthday) and Ashura. Here are the approximate future dates:

	Ramadan begins	*Eid-ul-Fitr*	*Eid-ul-Azha*	*Ashura*	*Mawlid un-Nabi*
1986	8 May	9 Jun	16 Aug	13 Sep	13 Nov
1987	28 Apr	29 May	4 Aug	2 Sep	2 Nov
1988	17 Apr	18 May	24 Jul	22 Aug	23 Oct

If you have a choice it's probably best to avoid travelling during Ramadan since people seem to go into a kind of hibernation, and many restaurants are closed between sun-up and sun-down. For accurate dates contact the Islamic Cultural Centre in London shortly before your departure (146 Park Road, London NW8 7RG; tel: 01-724 3363).

Sikhism

In the 15th century, a guru called Guru Nanak decided to reform Hinduism, mainly on account of the caste structure which he despised. Although they now represent only 2% of the population of India, Sikhs have become an influential minority both within India and outside. They are mostly concentrated in the state of Punjab in which there is a vocal movement to set up a separate state to be called Khalistan. It was the storming of the holy Sikh shrine in Amritsar (the Golden Temple) in June 1984 which immediately led to the new visa requirements for all travellers to India. After Indira Gandhi's assassination Hindus rose up throughout India to wreak vengeance on local Sikhs. The tension between Sikh extremists and the Indian Government persists.

Hinduism

Hinduism is virtually confined to the Indian subcontinent, though there are large immigrant Hindu communities in South-East Asia. Although as a religion Hinduism is very tolerant of other beliefs, it is internally strongly class structured. There are four traditional castes in Hinduism. At the top are the Brahmans, who are people such as teachers and priests. The next group, the Kshatriyas, are the warrior caste from which the princes and kings are descended. Vaisyas are the caste to which agriculturists and traders belong. The lowest group are Sudras, originally the native people of India who were mainly craftsmen and agricultural workers. Within these four castes developed hundreds of sub-castes corresponding to trades and crafts. The rest of the population — the forest dwellers and aboriginal Indians — were kept outside Hindu society and this group, once known as the "untouchables" is now labelled "scheduled caste", Harijans or "backward class". In recent years the government has tried to improve the position of the scheduled peoples by legislation in order to remove the traditional prejudice. This has met with some success, but also with strong resistance which resulted in serious rioting in the Indian city of Ahmedabad in 1985.

The religious observances of Hinduism are highly complex and in many cases colourful. It is interesting to spend time in a major temple and watch the *pujas* (acts of devotion) preferably in the company of an English-speaking Hindu who can provide some insights into the character of the gods and the symbolism involved in the rituals. The Hindu calendar is full of festivals and celebrations, many of which are localized. Dates change from year to year. For an introduction to the religion, read K. M. Sen's *Hinduism* (Penguin, 1970).

Buddhism

Buddhism has made a significant contribution to the cultural heritage of the Asian continent in excess of the number of its present adherents. Its teachings are based on the life and writings of Siddhartha, born in Lumbini (now in Nepal) who achieved Buddhahood or Enlightenment at Bodhgaya in eastern India. (An account of his life can be extracted from Herman Hesse's novel *Siddhartha* or from the film.) After renouncing the world and its pleasures in about 600 B.C. he taught that all life is suffering, that suffering arises from indulging in desires and perpetuating life, and that the only hope of salvation lies in the suppression of all earthly attachments. Despite this austere sounding belief, the Buddhists of Sri Lanka, Nepal, Burma, Thailand, Ladakh, Sikkim and the Tibetan refugees of Northern India are very cheerful people. Many experienced travellers have a decided preference for Buddhist countries, just as some might prefer to travel in Roman Catholic rather than Protestant Europe. A good introduction to Buddhist beliefs is Christmas Humphreys' *Buddhism* (Pelican, 1951, reprinted 1985 at £3.50).

COMPARISONS AND CONVERSIONS

Time Zones

On your journey to the East you will pass through several time zones. When calculating, bear in mind that British Summer Time will reduce the times given by one hour. The time differences are outlined below:

Turkey:	GMT+3
Iran:	GMT+3½
Pakistan:	GMT+5
India:	GMT+5½
Sri Lanka:	GMT+5½
Nepal:	GMT+5 hrs. 40 mins.
Bangladesh:	GMT+6
Burma:	GMT+6½
Thailand:	GMT+7
Malaysia:	GMT+7½/8
Singapore:	GMT+7½
Indonesia:	GMT+7/8/9

Electricity

If you must take an appliance, try to take a battery-powered one. Electricity supplies are uncertain in many parts of Asia, and voltage and plug fittings vary. Like Britain, all the countries in this book operate on a voltage of 220 (or thereabouts), though in parts of Turkey, Malaysia and Indonesia 110V predominates. Currents are D.C. rather than A.C. in certain areas of India. Plug fittings are far from standard. Altogether it might be a good idea to start brushing your teeth and shaving manually.

Metric Conversions

1 inch	=2.54 centimetres	1 centimetre	=0.39 inches
1 yard	=0.91 metres	1 metre	=3.28 feet
1 mile	=1.61 kilometres	1 kilometre	=0.62 miles
1 pint	=0.57 litres	1 litre	=1.76 pints
1 quart	=1.14 litres	1 litre	=0.88 quarts
1 U.K. gallon	=4.55 litres	1 litre	=0.22 U.K. gal.
1 U.S. gallon	=3.79 litres	1 litre	=0.26 gallons
1 pound	=0.45 kilograms	1 kilogram	=2.2 pounds

Temperature

To compute Fahrenheit, multiply Centigrade by 1.8 and add 32. To compute Centigrade, subtract 32 from Fahrenheit and divide by 1.8, e.g. 15°C=59°F, 20°=68°F, 30°C=86°F, 40°C=104°F etc.

SOURCES OF INFORMATION

A book of this scope cannot hope to answer all the questions a traveller might want to ask. Specific queries about the individual countries should be referred to the Embassy, Consulate or tourist office of the country concerned (London addresses below). See also the information under Maps and Guides above for

U.K. distributors of travel literature. A bibliography for further reading follows each chapter.

Travellers might also like to join a travel club offering an interchange of up-to-date information or read their relevant publications. Here are some sources of information:

Globetrotters Club — BCM/Roving, London WC1N 3XX. Publish their club newsletter called *Globe* six times a year. Membership costs £5 per year and entitles members to exchange information and hospitality with other members around the world.

Trailfinders Ltd. — 42-48 Earls Court Road, London W8 6EJ; 01-937 9631. Publish a quarterly magazine with articles and advice on travel worldwide. Operate as a travel agency, specializing in overland and adventure travel and longhaul flights.

WEXAS — 45 Brompton Road, London SW3 1DE; 01-589 3315. Published the excellent *Traveller's Handbook* in 1985 (bookshop price £9.95) for travellers planning expeditions of all kinds, which is sent free to new members. Club membership costs £17.58 and allows members to go on WEXAS off-the-beaten-track trips, to book WEXAS flights, to get specially devised travel insurance and to receive the quarterly magazine *Traveller.*

Business Traveller — 60/61 Fleet Street, London EC4Y 1LA. Although generally intended for the more affluent traveller, this monthly magazine contains many useful facts and reports on cheap air fares of interest to budget travellers.

Servas International is an organization begun by an American Quaker, which runs a worldwide programme of free hospitality exchange for travellers, to further world peace and understanding. To become a Servas traveller contact 77 Elm Park Mansions, Park Walk, London SW10 for an application form. You pay a fee of £10 plus a deposit on a list of contacts in the region of the world you want to visit. The list is not very extensive in Asia except for India.

The Tropical Traveller by John Hatt provides both invaluable practical information on travelling in hot countries and an entertaining introduction to the kinds of psychological surprises you might expect to encounter. The author also runs an original publishing house which reprints travel classics, most of which are superbly well chosen (Eland Books, 53 Eland Road, London SW11 5JX).

The most thorough guide to the sites of the Indian subcontinent is unfortunately very expensive (£25). Professor Rushbrook Williams' *Handbook for Travellers in India, Pakistan, Nepal, Bangladesh and Sri Lanka* (John Murray, 1982, 22nd edition) is an excellent and detailed guide to the civilization and art of southern Asia. For an interesting introduction to the flavour of travelling in Asia, Paul Theroux's *Great Railway Bazaar* and recently published *The Imperial Way: Making Tracks from Peshawar to Chittagong* are recommended. Also Dervla Murphy's books are entertaining as well as evocative (e.g. *On a Shoestring to Coorg, Where the Indus is Young* and others).

Consular and Tourist Office Addresses in London

Bangladesh

High Commission, 28 Queen's Gate, SW7 5JA. Tel: 01-584 0081/4.

Burma

Embassy, 19a Charles Street, Berkeley Square, W1X 8ER. Tel: 01-499 8841.

India
High Commission, India House, Aldwych, WC2B 4NA. Tel: 01-836 8484.
Government Tourist Office, 7 Cork Street, W1X 2AB. Tel: 01-437 3677.

Indonesia
Embassy, 38 Grosvenor Square, W1X 9AD. Tel: 01-499 7661.
Tourist Information Centre, 70/71 New Bond Street, W1Y 9DE. Tel: 01-409 3588.

Islamic Republic of Iran
Embassy, 27 Princes Gate, SW7 1PX. Tel: 01-584 8101.
Consulate, 50 Kensington Court, W8 5DD. Tel: 01-937 5225.

Malaysia
High Commission, 45 Belgrave Square, SW1X 8QT. Tel: 01-235 8033.
Tourist Office, 17 Curzon Street, W1Y 7FE. Tel: 01-499 7388.

Nepal
Embassy, 12a Kensington Palace Gardens, W8 4QU. Tel: 01-229 6231.

Pakistan
Embassy, 35 Lowndes Square, SW1X 9JN. Tel: 01-235 2044.

Singapore
High Commission, 5 Chesham Street, SW1X 8ND. Tel: 01-235 9067/9.
Tourist Office, 33 Heddon Street, W1. Tel: 01-499 0033.

Sri Lanka
High Commission, 13 Hyde Park Gardens, W2 2LX. Tel: 01-262 1841.
Sri Lanka Tourist Board, 52 High Holborn, WC1V 6RL. Tel: 01-405 1194.

Thailand
Embassy, 30 Queen's Gate, SW7 5JB. Tel: 01-589 0173.
Tourism Authority, 9 Stafford Street, W1X 3FE. Tel: 01-499 7679.

Turkey
Embassy, 43 Belgrave Square, SW1X 8PA. Tel: 01-235 5252.
Tourism Information Office, 172/3 Piccadilly, W1V 9DD. Tel: 01-734 8681.

Turkey

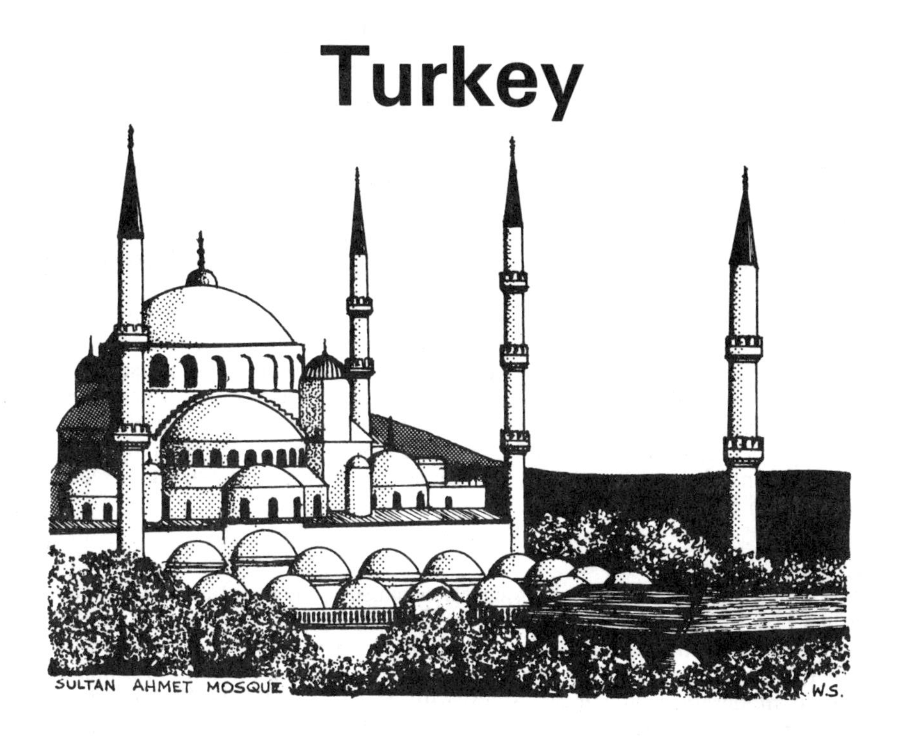

Capital: Ankara **Government:** Republic

Although only 3% of Turkey's vast area (nearly 300,000 square miles which is 3 times bigger than West Germany) is technically in Europe, the country's ambition is to model itself on Western Europe and perhaps some day join the E.E.C. In the cities of the western part, you will notice more similarities of attitude, cuisine, commerce, etc. with Greece than with India. A favourite image used of Turkey is as the "meeting place between East and West" and this aspect results in an interesting, sometimes bizarre, juxtaposition: handmade wooden ploughs and Mercedes-Benzes, nomadic tents and office skyscrapers, dust and concrete.

The Turkish Republic came into existence in 1923, after an extended struggle to dissolve the Ottoman Empire once and for all. The land has been host to many peoples, including the Hittites in the second millenium BC, the Greeks and Romans, the Byzantines, the Seljuks and the Ottomans. Many of the ancient sites in Turkey exhibit remnants of several conquering cultures and it is interesting to see how the architecture and fortifications were successively adapted. It may come as a surprise when you discover how many famous places from the Bible and history are located in Turkey, for example Ephesus, Antioch, and Tarsus. Continuity with the past is retained in place names such as Kayseri (once Caesarea) and Iconium (now Konya).

The man primarily responsible for the modernization of Turkey is Mustafa

Kemal, later given the name of Atatürk meaning father of the Turks. He was a shrewd general who organized a successful revolt against the post war occupation of Turkey and drove the Greek army off the mainland and onto the Aegean islands. He opened the Grand National Assembly in the modern city of Ankara rather than the traditional capital of Istanbul and was immediately voted leader. His important reforms include the creation of a secular state with religious toleration for all, and less importantly, the westernization of dress and the substitution of the Roman alphabet for Arabic script. Although he died in 1938 Atatürk is still universally revered; almost every public and private building has a picture of him prominently displayed.

After increasing instability during the 1970s the military took control in 1980. Soldiers and guns became a feature of every street, curfews were imposed, film-makers were imprisoned, etc. The Turkish people did not seem to resent these changes because of their tradition of military coups (for example Atatürk himself was a usurping general) and their appreciation of law and order. In November 1983, general elections were held. Many freedoms have been restored (though by no means all) and the stability continues. As a result tourism is increasing and earned $1.5 billion in 1985.

Climate

The climate of Turkey varies immensely because of the geographical contrasts. When it is quite balmy on the Aegean Coast in spring, the snow has not yet disappeared from the Anatolian hinterland. Severe Siberian winters are experienced in the central, northern and eastern regions, though the Black Sea has a moderating influence. Temperatures of –40°C (–40°F) are not uncommon. The average high for the summer months in Istanbul is a very pleasant 28°C (82°F) so the heat is rarely unbearable even if it is a little too humid. The annual rainfall varies from 10 inches in Central Turkey to about 100 inches on the Black Sea Coast. Smog is becoming a problem in the large cities between September and April.

Language

It is speculated that Turkish belongs to the language group which includes Finnish and Hungarian. English is increasingly being taught in schools, and many young people are eager to practise. The further east you travel the fewer English speakers you will find. This is one country where a good phrase book is a real asset. (Berlitz is good, though the binding doesn't stand up to rough handling by the numerous Turks eager to communicate by pointing at the relevant word or phrase). German is the most widely understood second language because of the number of Turkish migrant workers who have been in Germany and also because of the large number of German tourists who visit Turkey.

The change to the Roman alphabet from Arabic script in 1928 makes it easier for the English-speaking traveller, though the sentence construction is alien. Some of the rules of pronunciation are very tricky:

c like j
ç like ch
ğ like y
j like zh (as in azure)
ş like sh

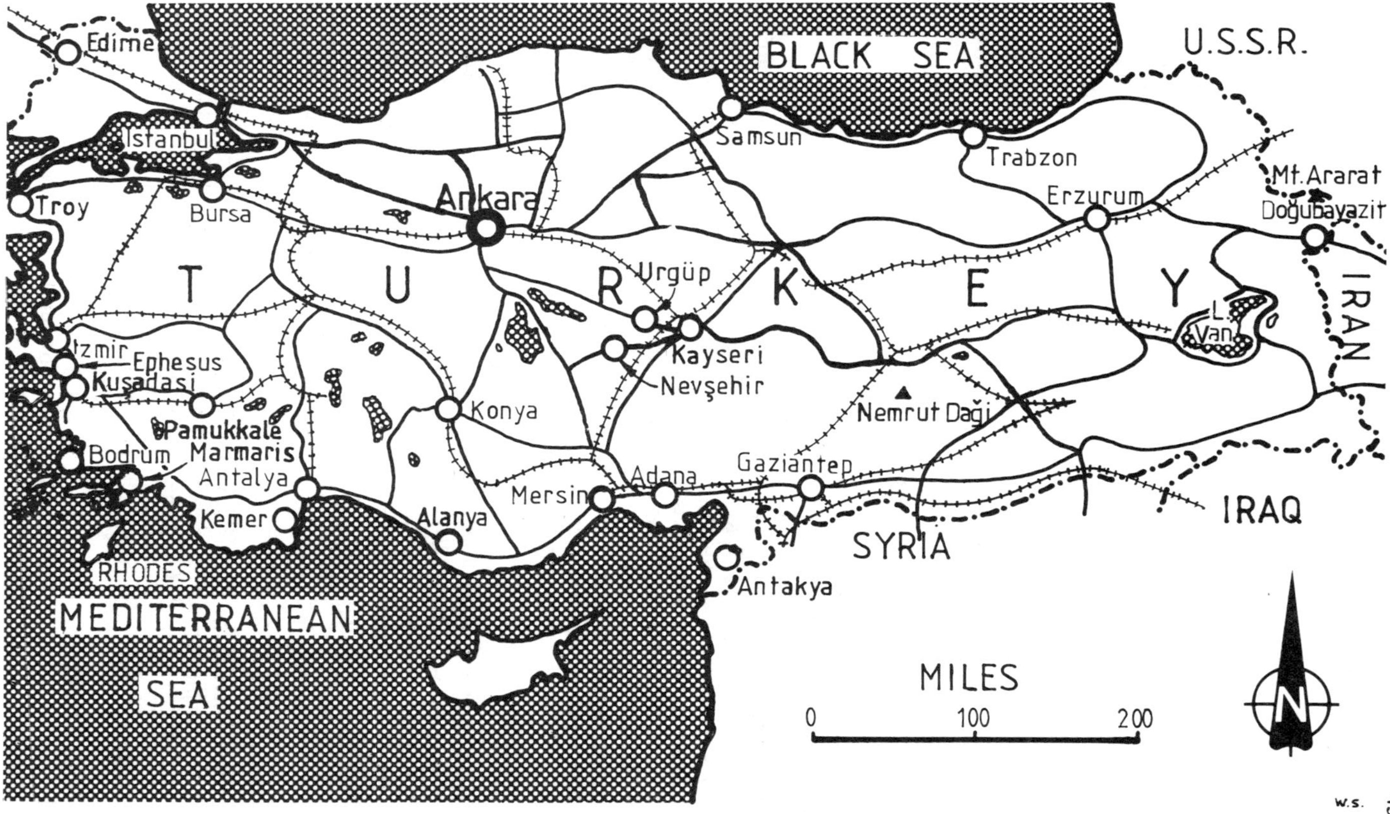

BLACK SEA
U.S.S.R.
IRAN
IRAQ
SYRIA
TURKEY
MEDITERRANEAN
SEA
RHODES
Edirne
Istanbul
Troy
Bursa
Izmir
Kusadasi
Ephesus
Pamukkale
Marmaris
Bodrum
Antalya
Kemer
Alanya
Konya
Ankara
Ürgüp
Nevşehir
Kayseri
Mersin
Adana
Gaziantep
Antakya
Samsun
Trabzon
Erzurum
Nemrut Dağı
L. Van
Mt. Ararat
Doğubayazit
MILES
0
100
200
N
W.S.

Useful Turkish Words

hello	— merhaba	1	— bir
good morning	— günaydin	2	— iki
please	— lütfen	3	— üc
thank you	— teşekkür (ederim)	4	— dört
yes	— evet	5	— bes
no	— hayir, yok	6	— alti
very nice	— çok güzel	7	— yedi
cheers!	— şerefe!	8	— sekiz
yesterday	— dn̈	9	— dokuz
today	— bugn̈	10	— on
tomorrow	— yarin	20	— yirmi
toilet	— tuvalet (pron. 'toilette')	100	— yüz
how much?	— bu kaçadir?	200	— iki yüz
hot	— sicak	1000	— bin
cold	— soguk		

good-bye (said by the person leaving) — allahaismarladik
good-bye (said by the person remaining) — güle güle

Red Tape

Visas

Visas are not required for British, Australian, American, Canadian, Irish or New Zealand passport holders. A valid passport is all that is required for visits of up to three months. If you want to stay longer than 3 months, you must obtain a residence permit which costs TL2250 (which lasts up to 6 months). If you fail to do so before the initial 3 months expires, you will be charged more than triple that sum. An easier alternative to getting a residence permit is to cross over to Greece every 3 months and get a fresh entry stamp in your passport.

Customs

Usually a verbal declaration is enough on entry and luggage is not searched. Valuable items may be registered in your passport to ensure that they are taken out of the country. The duty-free allowance is 400 cigarettes (twice the usual limit), 50 cigars, 200gr tobacco, a generous 5 bottles of spirits (though no more than 3 can be of the same brand) and $1\frac{1}{2}$kg of coffee.

Be very careful about buying old artefacts since export of antiquities is strictly forbidden.

Currency Regulations

There is no limit to the amount of foreign currency that may be taken into or out of Turkey, though there is an export limit of $1,000 worth of Turkish lira. Exchange slips showing conversion of foreign currency should be kept, though it is unlikely you will need them. You may reconvert $100 worth of lira on departure without showing exchange receipts.

Health Certificates

There is no check at Turkish immigration for certificates, so any shots you get are solely for your protection. A cholera vaccination is, as usual, a good idea.

Drugs
There is only one word of advice on the subject of drugs and smuggling in Turkey; DON'T. If you find yourself tempted, just go out and see the harrowing film *Midnight Express*. Sentences of 20 to 30 years for possession are not unknown. (There is no legal distinction between soft and hard drugs.) Even if you are innocent, it will take a long time for your case to be heard, and you will be held in a prison where conditions may not be quite as dreadful as they are in *Midnight Express* but will by no means be luxurious. Another strange quirk of Turkish justice is that the prosecution has the right of appeal against any sentence thought to be too lenient. The death penalty is enforced for certain offences involving large quantities, although this sentence has never been passed on foreigners.

There are a number of British nationals detained in Turkish prisons, all of them held in Izmir. If you seriously want to take them books or food or just visit them, contact the National Council for the Welfare of Prisoners Abroad (01-226 1668) who, after an interview, can supply a letter of introduction to the British Consul in Izmir, who can in turn arrange a visit.

Motoring Documents
National driving licences in English, French or German are now accepted in Turkey, but an International Driving Permit will be required if you wish to drive a vehicle with Turkish registration, e.g. a hired car. You may drive your own vehicle in Turkey for up to three months without a *carnet de passage,* but particulars of the vehicle will be entered in your passport. If your vehicle is severely damaged or completely wrecked while inside Turkey, and you have to abandon it, the customs office *(Gümrük Müdürlügü)*must see or take delivery of it, so that your passport can be suitably endorsed. A similar procedure is necessary if you leave your vehicle in Turkey while visiting a neighbouring country. If your vehicle is stolen, you will have to obtain a special certificate from the Governor of the province *(vali)*. For stays exceeding three months, a "tryptique" must be obtained from the Turkish Touring and Automobile Club (address below).

Third party insurance is obligatory. As in the United States many Turkish drivers are under-insured and it is therefore essential that foreign drivers have full cover. The best solution is to get an international green card from a specialist insurer in Britain (see Introduction). Make sure you specify that you want it endorsed for the Asian as well as the European part of Turkey.

You can buy Turkish third party insurance from the *Dogan Sigorta* office at the frontier or from TTOK (The Turkish Touring and Automobile Club, Halaskärgazi Cad. 364, Şişli, Istanbul; tel: 14 67 090). This costs TL10,000-TL15,000 per month, but is arguably less than adequate if you are involved in an accident. If you are involved in an accident, report it to the nearest police station and get a copy of the prosecutor's report.

Internal Travel Restrictions
Certain areas of Turkey are restricted for visitors, for example the areas which border the USSR, and Kurdish areas where there is unrest, for instance Hakkari in the south-east corner of Turkey. If you do try to approach an off-limits zone, you will probably encounter roadblocks and be turned back.

Mount Ararat, famous as the resting place of Noah's Ark, is strictly out of bounds. Mountaineering parties must apply a year in advance for permission to climb it.

As in Eastern European countries it is forbidden to photograph airfields, railway lines or anything in sensitive border areas. Look for signs "Yasak bolge" or "Yabancilara yasaktir," which indicate restricted areas.

£1 = TL770 TL100 = £0.13
$1 = TL530 TL100 = $0.19

Currency
The unit of currency is the Turkish lira (TL). The lira was once divided into 100 kuruş, but due to the high annual rate of inflation (25%-30%), kuruş are now virtually extinct. The smallest coin is now the TL5 coin.

Coins
5, 10 TL.

Notes
TL10 (green), TL20 (red/brown), TL50 (brown), TL100 (green/light brown), TL500 (blue/olive green), TL1,000 (purple), TL5,000, TL10,000. All notes have a picture of Atatürk on them.

Changing Money
The exchange rate doesn't vary much from bank to bank; even hotels use a rate which almost tallies with the official rate. The Iş Bankasi which has branches throughout the country seems to be generally willing to carry out exchange transactions. (The one at the Sirkeçi Railway Station in Istanbul is open on Saturdays). Many banks, which display the "Kambiyo/Change/Weschel" sign, change only notes, not travellers' cheques, so it might be wise to carry a few notes to prevent the frustration of having to search for another bank. With Barclays/Visa travellers' cheques, you may be asked to show a Visa cheque card. Eurocheque cards can be used at some banks in the major cities to support cheques drawn on British banks with the usual £50 limit.

The black market is a risky proposition, both because it is against the law and because the people in the business are often con artists. One of their favourite tricks is to end the transaction abruptly because they claim to have spotted a policeman, and in the resulting confusion you are left with a wad of worthless notes or some worth far less than the value of what you traded. In any case the profits to be made (reputedly highest in Istanbul) are not very great.

Emergency Cash
A few years ago there was a large demand for Johnny Walker whisky, Marlboro cigarettes and Levi jeans, especially at tourist centres such as Ephesus. However that market disappeared in May 1984 when the government lifted many import restrictions and so foreign goods became more widely available in the shops.

Several outlets in the Sultanahmet area of Istanbul buy second hand garments and possessions of all kinds from foreigners. Or you are always entitled to join the local market — daily near the Yeni Camii in Istanbul — to sell off your excess clothing.

Travellers who arrive at tourist centres and resorts early in the season (March/

April) may find work in carpet and souvenir shops. Merchants are eager to have fluent English speakers on the premises. Also there is a reasonable amount of yacht-related work in Marmaris, Kuşadasi, Bodrum, etc. in the tourist season; just ask around the marina. The wages, however, are not likely to cover more than your meals.

Opening Hours

Banks and most offices are open Monday to Friday from 09.00 (occasionally 08.30) to noon and from 13.30 till 17.00. The same hours apply to shops Monday to Saturday, though many stay open till 19.00. The fact that Friday is the Moslem holy day does not affect commerce. Along the Aegean and Mediterranean coasts during the summer, some shops and banks observe the afternoon siesta and open again for the evening.

Museums are open every day except Mondays. Entrance fees for museums vary from a few lira to TL400 at the Topkapi Palace in Istanbul. Photography charges at museums and archaeological sites are often twice as much as the entrance fee.

Public Holidays

1st January	New Year's Day
23rd April	National Independence Day, and Children's Day
19th May	Youth and Sports Day, and Ataturk's Birthday
30th August	Victory Day (to commemorate the final rout of invading forces 1922)
29th October	Republic Day

There are also two religious festivals each year: Şeker Bayrami, the Sugar Festival, which lasts for three days at the end of Ramadan, the month of daytime fasting. The other one is Kurban Bayrami, the Festival of Sacrifices, lasting four days. For the dates see page 36.

Arrival and Departure

The cheapest way to get to Turkey is to take a coach from London bound for Athens (about £35), alight at Thessaloniki (thereby cutting off nine hours from the three day journey) and change to a local bus bound for the border post of Ipsala/Edirne in Turkey. Coach companies in London advertise straight through fares to Istanbul of £55 one way, £105 return, but check to see if you have to go all the way into Athens first. The Turkish officials now want to see that you are carrying enough money; $75 should be enough. There is now a Greek departure tax of about £2.50.

A better route for hitch-hikers than through Northern Greece is along the E-5 from Belgrade, Nis and Sofya to Edirne and Istanbul. You will have to get a transit visa for Bulgaria on this route, preferably before you set off, since the border officials charge four times as much as the consulates. If hitching out of Istanbul towards Europe, take bus 84 from Sultanahmet to Topkapi and walk to the E5.

Non-hitchers will want to compare bus prices from Istanbul to European cities; most offices are in Sultanahmet or in Laleli (the area just west of Sultanahmet). Because of all the Turkish *gastarbeiter* in Germany, there are many services to Munich. The most upmarket and best known coach company is Bosfar Turizm (Mete Caddesi, Taksim, Istanbul; tel: 143 25 25). Unfortunately they only go as far as Paris.

The bus service between Turkey and Iran is discussed in the Iran chapter. You can buy a bus ticket for Tehran in Erzurum (at the Ornek Hotel) as well as in Istanbul, provided there are spare seats. It is rumoured that it is possible to get permission from Ankara to cross the border into Soviet Armenia, though you would have to obtain a visa from the USSR first and prepare a detailed itinerary.

The train departs both from Athens and Istanbul in the evening and arrives 33 hours later. Most claim that it is cheaper and faster to go by road.

You can also of course fly directly from London to Istanbul. Bucket shop fares are in the region of £100 single, £200 return. Turkish Airlines (THY) is not one of the world's most jolly airlines. They do offer a seemingly generous discount to students of 60%, however this is only on the scheduled return fare of £620. The specialist in arranging Turkish flights in London is Suncrest (01-749 9933). To get from Yesilkoy Airport to downtown Istanbul, take bus 86 to Aksaray.

Finally you might want to arrive by sea. Libra Maritime sails between Piraeus and Izmir during the summer (ring David Walker Travel in Oxford for more details: 0865 728136), and Turkish Maritime Lines operate in the summer to Italy and Syria (ring 01-480 5621 for further information). There is now more traffic between the Greek islands and Turkey's Aegean coast than there was four or five years ago. There are frequent summer crossings between Rhodes and Marmaris, Kos and Bodrum, Chios and Çeşme, Samos and Kuşadasi and Lesbos and Ayvaçik. The first two operate all year round; the others cease or curtail operations in the winter. Prices range from $10 (Bodrum to Kos, which is 50% cheaper than the same trip in the opposite direction) to $25 Kuşadasi—Samos. You can always try to get a crewing job or a straight lift on a private yacht instead of paying for the ferry.

Motoring

There are over 15,000 miles of fairly good asphalt roads in Turkey. There are three major highways: the E5 Istanbul/Ankara to Syria and Jordan, the E24 to Iraq and the E23 to Iran. The government plans to complete a 4-lane motorway from Edirne to Iskenderun by 1993, and all roads are to be paved. In winter certain passes, such as the Tahir Pass (between Erzurum and Ağri) and the Kopdaği Pass (between Trabzon and Aşkale) are closed due to heavy snowfalls. Turkish road signs conform to international standards and driving is on the right. The maximum speed is 90km per hour. Free road maps are available from National Tourist Offices, and in fact their maps are not bad. (Roger Lascelles also publishes a map of Turkey for £3.95).

Cautious driving is essential to avoid an accident. Public transport tends to stop suddenly and without warning, and the general standard of driving is not high. Except for the Istanbul/Ankara highway, the roads tend to be fairly empty, which leads to a relaxation of motorists' guard. Follow the local example of using your horn liberally, whenever you're in the vicinity of pedestrians and cyclists. Night driving is especially dangerous since not all local vehicles are illuminated. Involvement in an accident often leads to imprisonment until a hearing can be scheduled.

There are many garages in the towns, usually grouped together in one street. There are agents for most foreign makes of car in Ankara, Istanbul and Izmir;

Renault is the most easily found. The official motoring organization is the Turkish Touring and Automobile Club, Halaskãrgazi Cad. 364, Sisli, Istanbul which has an information office at the Topkapi Gate. There are also offices in Ankara, Izmir, several other cities and at all frontiers.

There are road rescue services stationed at strategic intervals on the Istanbul-Ankara road. The emergency numbers for this service are: 146 70 90 in Istanbul or 353 35 11 and 31 76 49 in Ankara.

Petrol is sold in litres and costs about TL235 per litre, or TL1075 (£1.40) per gallon. There are sometimes shortages in Eastern Turkey, so keep a spare supply in the boot. Diesel tends to be considerably cheaper.

Car Hire

Hertz has an office on Cumhuriyet Caddesi, 295 Harbiye, Istanbul (tel: 141 20 36) as well as at Yesilkoy Airport. Avis's head office is at Tramvay Caddesi 72, Istanbul (tel: 163 65 42). Apart from Istanbul, the other cities which have car hire facilities are Ankara, Izmir, Antalya, Adana, Alanya, Bodrum, Kuşadasi, Marmaris, Mersin and Samsun. One week's rental of a small car with unlimited mileage will be about $260. Considering how reliable, extensive and cheap public transport is, hiring a car is only for the affluent.

Bus

The bus network of Turkey is very highly developed with fast and frequent services. Long distance travelling is cheaper than a series of short hops, so that a journey of 80 miles will cost about TL700 whereas a journey 7 times as long will only cost 4-5 times as much. There are many private bus companies in competition with one another, which will become abundantly obvious if you visit the Istanbul bus station at the Topkapi Gate. Prices vary and it is worth comparing them. By law the companies should post the prices in their offices. When looking for the bus station, ask directions to the *otogar* or *garaji,* though *otobüs* will convey your meaning. If you buy a ticket in advance (which is possible though usually not necessary) make sure that you get on a bus belonging to the company who issued the ticket. For more comfort and slightly higher prices look for Varan Bus Co. who offer air-conditioned and video entertainment on some routes. But even without any frills, bus travel is convenient and pleasant. Many ordinary buses carry supplies of iced water and splash around a refreshing eau de cologne every so often. There are frequent rest and refreshment stops, so even long journeys are not too gruelling.

Dolmuş

A dolmuş is a minibus or transit van which operates as a collective taxi and connects even remote villages with the larger centres. They can always be distinguished by the belt of yellow paint below the windows. Fares run about TL5-6 per mile, often little more than buses. Dolmuşes which operate in cities wait until they are full before setting off; dolmuşes in rural areas have fixed schedules. Often the country services are alarmingly oversubscribed, though the local people usually defer politely to foreigners and leave the seats vacant. If you are early enough, claim the back corner, as far from the crush and jostling as possible.

Train

Travelling second class on the trains is even cheaper than buses: on longer journeys just over half the price. Both first and second class seats are bookable in advance. "Ekspres" trains can be slower than their name indicates, though this might be to your advantage on an overnight journey. Couchettes are perfectly comfortable; for a small surcharge of TL10-TL15 you can have a pillow and sheets, though no blankets. All trains have a dining car ("Lokanta") where the food is unexciting but the old-fashioned decor creates an interesting atmosphere. The main disadvantage of the trains is that they are more likely than buses to be late. There are 10% student discounts on trains and a 20% discount on return tickets.

There are two railway stations in Istanbul. The European trains depart from Sirkeçi in the old city (tel: 527 00 50/1); trains to the rest of Turkey and on to Asia depart from Haydarpaşa (tel: 336 04 75). You must cross the Bosphorus to get to Haydarpaşa which is on the Asian side; ferries leave regularly from the far side of the Galata Bridge and the journey costs TL50. If you arrive at Haydarpaşa station by train, follow the throng to the dock waiting area and pass through the gate marked "Köprü" meaning Galata Bridge.

Boat

Turkish Maritime Lines offer a very affordable alternative to land travel. Boats sail from Istanbul down along the Mediterranean coast, via Izmir and Antalya to Mersin near the Syrian border (first class fare TL23,000), and also along the Black Sea coast to Trabzon (TL8,000). The booking office in Istanbul is clearly labelled "Denizcilik Bankasi T.A.O." and is located just east of the Galata Bridge on the Galata side. Student discounts of 50% are available. Services are reduced in the winter months.

For service between the Greek islands and Turkey, see the section on Arrival and Departure. The agent in Bodrum is Duru Yachting (tel: 61 41 18 68) and in Marmaris, Yeşil Marmaris, Kordon Caddesi (tel: 61 21 10 33). There are many yacht charter companies based in Marmaris and Kuşadasi.

Hitch-hiking

The prospects for the hitch-hiker in Turkey are very good. Because of the hospitable nature of the people and because young hitching travellers are a relative novelty, there is no trouble in getting lifts. All manner of vehicles, including carts and tractors, are likely to stop, so this is not guaranteed to be the most rapid means of transport. It is highly recommended for travelling between the archaeological sites between Kuşadasi and Bodrum, and in the Göreme Valley.

Especially in the east of the country, you may be asked to share costs with the driver. Many hitch-hikers have recommended "Londra Camping", a truck stop on the outskirts of Istanbul for getting long distance lifts in both directions. It is sometimes possible to chat up the drivers and arrange a lift. In other towns, it may be better to catch a dolmuş a mile or so out of town to avoid heavy local traffic and curious passers-by surrounding you thereby making it impossible for potential lifts to see you.

City Transport

There is a slightly complicated bus system in Istanbul. Along with the red municipally operated buses (always marked I.E.T.T.) there are privately run buses, usually blue. All journeys cost TL10 which is true of municipal bus fares in other cities in Turkey as well. Tickets for municipal buses in Istanbul are not sold on the bus but at various kiosks including one just outside the Covered

Bazaar. If you haven't managed to obtain a ticket in advance, it is always worth asking other people in the queue or even on the bus to sell you a ticket from their stock. Tickets may be bought from a conductor on the private buses. To get from Sultanahmet across the Golden Horn to Taksim, take buses numbered L2, L2A, G2, OK 2 or T4. To get from Yesilkoy Airport to Aksaray take bus 96, from the Domestic Terminal.

Taxis are numerous in all towns and are marked with a black and white or yellow checked markings. Meters are being introduced in Istanbul as they have been in Ankara, but otherwise you should settle on a fare before getting in.

City dolmuşes are not always easy to distinguish from taxis so be careful not to confuse them. They follow a prescribed route but will pick you up and set you down at any point on the route; you pay for the distance travelled. The main dolmuş ranks in Istanbul are at Eminönü Square, Sirkeçi, Taksim Square and Usküdar. In other towns, dolmuşes are usually parked in the vicinity of the bus station.

Traffic congestion may be eased by the building of a second bridge over the Bosphorus.

Trekking

There is ample opportunity for hiking in the mountains (*dağlari*) of Turkey. The best areas for amateurs are Uludağ (which is also an important ski resort, south of the Marmara Sea), Hasandağ in Cappadocia, and Munzur Dağlari (south of Trabzon). Experienced mountaineers might consider the Aladağlar area north of Adana which reaches about 13,000ft in altitude.

A group of serious climbers should first apply to the nearest Turkish Embassy or Consulate for permission to organize an expedition; it in turn seeks permission from the Department of Cultural Affairs. The Turkish Mountaineering Club (Dağcılık Federasyonu, B.T.G.M.) may be contacted at Ulus Işhani, A-Blok, Ulus-Ankara; tel: 10 85 66, ext. 356.

Post

Post offices are recognizable by their yellow P.T.T. signs, meaning Post, Telegraph and Telephone. The major ones are open 08.00 - midnight, Monday to Saturday. A poste restante service is available from the central post office in all towns of a reasonable size. You may be asked for your passport when collecting mail, but this is usually just so there will be no doubt as to the spelling of your name. There may be a small fee for each piece of mail collected. Poste restante letters should be sent to you at the Merkez Postanesi (i.e. Central Post Office). The central post offices in the three major cities are at the following addresses:

Istanbul: Erminönü.

Ankara: 59 Atatürk Bulvari.

Izmir: Atatürk Caddesi (near the Monument to Atatürk).

Air mail letters should be marked "Uçak Ile," in the absence of an air mail sticker. When enquiring about the up-to-date postal charges, do not be surprised to find an utter lack of consensus. Take the average and stick to it!

Telephone

Public telephones take a TL20 or TL50 token called a jeton, available from any post office and some newspaper kiosks. The jeton is dropped into the machine after you have satisfied yourself that the telephone is in working order and before dialling. The cost of a long distance call to Britain is TL450 per minute if operator-controlled and TL375 if dialled direct. There may be a wait of several hours, even if you are dialling from a big city. Reverse charge calls are called *odemeli*. You can make direct dial calls between most cities within Turkey: dial 9, then the city code and then the number. Some city codes are: Istanbul 1, Ankara 41, Kuşadasi 6361, Erzurum 011. It can sometimes be difficult to get a line. If it is urgent you can book a "flash call" or *yildirim*. Prime Minister Ozal has promised telephone connections to most villages by 1988, as well as electricity by the end of 1987.

Newspapers

The *Daily News,* published in Ankara, is the only English language daily. It is sold at a few outlets in most cities and in the tourist areas of Istanbul (Sultanahmet and Istiklal Caddesi). It costs about a fifth of the price of a 2-day-old *International Herald Tribune* and provides some interesting insights into Turkish politics.

Broadcasting

Although much of the television programming is imported from America, all of it is dubbed into Turkish.

There is a meterological bulletin in English broadcast daily on the short wave band (25 m.) from 07.30-08.00 and at 10.00, 12.00, 14.00 and 19.00. It may be easier to catch the television weather report at 21.00 with charts covering the whole country which are easily understood.

The BBC World Service can be picked up in Turkey at the following times and on the following wavelengths in MHz:

05.30-07.30 (GMT)	11.76, 9.58, 12.095, 9.41, 6.18 or 6.05
07.30-17.45 (GMT)	21.71, 17.79, 15.07 or 12.095
17.00-23.15 (GMT)	9.41, 7.325 or 6.18

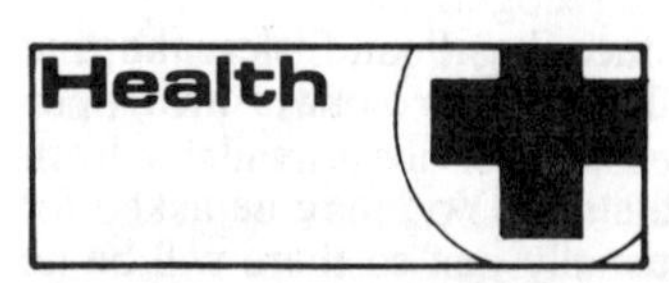

Despite claims made in the Turkish tourist literature, there is still a risk of malaria especially in the south and south-east of the country. The World Health Organization reports that potential risk exists from March to the end of November in the provinces of Adana, Hatai, Icel, Hakkari and Siirt. There is no chloroquine resistance as yet.

Treatment is free or cheap in government-run hospitals, though there are also many private foreign hospitals and IAMAT recommended clinics, where medical costs will be at least £15 a day.

Istanbul

Admiral Bristol Hastanesi (American), Güzelbahçe Sokak, Nişantaşi. Tel: 148 60 30.

Fransiz Pastör Hastanesi (French), Taşkişla Cad. 3, (behind Divan Hotel), Taksim. Tel: 148 18 32 or 148 47 56.

German Hospital, Siraselviler Cad., Taksim. Tel: 143 55 00.

Ankara
IAMAT Center, Necatibey Cad. 22/5. Tel: 29 57 64.
American Hospital, Güniz Sok. 30. Tel: 27 14 84.

Izmir
Franciz Hastanesi (French Hospital), Ali Cetinkaye Bulvari. Tel: 3 39 34.

Adana
IAMAT Center, Abidinpaşa Cad., Kurttepeli, Apt. Kat. 1. Tel: 1 75 99.

Gaziantep
American Hospital. Tel: 10 69/34 20.

Vaccinations are available free from the Vaccination Centre, Sahil Sağlik Merkezi, Karaköy, Istanbul (just across the Galata Bridge). Tel: 45 40 27.

Water

Only in major cities is the water chlorinated, thereby reducing the risk of disease. Purification tablets should be used on tap water in the provinces, or else drink the very cheap bottled water (*su*). Restaurants sometimes use bottles instead of pitchers for tap water, so make sure your bottle of water has a foil cap.

There is a great tradition among Turkish men of eating out, both for lunch and dinner, so there is never a shortage of eating places. The most popular establishments are *kebapçis* and *köftecis* where the standard meal consists of soup followed by kebab and salad and eaten with a great deal of white bread. All of this costs about TL300. There are of course fancier places which may feature fish, tripe soup or even whole sheep's heads. Much of Turkish cuisine overlaps with Greek, as does the habit of inviting the customer into the kitchen to choose his dishes by pointing.

Below is a basic vocabulary for eating out:

balık — fish (varies from place to place; basic kind is çinakop, a variety of seabass; also look for *kiliç* or swordfish)
piliç — chicken
et — meat (usually lamb, served stewed with vegetables)
köfte — spiced ground meat rissoles
arnavut cigeri — spiced lamb's liver fried with onions
işkembe çorbasi — mutton tripe soup with garlic and lemon (eaten by the locals to cure hangovers)
dolma — stuffed vegetables (vine leaves, peppers, tomatoes, etc.)
imam bayıldı — cold aubergines stuffed in olive oil (means "the priest swooned")
pilaf — rice
zeytınyağli — cold vegetables in olive oil
cacık — cucumber in yoghurt with garlic and olive oil
börek — flaky pastry filled with cheese or spinach
ekmek — bread
sütlaç — cold rice pudding
baklava — filo pastry with nuts and syrup

süt — hot, sweet milk
şeker — sugar
tuz — salt
ayran — salty yoghurt drink like buttermilk
bira — beer (Danish lager type)
şarap — wine (sek-dry; tatlı-sweet)
rakı — aniseed liqueur like ouzo, the national drink, drunk with meals, (*yeni* means weak, *kulüp* means medium and *altinbas* means strong).

Tea *(çay)* is the universal drink. It is grown in abundance on the shores of the Black Sea, is very cheap, and is drunk in small tulip-shaped glasses with two sugars and no milk. Coffee is again available but is very expensive.

The wines are good (and cheap). Try Doluça, Kavaklidere or Buzbağ.

The places discussed here are roughly on a route heading south from Istanbul, up to Ankara and then east.

ISTANBUL

Istanbul has a population of about 4.8 million and is the commercial and tourist capital of Turkey, even though the government transferred to Ankara in 1923. There is continuous modernization, so you must wander along some of the steep back streets to find the traditional wooden houses with overhanging porticoes. There are over six hundred mosques in Istanbul — many built by the famous architect Sinan in the 16th century — with beautiful decorations, interesting domes and peaceful courtyards. When visiting an active mosque, women must remember to cover their heads, and everyone must remove their shoes, behave modestly and try to avoid the five daily prayer times.

After a round of sightseeing, visit a *hamam* or Turkish bath (especially if your hotel doesn't feature hot water). A famous one, much visited by tourists, is the Cağaloğlu Hamam on Yerebatan Caddesi, near Sultanahmet Square. Even better is the one located on Gedikpaşa Caddesi, halfway between Sultanahmet and Aksaray. Self-service washing will cost TL200-300 with tip, but you might want to pay an extra TL100 for the experience of being professionally scrubbed (called *kese*).

What to See

The Blue Mosque — the Sultanahmet Camii is probably the most famous mosque in Istanbul and is distinguished by its six minarets. It took seven years to build, being completed in 1616. The popular name of the mosque comes from the blue glazed tiles that cover the inside walls.

Ayasofya — built in the 6th century as the greatest cathedral in the Byzantine Empire and used as a model by subsequent architects. Later became a mosque, then in 1935 a museum. Entrance fee TL200, closed Mondays.

Topkapi Sarayi — great palace of the Ottoman sultans built in the 15th century and continually added to until the 19th century. Now houses an outstanding collection of Oriental porcelain, manuscripts, mosaics, costumes and jewellery. Interesting to see the harem, though for an extra charge. Entrance fee TL400, closed Tuesdays.

Archaeological Museum, Museum of the Ancient Orient and *Ceramic Museum* — surrounding a courtyard in Gülhane Park. Contain respectively: Greek and Roman tombs and sculpture; Syrian, Mesopotamian and Egyptian relics; Iznik and Seljuk tiles displayed in a charming 15th century pavilion. Entrance fee (combined) TL100, closed Mondays.

Museum of Turkish and Islamic Art — in the old kitchen of the Suleymaniye Mosque. Houses a collection of carpets, prayer rugs, Persian miniatures and manuscripts including the Sultans' proclamations.

Kariye Camii — an ancient church turned mosque turned museum, out by the land walls in Edirnekapi (take buses 37, 38, 39 or 86 from Sultanahmet). Contains Byzantine frescoes and mosaics in an outstanding state of preservation. Entrance fee TL100, closed Tuesdays.

Kapali Çarşi (Covered Bazaar) — a bewildering collection of 5,000 shops, located between Sultanahmet and Aksaray. Predictably sophisticated with no real bargains.

Misir Çarşisi (Spice Bazaar) — near the Yeni Camii. A more genuine and colourful market, which sells far more than just spices.

Accommodation

The cheapest hotels are in the Sultanahmet area near many of the sights worth seeing, as well as the budget travel agencies.

Hotel Güngör — 4 Divan Yolu Cad., next door to Lale's Pudding Shop. Tel: 526 23 19. TL800 for dormitory bed, TL2,000 double; 25% discounts in off-season (November to March). Helpful manager named Manuel. Recommended.

Sultan Tourist Hotel — Yerebatan Cad. behind Pudding Shop. Dorm beds, singles and doubles. Cheap and homely.

Yucelt y Hostel — across from Aya Sofya. Cheap but spoiled by its popularity.

Also try the Yeni Tourist Pensyon (near the Blue Mosque).

If you don't want to dine in the passé hippy hang-outs of Sultanahmet (the Pudding Shop, Yener's, etc.) then try the Vitamin Restaurant on Divan Yolu Cad. Friendly service and varied menu.

Useful Addresses

Tourist Information (Danişma) — Sultanahmet Square, Grand Bazaar, both railway stations and Karaköy docks next to the Turkish Maritime Lines office. Sultanahmet phone number: 527 21 88.

British Consul — Meşrutiyet Cad. 34, Tepebaşi. Tel: 144 75 40.

British Council Library — Kat 3, Ege Han, 22/24 Cumhuriyet Cad., Elmadag. Tel: 146 71 25.

American Consul — Meşrutiyet Cad. 106, Tepebaşi. Tel: 143 62 00.

Iranian Consul — Türkocagi Cad. 2, Cagaloglu. Tel: 28 50 53.

American Express (called Turk Ekspres!) — Cumhuriyet Cad. 91, Kat 6, Elmadag. Tel: 141 02 74.

Thomas Cook — Rihtim Caddesi, 101 Nesli Han. Tel: 144 40 76.

THY (Turkish Airlines) — Meşrutiyet Cad. 30, Sişhane Terminal. Tel: 144 02 96.

Gençtur Youth Tourism and Travel — Yerebatan Cad. 15/3, Sultanahmet. Tel: 528 07 34.

Tourist Police — corner of Alemdar Cad. and Yerebatan Cad., Sultanahmet. Tel: 528 53 69.

TRUVA (Troy)

The discovery of the Trojan city in the 19th century by the German self-taught archaeologist Heinrich Schliemann who used Homer's epics to guide him has been popularized by Michael Wood's telvision series *In Search of Troy*. The city once dominated the narrow entrance of the Dardanelles and was used as the site for nine successive settlements, the earliest about 3,500 years ago and the last in 400 A.D.

To reach Troy, take a bus south from Çanakkale or north from Izmir and get off at the Truva turn-off called Gökçali. It is a pleasant 3 mile walk to the site, though you are quite likely to be offered a lift in the summer. There are no hotels in Truva, so you will probably stay in nearby Çanakkale across the straits from Gallipoli.

BEHRAMKALE (Assos)

About 30 miles south of Troy is the magnificent site of Assos. In the 4th century B.C. it was an important city in the Greek world where Aristotle came to teach, and later a Byzantine and then Ottoman town. The clifftop setting overlooking the Greek island of Lesbos makes up for the ruined condition of the remains.

To reach it take the coastal bus to Ayvaçik and then by dolmuş in the afternoon to Behramkale. There are more tourist amenities than there used to be, but it is still relatively unspoiled. If you eat at Mustafa's ask to see his scrapbook of visitors' comments.

IZMIR

A big modern sprawling city, the third largest in the country. It has been so often destroyed by fires, earthquakes and wars that its history as Smyrna is no longer visible. Homer is reputed to have come from Smyrna (among other places).

It is now an important NATO base, full of Americans, so if you derive pleasure from shopping at "Foodland" you might enjoy Izmir. Try the large open bazaar for a more indigenous shopping venue, at Konak Square. Otherwise Izmir is useful only as a base for visiting the archaeological sites and beaches further south.

Accommodation

Pension Fa — 1375 Sokak No. 24/2. Often full.
Otel Babadan — 50 Gazi Osman Paşa Bulvari, Çankaya. Much more expensive (£8+ for bed and breakfast) but with lots of facilities.

Useful Addresses

Tourism Information Office — Atatürk Cad. 418, Alsancak. Tel: 22 02 07. Also an office at Gazi Osman Paşa Bulvari No. I/C. Tel: 14 21 47.
British Consul — Mahmut Esat Cad. 49. Tel: 21 17 95.
U.S. Consul — 386 Atatürk Caddesi. Tel: 13 21 35.
American Express — Egetur Travel Agency, Nato Arkasi, Talatpaşa Bulvari 2B. Tel: 521 79 21.
Thomas Cook — Key Tours Turizm Ltd., 212/2 Atatürk Caddesi. Tel: 21 78 40.

SELÇUK (Ephesus)

Apart from the splendid ruins at Efes 2 miles away, Selçuk is a charming town with a Byzantine citadel, a 14th century mosque, an interesting little museum with mosaics and statuary and a lively Saturday market. Five miles from the town is a chapel built on the spot where the Virgin Mary is said to have died. The setting and view are both very pleasant.

The site at Ephesus dates from the 13th century B.C. and was settled by Greeks, Romans, Byzantines and Ottomans. There is a Hellenistic amphitheatre capable of holding 24,000 people, a magnificently restored library, temples and houses. From the southern gate you can walk to a spooky necropolis (burial place) which includes the Cave of the Seven Sleepers, 7 Christian youths who were walled up by persecuting Romans in the 3rd century and who awakened 200 years later to discuss resurrection with their fellow Christians. Entrance fee to Ephesus TL200.

Accommodation

Pension Akbulut and Pension Mengi — both on Spor Sahasi Ikinci Sk.4, just off the main road (E24) two streets south of the Kuşadasi Road. Very clean with hot showers, TL1600 double. Breakfast TL300.

BODRUM (Halicarnassus)

Birth-place of Herodotus (father of history) in 484 B.C. The town was much fought over by Alexander the Great, the Romans, the Byzantines, the Seljuks and the knights of St. John of Rhodes. The Knights landed here in 1402 and built the fortress which now houses a tremendous collection of objects found on the sea bed. Bodrum is now a booming holiday resort and is a port of call for the Turkish Maritime Lines' cruise down the Aegean coast.

Accommodation

Nereid Pansiyon — Cumhuriyet Caddesi. A short walk from the bus station. Usually full. If so try others on this road, e.g. *Gozcen Pansiyon* at number 13.

PAMUKKALE

This is one of the most famous spas in Turkey. Remarkable deposits of calcium give the cliff the appearance of a frozen white waterfall. The warm health-giving mineral waters are piped into several hotel swimming pools, including the Government hotel, most of which are open to non-residents for about TL200 per hour.

Pamukkale was also an important city in Hellenistic times and there are some existing remains. Ancient columns and tablets litter the bottom of the pool at the Turizm Motel.

Accommodation

The accommodation at Pamukkale itself is more expensive than the hotels in Denizli, a large city 13 miles away. In Pamukkale, pensions at the bottom of the cliff are resonably priced, such as the Konak Sadez and Ali's. In Denizli, try the Otel Kismet near the railway station for TL2000 double.

THE TURQUOISE COAST

The stretch of 500 miles of Mediterranean coast facing due south is known as the Turquoise Coast or the Turkish Riviera. With the recent completion of the coastal road from Marmaris to Antakya near the Syrian border, visitors no longer have to depend as much on the twice-weekly service of Turkish Maritime

Lines. The new ease of access also means that this coast is acquiring more and more tourist developments. The combination of interesting remains of the ancient world, associations with Alexander the Great, St. Paul and Antony and Cleopatra, together with warm clear seas, cannot fail to attract increasing numbers of visitors.

Antalya is the principal resort of the area and has Roman and Byzantine ruins as well as an excellent archaeological museum and old wooden houses. The city (population 170,000) is too large to stay in just for its beaches, though there are many pleasant pensions off the seafront (try the Hassan, or others near the Stadium). Surrounding villages such as Kemer and Side have magnificent beaches (though some are stony), but also discos and souvenir shops. There are many campsites along this coast, and it is easy to find empty beaches. Ninety miles further east of Antalya, Alanya is distinguished by its Seljuk fortress set high above the town.

Useful Addresses

Tourist Information Antalya — Cumhuriyet Cad. 91. Tel: 11747.
Tourist Information Alanya — Iskele Cad. 56/6. Tel: 1240.
Turkish Touring and Automobile Club — Yetkili Acenta, Hitit Turizm, Mersin. Tel: 16 33.
American Express — Pamfilya Travel Agency, 30 Agustos Cad. 57B & C, Antalya. Tel: 11698.

ANKARA

Although there has been a settlement on the present site since the Bronze Age it wasn't until Atatürk made Ankara the capital of the new Republic in 1932 that it became important. There is now a population of about three million, with government offices and many firms providing work. The town is surrounded by a green belt and, unlike in Istanbul, the roads were built for cars.

What to See

Museum of Anatolian Civilizations — outstanding collection of Neolithic and Hittite remains, housed in a former covered bazaar at the base of the Citadel. Largest collection in the world of Hittite arts and crafts, dating back to 6000 B.C. Well presented. Closed Mondays.

The Citadel (Hisar) — inside the walls, built in the 7th and 9th centuries, is a warren of narrow lanes which resemble an Ottoman town more than the bustling capital outside the walls.

Ethnographic Museum — houses a collection of Turkish crafts including musical instruments, weapons, tools, household objects and costumes. Located on Talâpaşa Bulvari.

Atatürk's House and Museum — on Çankaya Hill. Full of Atatürk relics. Open Sunday afternoons only.

Accommodation

The best area is north from Ulus Square on Çankiri Caddesi or on side streets such as Sanayi Caddesi. Look for the As Oteli, the Otel Devran, the Bulduk, the Akman and the Taç. More luxurious accommodation can be found in the Yenişehir area (meaning "new town"); try the Gül Palas, 15 Bayindir Sokak or the Yenişehir Sağlik Koleji at Tuna Caddesi 41.

Useful Addresses

British Embassy — 46A Sehit Ersan Caddesi, Çankaya. Tel: 27 43 10.
British Council Library — 50/52 Güniz Sokak, Kavaklidere. Tel: 28 31 65.
American Embassy — 110 Atatürk Bulvari. Tel: 26 54 70.
Tourist Information — 33 Gazi Mustafa Kemal Bulvari, Demirtepe. Tel: 29 09 65.
American Express — Turk Ekspres, Sehit Adem Yavuz Sokak 14/5, Kizilay. Tel: 25 32 82.
SILA (Youth & Student Travel Center) — Emek Işhani (Gökdelen), Kat. 11 No. 1109. Tel: 41-181326. Arranges voluntary workcamps, though if the 1986 summer venue (i.e. Kuşadasi) is typical, not necessarily in the most underprivileged locations.

CAPPADOCIA

Cappadocia refers to the ancient province of the Roman Empire stretching east and south of Ankara, whose capital was Caesarea (now Kayseri) and whose principal places of interest nowadays are the subterranean dwelling places of the early Christians at Urgüp and the nearby Byzantine rock chapels decorated with frescoes in Göreme. The landscape in this part of Anatolia is as striking as the Badlands of South Dakota, but it is even more bizarre because these strangely eroded rock cones have been inhabited for centuries, first by Byzantine hermits and other Christians escaping persecution, and now by modern Turks who erect TV aerials on their rock towers. Some of these cave-like dwellings have had to be abandoned after being pronounced unsafe, but this does not mean that visitors are not allowed to explore the underground structures and clamber over the sandstone outcroppings. A torch is essential whereas joining a tour (which the local guides will urge you to do) is not. It is easy to hitch and possible to take dolmuşes between Urgüp and Zelve or Nevşehir and the 8-storey underground city of Kaymakli.

Accommodation

Pensions are concentrated in Nevşehir, capital of the province, and in Urgüp. Conditions are generally austere but prices are usually not much more than £1. The tourist offices in the area are at Lale Cad. 22, Nevşehir (tel: 1137) and at Kayseri Cad. 37, Urgüp (tel: 159).

EASTERN TURKEY

The further east you go the wilder and less European Turkey becomes. The climate and landscape are much harsher than in the west, and the people are correspondingly tough and unsophisticated. For a gripping introduction to some of the primitive customs still practised, see Güney's film *Yol*.

The largest town in Eastern Anatolia is Erzurum, once the eastern bastion of the Byzantine Empire, now a dreary place with two buildings worth viewing: the Museum and the Ulu Cami, an unadorned mosque built in the 12th century.

Not many people journey to Doğubayazit in the extreme east unless they plan to go to Iran, but it is a town with character in a magnificent setting. The twin peaks of Mount Ararat can be seen clearly from Doğubayazit. This is a strongly Kurdish part of Turkey, so avoid making inflammatory statements.

About 200 miles southwest of Doğubayazit is the beautiful inland salt lake, Lake Van, which you can cross by ferry at very low cost. This area was traditionally shared by nomadic Kurds and settled Armenians. There are some ancient Urartu (the same derivation as Ararat) remains throughout the area as well as Armenian buildings, although the Armenian population was expelled early in this century. A tiny island in the south of the lake called Ahkdamar is the setting for the beautiful 10th century Armenian Church of the Holy Cross, richly ornamented with carved angels, saints and biblical characters.

Another 350 miles west is the remarkable mountain of Nemrut Daği (over 7,000 ft) on which are perched colossal statues of the king who commissioned them (King Antiochus I) in the first century B.C. and of his favourite gods. There are also ruined temples, all of which were discovered just a century ago.

Bibliography

Noel Barber, *Lords of the Golden Horn* (Macmillan, 1973).
Tom Brosnahan, *Turkey: A Travel Survival Kit* (Lonely Planet, 1985).
Rose Macaulay, *The Towers of Trebizond* (1956, Fontana reprint 1984).
Jeremy Round, *Turkey* (Lascelles, 1986).

Iran

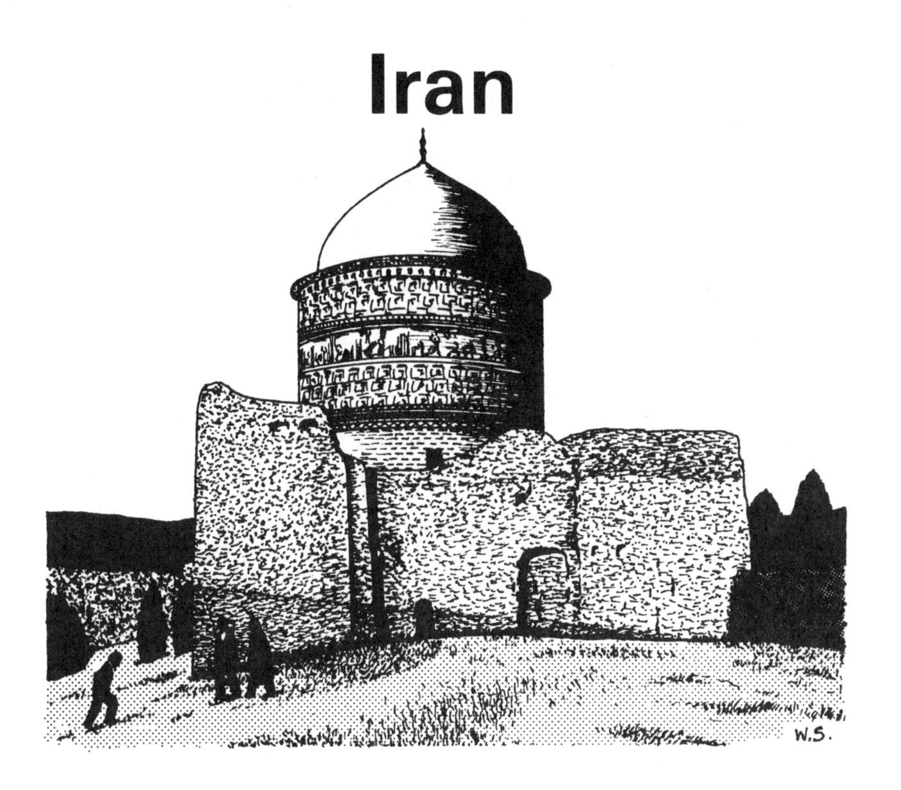

Capital: Tehran **Government:** Islamic Republic

The Islamic Republic of Iran has had an unfavourable press in the past few years, and many people assume that it is off-limits to travellers. But recently a minority have begun to realize that Iran is not difficult to enter nor are its residents hostile to visitors from the West. There are of course hazards and difficulties, but they need not intimidate the adventurous.

The desert-like interior plateau was once inhabited by nomads though most have now settled. The majority of the population lives in the prosperous western provinces or on the fertile shores of the Caspian Sea. The oil boom produced vast wealth for the country, although under the Shah much of it went towards arms deals and a too-rapid westernization of the urban areas. Since the Shah fled in January 1979, an enthusiasm for Islamic reform has prevailed. Religious fanatacism is not confined to the Ayatollah and his revolutionary guard; it is ubiquitous.

But anti-western feelings do not run as high as might have been expected. The ancient Persian habits of hospitality to strangers cannot be destroyed overnight. Because Iran has isolated itself so completely from the international community, many citizens are curious about what is going on abroad and are therefore eager to meet travellers. In some ways, the Revolution has made travelling easier, for example women are no longer bothered on the street by lascivious youths, who would be severely punished for such behaviour.

Much is made of the ruthlessly enforced dress code as symbolic of the repressiveness of the regime. The law is most resented by rich and sophisticated Tehran women — the ones who didn't flee Iran after the overthrow of the Shah — who do not want to be swallowed up in a *chador,* the tent-like garment approved by the authorities. There have been counter-demonstrations (which itself demonstrates that the present government is not completely tyrannical) but most Iranians have now adjusted to the new rules. Conflicts are less sharp and less frequent than they were a couple of years ago. But certainly any travellers to Iran, particularly women, should keep legs and arms covered by as shapeless a garment as possible, and endeavour not to offend in any way. Tracksuits, and other ostentatiously Western garments, should be avoided.

The war with Iraq is a more serious disincentive than the inconvenience of wearing long-sleeved shirts. Until May 1985 most of the action was confined to the south-west near the Persian Gulf. But in 1985, Iraqi planes dropped bombs on Tehran and Isfahan, damaging the magnificent Friday Mosque in the latter city. This resulted in the discontinuation of British Airways flights to Iran, not to mention international condemnation. Since then the Iraqis have retreated to the more familiar battle ground. As in all these cases, reading the newspapers leads to far more anxiety than travelling does. The only evidence of war which you are likely to see (besides the damaged Friday Mosque) are posters of martyrs, many thousands of whom have been killed in the "holy war".

Climate

Iran has a continental climate with extreme fluctuations of temperature. Temperatures of 55°C (131°F) have been recorded in the interior, possibly the highest in the world. The monthly highs for July and August often average over 44°C (111°F). Because of this you may be tempted to ignore the dress proprieties but the authorities mean what they say when they stipulate that women are to wear a "loose and long dress with trousers or long thick socks". During the cold winters, the temperatures stay consistently below freezing, and communication with remote areas is often impossible. On the other hand humidity is generally low and these extremes may not be as keenly felt as in a more humid climate. There is virtually no rain between April and October. The dreaded "Wind of 120 Days" is an impediment to summer travel in the south east of the country (see Pakistan — Climate).

Language

The official language is Farsi (formerly Persian) which is spoken by only half the population. Other regional and tribal languages account for the rest, including Kurdish, Armenian, Azarbaijani, Arabic, Turkic and Baluchi.

Although most educated people speak English in the large towns (or sometimes French), it is worth knowing the Farsi numerals, so that you will know what you are being charged for meals; also they are useful when looking for street numbers, identifying buses, etc.

1 — yek	— ۱		6 — shish	— ۶		15 — punzdah	— ۱۵	
2 — do	— ۲		7 — haft	— ۷		20 — bisto yek	— ۲۰	
3 — seh	— ۳		8 — hasht	— ۸		30 — si	— ۳۰	
4 — chahar	— ۴		9 — noh	— ۹		50 — panjah	— ۵۰	
5 — panj	— ۵		10 — dah	— ۱۰		100 — sad	— ۱۰۰	

SYRIA
TURKEY
Dogubayazit
Bazargan
U.S.S.R.
Djulfa
IRAQ
Tabriz
AZERBAIJAN
CASPIAN SEA
Kermanshah
Tehran
U.S.S.R.
Kuwait
Abadan
Isfahan
PERSIAN GULF
I R A N
Persepolis
Yazd
Mashhad
Shiraz
Kerman
Bam
AFGHANISTAN
U.A.E.
Zahedan
Mirjaveh
Taftan
GULF OF OMAN
PAKISTAN
OMAN
MILES
0 250 500
ARABIAN SEA
W.S.

Useful Farsi Words

please — lotfan
thank you — motshakkeram
hello — salam aleikom
good-bye — khoda hafez
yes — baleh
no — nakheir
how much?— in chande?
excuse me — bebakhshid
tea house — chai khaneh
station — istgah
airport — foroudagah
chemist — davakhane
hospital — bimarestan
today — emrouz
yesterday — dirouz
tomorrow — farda

Visas

Visas are now obtainable without much difficulty, though the fee of £8 to British passport holders is steep. The Embassy in London (50 Kensington Court, W8) promptly sends out two application forms for a "transit visa" with a maximum validity of two weeks. This visa is intended for overlanders, since it is not valid for travellers flying into Iran. Before applying you must obtain a letter of recommendation from the British passport office (which charges £3 for the service) or, if you are not a UK citizen, from your own Embassy. It may be possible to get an Iranian visa in Ankara, Delhi and Istanbul but this will take considerably longer than the two to seven days which it takes in London. Make sure there are no changes on your visa, since it may not be honoured if they suspect you have tampered with it.

Customs

Whereas passing through Customs is a mere formality in most countries, it is taken very seriously in Iran. Thorough searches are made at frontier crossings and Tehran airport by Revolutionary Guards. Be prepared for delays of several hours while they rip up playing cards or scrutinize your books. The list of prohibited articles includes all alcohol, "vulgar films, unpleasant records, cassettes and books with indecent photographs and any kind of fashion magazine."

The duty-free tobacco allowance is 200 cigarettes or 250 grams of tobacco. You are also searched on the way out though this is likely to be more cursory. Sometimes border formalities are supplemented by road block searches further on. They are especially concerned about drug smuggling and have been known to open cameras, thereby spoiling the film.

Currency Regulations

The import and export of Iranian currency is limited to 20,000 rials. If you don't manage to change your money at a favourable rate of exchange before entering Iran, try to prevent all your cash from being entered on your passport, thereby facilitating black market exchanges. Customs are normally particular about comparing your remaining hard currency with your bank receipts.

Health Certificates

Cholera and yellow fever certificates are required only if you have been travelling from an infected area within 5 days of arrival. Countries which are considered cholera-risk areas are Afghanistan, Bahrain, Bangladesh, Burma, India, Iraq, Malaysia, Pakistan, Saudi Arabia, Singapore and Thailand.

Drugs
The penalties for being caught are not attractive: up to 3 years for possession, 3 to 15 years for selling or smuggling (up to life for a second conviction). The death penalty is enforced for dealing in large quantities of opium, heroin, morphine or cocaine.

Motoring Documents
Motorists have two options, either to obtain a *carnet de passages* for which they must pay an indemnity worth five times the price of the car, or they must be accompanied by a customs official through their whole trip which costs about £50. Because of the high cost of a *carnet,* it is difficult to find a company to insure you against theft. Most recent travellers choose the latter course, though one of the disadvantages is that these officials will chivvy you across Iran more quickly than you would choose. One of the advantages is that you have a mediator and interpreter who might smooth the way if you want to camp by the roadside or if you run into any trouble.

In addition to an IDP and a *carnet* or an accompanying official, you must have an insurance policy accredited by Bimeh Iran (the Green Card bureau of Iran) or buy a third party insurance policy at the border. There are insurers at Bazargan (at the Turkish border) and at Djulfa (the USSR border). Bimeh Iran is located on North Saadi Avenue in Tehran.

£1 = IR 124
$1 = IR 90

IR 100 = £0.80
IR 100 = $1.11

Currency: 100 dinars=1 rial (IR); 10 rials = 1 toman.

Notes
50, 100, 200, 500, 1,000, 5,000, 10,000.

Coins
1, 2, 5, 10, 20, 50.

Changing Money
You get a much better rate on the black market, as much as four or five times greater than the official rate. The best place to buy Iranian rials is on the Pakistani side of the border where you get up to IR 400 to the dollar. Travelling in the opposite direction, you get a bad rate for Pakistani rupees if you try to buy them with rials, so try to spend your Iranian currency before departure. The rate is slightly worse in Turkey (Dogubayazit is preferable to the border post) but still very worthwhile. The black market inside Iran is about half of what it is outside and you have to seek out the sellers rather than wait for them to find you. Of course you will have to exchange a certain amount of money at a bank to satisfy the Customs Official on departure, though even travellers whose figures don't tally have not encountered much difficulty at exit points.

Do not try to use American Express travellers cheques in Iran.

Opening Hours
Banks, shops and public offices are open from 08.00 (sometimes earlier) to 13.00 or 14.00 Shops then reopen 16.00-19.00. Everything closes on Fridays, and

Thursday is often early closing. Government offices have a half-hour break for prayer at 12.00.

Public Holidays

The following dates are fixed public holidays:

11th February	Victory of the Islamic Revolution*
20th March	Nationalization of the Oil Industry
21st-24th March	Nowruz — Iranian New Year
1st April	Islamic Republic Day
5th June	Anniversary of uprising against Shah

*The Anniversary of the Revolution is celebrated over a 10-day period coming to a climax on 11th February when over a quarter of a million people pour into Azadi Square in Tehran.

The numerous other holidays are fixed according to the Islamic calendar and may be out by a day or two for 1986 according to sightings of the moon. For 1987 holidays, subtract 11 days:

24th March	Birthday of Imam Ali
7th April	Anniversary of the Revelation of Prophethood
25th April	Birthday of Imam Mehdi
31st May	Martyrdom of Imam Ali
9th June	Eid-ul-Fitr
3rd July	Martyrdom of Imam Jaafar Sadegh
19th July	Birthday of Imam Reza
16th August	Eid Ghorban (Hajj)
24th August	Eid Ghadir Khom
14th September	Tasua
15th September	Ashura (Martyrdom of Imam Hussein)
24th October	Arbain
1st November	Death anniversary of Prophet Mohammed
19th November	Birthday of Prophet Mohammed Imam Jaafar Sadegh

Arrival and Departure

The two most popular points of entry are Dogubayazit/Bazargan (Turkey/Iran border) and Kuh-i-Taftan/Mirjaveh (Pakistan/Iran border). Customs and currency formalities will probably take several hours at both. There is an interesting third option which is to enter by train from Moscow at Djulfa near Tabriz. Border formalities here will take the better part of a day and you will be required to press straight on into Tabriz, since this is a sensitive border area.

Many people will consider Istanbul as the starting point of their trans-Asia journey. Several private bus companies try to sell tickets through to Zahedan or even to India. Do not buy a ticket beyond Tehran, since it is virtually impossible to find a transport company in Tehran which will honour your ticket any further. Istanbul to Tehran takes between 3 and 4 days and tickets should not cost more than TL10,000 (about £13.50). Compare prices of Akdeniz Tourism (round the corner from the Pudding Shop), Ozsell Koll next door and Erkan Tour up the road. It is also possible to travel by local bus or train (in stages or continuously) from Istanbul to Erzurum and then Dogubayazit, which may work out cheaper than buying a straight through ticket. You can walk over the Turkish border and then pick up a local Iranian bus in Maku.

There used to be a rail service which connected with the ferry across Lake Van between the town of Van and Tabriz, crossing at Kapikoy, but this has been suspended.

Entering Iran at the Pakistani border involves arriving at Kuh-i-Taftan by bus or train. The Baluchistan Road Transport Board covers the 380 mile distance from Quetta in from 16 to 24 hours (cost about Rs80) and operates 3 or 4 services daily. You must plan ahead if you want to travel by train since it is a weekly service, departing Quetta at 09.50 on Saturdays only. The cost of the 26 (sometimes 36) hour trip is Rs65 second class, and Rs150 first class.

You may then have to take a taxi to the border which will cost about 15 Pakistani rupees or you may be lucky enough to find a local bus. After you have crossed the border, you will be charged an exorbitant IR 1,550 for the $1\frac{1}{2}$ hour bus journey Mirjaveh to Zahedan. (Locals pay about a tenth of this price.) Buses are normally searched several times for smuggled goods on this stretch; Western foreigners get off more lightly than Pakistani pilgrims. Services leave in the afternoons.

Leaving Iran is no more difficult than entering. Buses leave Tehran regularly in both directions though from different bus terminals (see *Bus* below). Buses are overcrowded as well as overpriced on the Zahedan-Mirjaveh leg, so queue as early in the morning as you can for a ticket.

Mehrabad International Airport is about 6 miles from Tehran's city centre. But unless you are going to Iran on something other than a transit (i.e. tourist) visa, you will not be flying into the country.

Motoring

All main roads are now paved and most sturdy vehicles should be able to cross the country without serious problems. The road between Kerman and Mirjaveh is the roughest. Petrol is no longer rationed and, if bought with black market money, costs very little. The map of the country distributed by the consulate in London indicates the location of petrol pumps. Outside Tehran (where the traffic is hair-raising) roads are not usually crowded. None of the international car rental chains has an outlet in Iran and car hire from domestic firms will be expensive, since the places of interest are so far distant from Tehran.

The Touring & Automobile Club is located at 37 Avenue Martyre, Dr. Fayaz-Bahkche, Tehran 11146, (B.P. 1294 Tehran); tel: 679 142.

Bus

Buses are by far the cheapest and most versatile form of transport with destinations all over Iran. Services between Tehran and Isfahan (8 hours), Shiraz (15 hours), Tabriz (12 hours) and Zahedan (24 hours) are express and relatively comfortable. Many are even air-conditioned. Be sure to make a booking as early as possible, since the services are crowded (often with soldiers). If you have difficulty getting a seat tell them your visa is about to expire (which it probably is). There are many rival bus companies, principally Tehran Bus Transport (TBT), Mihantour (who have recently reduced their range of tours) and Payma. The bus terminals in Tehran are inconveniently distant from the centre. Buses for Isfahan and the south-east leave from Terminolojunu (near the airport — take bus 141). Buses arriving from Turkey and Tabriz drop you in Azadi Square, though try to get them to drop you in town near Ferdowsi Square. Ask for the Iran Payma bus office (which is near Ferdowsi Square) if you want to continue south. In Tabriz there is a single bus station and in Isfahan the different company terminals are on one major road. A journey of 250 miles (e.g. Tehran to Isfahan) will cost about IR 500. Tehran-Zahedan costs IR 1,500.

If you can't get onto a bus, consider taking a collective taxi, comparable to the Turkish dolmuş. Private taxi services are widespread and fast, and usually cost about twice as much as the bus.

Train

The rugged terrain of the country made the building of the line between the Caspian Sea and the Gulf before World War II very difficult. Although the rail network is still not large, it does serve some otherwise isolated provinces, e.g. Mashhad in Khurasan and oil-producing Khuzestan on the Persian Gulf. The section east of Kerman is under construction and is due to meet up with the now existing section Zahedan-Mirjaveh in the late 1980s.

It is not as difficult to get a booking on the trains as on the buses, even though services are less frequent. There are no couchettes except on the international trains to and from the USSR. Nevertheless the overnight service (in both directions) betwen Tehran and Mashhad is a good option. It takes 17 hours and costs about IR 2,500.

Hitch-hiking

Lorry drivers and some car drivers expect payment for giving lifts. But if you simply want a lift out of town to a farflung hotel or bus terminal, Iranians will eagerly help you out.

City Transport

Urban service taxis in Iran are distinguished from ordinary taxis by their orange or occasionally blue bodywork, depending on the city in which they operate. These taxis are usually shared; the idea is that if you shout out your destination as the taxi passes, the driver will stop for you and then drop you off accordingly. You may have to take several different taxis to reach your destination. Short runs will cost as little as 15p or 20p, which is far cheaper than the flashy taxis parked outside the plush hotels, which are provided with radio-telephones. All taxis in Tehran are metered, though you'll have to be familiar with Farsi numerals to read them.

A Tehran underground system was started using a French design, however building has ceased since the Islamic revolution, and the project is being reconsidered. Instead there are many city buses.

Post

Letters to addresses in Iran should be clearly written, as Roman letters can create problems. When in Iran, it is advisable to post letters at the main post offices in large towns. Facilities for poste restante are not too reliable, especially in rural areas. Naturally there are no American Express offices in Iran. The Farsi for post office is *postkhaneh.* Stamps and aerogrammes can sometimes be bought at tobacco kiosks. Post boxes are painted yellow.

Telephone

Iran has a fairly good telephone system, with automatic exchanges in the large cities. It is possible to make international calls not only from telegraph offices *(telephone khaneh)* but also from private telephones. The Chief Telegraph Office is located on Imam Khomeini Square, although public communications services are far from infallible.

Newspapers

The two main English dailies are the *Tehran Times,* and *Kayhan International,* both pro-Islamic papers (understandably enough). There is also a French newspaper called *Le Journal de Téhéran.*

Broadcasting

For frequencies and times of BBC World Service programmes, please see the complete listings in the "Communications" section of the Introduction. If you try to carry in a short-wave radio to hear the World Service, border officials may try to confiscate it because they loathe the BBC. You are advised to be politely but persistently firm about your rights.

Malaria risk exists from March to November in the province of Baluchistan (in which Zahedan is located), and along the Persian Gulf and Iraqi border. There is no malaria above 5000 feet and urban areas are reputed to be free of it.

Although there is a national health system in Iran, treatment for foreigners will have to be paid for. This can be expensive. There are hospitals in all large towns. I.A.M.A.T. do not run any clinics at the moment.

Gamma globulin shots for hepatitis are recommended.

Water

The water is heavily chlorinated in Tehran, Tabriz, Shiraz, Isfahan and Abadan and therefore probably safe to drink. This is not true of other cities such as Mashhad and Kermanshah, nor of rural areas. Here water should be purified or tea and fruit juices drunk exclusively.

There seems to be little variety in food. Most cafés sell kebabs, bean stews, rice, yoghurt and black tea. Fruit, such as pomegranates and dates, abounds. A meal in a tea house will cost between IR 100 and IR 400.

chelo-kebab — grilled spiced lamb or chicken with rice *(chelo)*
chelo-khoresh — meat (usually mutton) and lentil sauce on rice
ab-gousht — chickpea, onion, potato and meat soup-cum-stew
ash-sak — thick vegetable soup or stew with meatballs
ab-dogh — yoghurt drink, sometimes fizzy
mast — yoghurt
halva — sweet made from sugar, butter, flour and nuts

Omelettes are often available and are more interesting than the English equivalent because of the spices used. Watch for *kuku,* a baked omelette.

Food shortages have been a problem since the revolution (sugar, eggs, etc.) though this is more irritating for the Iranian populace than for travellers.

TABRIZ

This is the first major city in the north after Erzurum in Turkey, and only 85 miles from the Soviet border. With a population of 650,000, it is the second largest city in the country and capital of the province of Azarbaijan, which the Russians unsuccessfully attempted to seize in 1946. It is at the centre of an important dried fruit industry. The Blue Mosque, which has been restored extensively, is worth visiting; next door is the Archaeological and Historical Museum of Tabriz.

Accommodation

There used to be plenty of cheap hotels and pensions down the back streets, but many closed after the Revolution. Good places to try are the alleys off Ferdowsi Avenue. Enquire locally since there may be hotels which do not display a sign. Apparently the Tourist Information office operates; ask in the central bus depot.

TEHRAN

There is evidence of a settlement in Tehran 3,000 years ago, though a 12th century source describes it as a small village, situated on the caravan routes to the East. During this time it developed as a rest halt for the merchants and pilgrims, partly due to the wooded hills of Shemiran, which offered good grazing and protection from the sun during the summer months.

A great deal of modernization took place under the Shahs, so you now must hunt to find a house more than 50 years old. Since the Revolution Tehran has begun to look derelict; buildings gutted by counter-revolutionary attacks have been left to rack and ruin, and many shops and bazaars are closed. Not a place to linger.

What to See

The Archaeological Museum — 30th of Tir Avenue, open every day except Mondays, from 09.00 to 12.00 and 15.00 to 18.00.

Museum of National Arts — Baharestan Place and Kamal-ol-Molk Avenue. Closed Tuesday.

The Decorative Arts Museum — (Honarhaye Tazini) Amir Kabir Avenue open from 08.30 to 12.30 and 18.00 to 19.00, except Tuesdays and Fridays.

Madraseh-e-Shaheed Motaheri (formerly the Sepah Salar Mosque) — Baharestan Place. Has eight minarets which afford a view of the city. Open to Moslems only.

Imam Khomeini's Mosque — 15th Khordad Avenue, not open during religious festivals.

The Shahyad Monument — on the road from the airport. Now defaced with anti-royalist slogans. The film of the Shah's coronation has now been replaced by a film of Khomeini's arrival and the glorious successes of the Revolution.

Accommodation

The Amir Kabir Hotel on Amir Kabir Avenue which was once the headquarters of overlanders is still open, but much reduced. Dorm beds cost IR 300 and doubles about IR 750. There are other cheap hotels nearby. Try also around Imam Khomeini Square, although during the recent upheavals, the pattern of opening and closing has been somewhat random. Although more expensive, the youth hostel on Kusht Road (off Ferdowsi Street) is recommended. The price here is IR 1,150 for a double. Cheap meals are available.

Useful Addresses

Indian Embassy — 166 Sabah North Avenue. Tel: 89 88 14.
Pakistan Embassy — 199 Iranshdu Avenue. Tel: 93 43 31.
Main Post Office — Imam Khomeini Square.

Both the British and American Embassies are closed. British interests are being looked after by the Swedish Embassy (Avenue Ferdowsi; tel: 67 50 11/ 20).

Tourist information offices have all but disappeared, no doubt due to the severe shortage of tourists. The Office of Tourism is now called the "Ministry of Islamic Guidance".

MASHHAD

Once on the Silk Route to China, Mashhad is now the second most holy city in Iran and an important pilgrimage centre for Moslems. Much of its wealth derives from the shrine, as well as from the surrounding fruit-growing industry. The centre of the town contains the mausoleum of Imam Reza (whose birthday is a national holiday) and a museum which has good examples of the Shias' contribution to Islamic art. Tourists are allowed to wander in the bazaars and up to the gates of the domed shrine with adjacent twin blue-tiled mosques, but may not enter.

In the town of Neyshabur, about 80 miles west, Omar Khayyam was born and buried. In addition to being author of the famous *Rubaiyat,* Persian quatrains in praise of wine and beauty, he was also an astronomer, and flourished in the eleventh century.

Accommodation

Sadaf Hotel — Railroad Square.
Jouharie Hotel — Shohada Avenue.
Government Hotel — Imam Reza Avenue.
It used to be possible to pitch a tent in Mellat Park.

Useful Addresses

Office of Islamic Guidance — 44 Jahanbani Avenue. Tel: 5878.
The Hospital — Imam Reza Avenue at Jahanbani Avenue. Tel: 4862.
The Post Office — Ark Avenue.

ISFAHAN

This is the most beautiful city in Iran and of great interest to admirers of Persian art and architecture. It has lovely bridges (including one with 33 arches), gardens, mosques and bazaars, especially good for textiles.

What to See

The Maidan Jomhuri — is a grand square with backdrop of cupolas, minarets and columns. The Maidan has been used for many events, including executions and polo.

The Friday Mosque — (Masjid-e-Jomah) was begun in 1612 and completed in 1628. It is not clear how much of the breathtaking Persian decorations were irreparably damaged in the Iraqi bombing. For those who like statistics, it took more than 18 million bricks and half a million tiles to complete it.

Accommodation

Amir Kabir Hotel — Chahar Bagh and Enghelab Avenue. Singles IR 600, doubles IR 1,000.
Toos Hotel — welcoming.
Young Tourists' Inn — IR 500 per person.
Shar Abbas Hotel — IR 5,000 double. Lavish decorations and dining room.
Mihantour Hotel — IR 900 double.
Shahzad Inn — near bus terminals. IR 400 per person.

Useful Addresses

Office of Islamic Guidance — corner of Chahar Bagh and Shah Abbas-i-Kabir Avenue.

YAZD

The town is situated on a large oasis, over 4000 feet above sea level. It is an important textile centre and bustling market and trading town. Places of interest include the 14th century Friday mosque, the cobbled streets of the Zoroastrian quarter and the Towers of Silence (see the section on Bombay).

SHIRAZ

Once the capital of Persia and now an important pilgrimage centre, Shiraz is a town worth visiting. To see most of the buildings of interest, walk down the Karim Khan Zand Avenue, which passes the Citadel of Karim Khan (Regent of Persia in the 18th century), the Fars Museum (only the building's exterior is of interest) and the Mosque of the Regent. The Masjid-e-Shah Cheragh ("King of Light Shrine") containing the tombs of Caliph Ali's sons, is lined with spectacular mirror-work. Since this is a Shia shrine, dress appropriately.

The bazaar is famous for its rugs, some of which are woven by the nomadic Qashqais tribe.

The ruins of Persepolis are 30 miles north of Shiraz and accessible by minibus from the Darvazeh-e-Isfahan at the cost of IR 35. Persepolis, meaning "City of Persia", was the capital of the empire of Darius and Xerxes in the sixth century B.C. After having been ignored for some time because of its pre-Islamic importance, the site is now being restored. Entrance is IR 50, which includes admission to the museum.

CASPIAN COAST

Few travellers go north from Tehran, though this would be an interesting alternative route to Mashhad. The Caspian coast has a milder climate than the interior uplands and boasts many resorts, primarily for Iranian holiday-makers. Fish plays a large part in restaurant menus.

Bibliography

Robert Byron, *Road to Oxiana* (1931, Picador reprint 1981).
Sylvia Matheson, *Persia: An Archaeological Guide* (Faber, 1976).
Nagel's Encyclopaedia Guide to Iran (Geneva, 1977).
Freya Stark, *Valleys of the Assassins* (Century, 1982).

Afghanistan

Capital: Kabul **Government:** People's Republic

The deplorable political situation in Afghanistan means that the country must for the present be omitted from any travellers' guide to Western Asia. This is sad in view of how intensely those lucky travellers of the 1960s and 1970s enjoyed Afghanistan. It is even sadder for the dispossessed millions of Afghanis: the traveller's disappointment at being unable to visit is as nothing compared to that of the refugee.

There are over two million refugees in the Northwest Frontier Province of Pakistan and a further third of a million in Baluchistan. The poor and the prosperous together have fled over the mountains, some carrying with them all their belongings. One of the Soviet tactics is to burn crops and blow up dams and irrigation equipment in an effort to subdue the people. Instead this drives more of them over the border, with reinforced determination to resist. Although a remarkable number of refugees are economically active (in the bazaars, in the transport business, since their trucks have the reputation for being more reliable than Pakistani ones), many languish in their tents in huge refugee camps. More refugees arrive every day. One learns to pick them out on Pakistani trains, by their proud yet cheerful bearing and their distinctive clothing. If you look under their seats there is a strong probability of seeing a large roll of canvas and tent poles. The huge influx creates many problems for the government and people of Pakistan, but since they share a religion and, in many cases, a language

(Pushto, the language of the Pathans), there is less conflict than might have been expected.

It is estimated that there are over $2\frac{1}{2}$ million Afghanis whose way of life is still mainly nomadic. Since the Soviet invasion on Christmas Eve 1979, a new kind of nomad has been created, one who roams the wild and mountainous terrain in order to destroy Soviet outposts and garrisons. These rebels (a term they reject) are called *mujaheddin,* which literally means warriors (or martyrs) engaged in a holy struggle. According to many reports the *mujaheddin* have been astonishingly successful against full scale Russian military equipment. (Of course this is what the West would like to believe.) Certainly the occupying Soviets have sustained terrible losses. But so have the *mujaheddin* forces who, when attacked and wounded, have none but the most primitive health care available.

The International Committee of the Red Cross (called Red Crescent in Moslem countries) runs two hospitals for the war-wounded in Quetta and Peshawar. Most of the victims who arrive are *mujaheddin* who have been wounded either at the hands of the Soviets or by rival resistance movements. Few will have been travelling for less than a week since sustaining their injuries. Many of the injuries result in amputation.

In addition to tending the wounded, the Red Cross run first aid courses. The pupils are mostly *mujaheddin,* often commanders, who want to be able to assist their comrades in battle. They are taught how to disinfect and dress wounds, how to immobilize fractures, etc. At the end they are sent back over the border not only with a first aid kit but also with a dossier explaining humanitarian principles of war, e.g. the obligation to look after the wounded enemy rather than kill them (which is a very difficult business when the *mujaheddin* have no settled bases in which to keep prisoners of war.)

Surprisingly it is not impossible to get an Afghan visa, but it is pointless. You will not be allowed in by land from Iran or Pakistan, and besides it would be very dangerous. So you must fly into Kabul. All the old travellers' hotels in and around Chicken Street are now closed. Of necessity you must stay and also eat at the Intercontinental Hotel (about £20 double). Unless you have contacts in the Afghan Armed Forces willing to find a place for you on an army convoy, you will not be allowed to leave Kabul. You will be trapped in a city in which almost everything (except the museum) is closed. It seems a better idea to sample as much Afghani culture as possible in and around Peshawar and Quetta. There in the safety of Pakistan, you will be able to buy Afghani handicrafts (woven salt bags for mules, carvings, metal work, etc.) and eat Afghani food at refugee restaurants (e.g. in the Qandhari Bazaar of Quetta where, just like Tibetan restaurants in India, the rooms are decorated with carpets).

Bibliography

Robert Byron, *Road to Oxiana* (1931, Picador reprint 1981).

John Fullerton, *The Soviet Occupation of Afghanistan* (Far Eastern Economic Review).

Peter Levi, *The Light Garden of the Angel King: Journeys in Afghanistan* (Collins, 1972).

Mike Martin, *Inside a Rebel Stronghold: Journeys with the Mujaheddin* (Blandford, 1984).

Eric Newby, *A Short Walk in the Hindu Kush* (1958, Picador reprint 1981).

Pakistan

Capital: Islamabad **Government:** Islamic Republic

Pakistan is an artificial creation. The Moslems of the Indian subcontinent, discontented with Hindu supremacy, wanted a national home and, under the leadership of M. A. Jinnah, set up a self-governing state in 1947 at the same time as the British relinquished India. During 1947 12 million Hindu and Moslem refugees crossed the border, dividing families and communities. A large number of Pakistanis have vivid memories of life in India before Partition and some still have family members across the border.

Within the present (disputed) borders of Pakistan there is an astonishing variety of races, tribes and languages; the name Pakistan is thought to be an acronym combining Punjab, Afghan, Kashmir, Indus and (Baluchi)stan. Whereas sophisticated Punjabis in Islamabad tell terrifying tales of wild and fierce tribesmen in the mountains a few hours away, the gentle mountain people roll their eyes in contempt of hoity-toity Punjabis. What unites Pakistan is Islam. All but a tiny proportion of the population is Moslem, from Lahore's intellectuals to Swat's nomads.

Many travellers, especially women, shy away from Pakistan, and so miss out on this fascinating ethnic diversity. People flock to India to see the Himalayas, the great Mogul monuments and the railways, without realizing that Pakistan can offer many of the same pleasures in abundance. Whereas trekking in Nepal has become almost a commonplace, the Karakoram Mountains (which include Nanga Parbat and K2) are a relatively undiscovered destination.

At one time, it was impossible to visit the northern mountain valley regions of Hunza, Swat, etc. without a permit and without getting a seat on heavily overbooked flights. But Pakistan has been encouraging tourism in recent years and roads have been built, so access is much easier now. Large tracts of the country remain undeveloped for tourists, however, and regions like the Makran district west of Karachi are reputed to be populated with smugglers and bandits. Since most of Pakistan comprises featureless and virtually unpopulated desert, the majority of travellers are not interested in visiting these areas in any case. You are also not permitted to get too close to sensitive borders, such as the Chinese border at the head of the Karakoram Highway or the Kashmiri border. There is an active war being carried on along the border between Indian Kashmir and Azad (i.e. Free) Kashmir in Pakistan and foreigners are not permitted within 16 miles of the so-called ceasefire line. Finally you need a permit from Islamabad to go trekking in certain tribal areas of the Northwest Frontier Province adjacent to Afghanistan.

Politically Pakistan is fairly stable, despite occasional rumours of a coup. President Zia ul Haq, who has led Pakistan since 1977, declared an end of martial law at the beginning of 1986. This may reduce local resentment of police powers and especially of their abuse, which resulted in rioting in Karachi in the spring of 1985. But on the whole Pakistan is no more dangerous nor difficult for travellers than the other countries of Asia.

Climate

Summers on the plains are extremely hot, though the heat is so dry that it is easier to bear than expected. Whereas one normally expects a moving train to generate a cool breeze, the moving air on a train across the provinces of Sind or Baluchistan in June is scorching. A further impediment to summer travel is the dust which settles everywhere, especially when the blistering "Wind of 120 Days" begins to blow across from Iran in June, a wind so powerful that it is thought to have killed off most of Alexander the Great's Army in the fourth century B.C. and to have been partly responsible for the failed American attempt to rescue their hostages in Tehran during the summer of 1980.

Summer (May-September) is the ideal time to visit the mountainous north; even Quetta at 5,500ft makes a delightful change. When it's 90°F (32°C) in Karachi, it is only 73°F (23°C) in Quetta. If you visit these elevated places in winter, be prepared for extreme conditions. (For a graphic account of a winter in the Karakoram, read Dervla Murphy's *Where the Indus is Young.*) Many of the residents of Upper Swat and Upper Hunza migrate south for a few months in winter while their own communities are completely cut off by snow.

The rains provide some relief from the summer heat, though the monsoon in Pakistan is not nearly as pronounced as it is in India and Bangladesh. For example only 7 inches of rain fall annually in Karachi, on just 10 days of the year mostly in July and August. The rains come early to Quetta (January-March) and to Peshawar (March-April). The mountain valleys rarely receive any precipitation whatsoever. Their fields are watered by diverted rivers or glacial run-off rather than by rain. Occasionally there will be a heavy rainfall which will disrupt travel, especially in and around Rawalpindi where it rains on 60 days of the year.

Language

Next to Islam, Urdu is the most important unifying element in Pakistan. Together with English, Urdu is the official language, though for most people it

W.S.
Mirjaveh
IRAN
Taftan
MILES
0
200
400
BALUCHISTAN
AFGHANISTAN
Quetta
PAKISTAN
Ziarat
U.S.S.R.
Chitral
Khyber Pass
SWAT
Peshawar
Kalam
Mingora
Gilgit
HUNZA
Mohenjo Daro
Karachi
ARABIAN SEA
Thatta
Taxila
Rawalpindi
Hyderabad
Islamabad
Besham
Passu
Nanga Parbat
CHINA
Skardu
K2
Lahore
INDIA
Amritsar

is a second language. Punjabi is spoken by 66% of the population, Sindhi by 13%, Pushto (the language of the Pathans) by 8.5%, Baluchi by 2.5%, and so on. Only a small percentage of children learn Urdu in their homes. Uneducated or remote people speak only their own languages of which there is a very large number. Spoken Urdu is indistinguishable from spoken Hindi but is written in Arabic characters rather than the Hindi script. So all the words you learned in India from *pani* (water) to *gari* (train) can be used in Pakistan (see vocabulary in chapter on India). The standard greeting in Pakistan is *salaam-o-alehku* or simply *salaam* rather than *namaste.* "Please" is *merbonay* and "thank you" *choucria.*

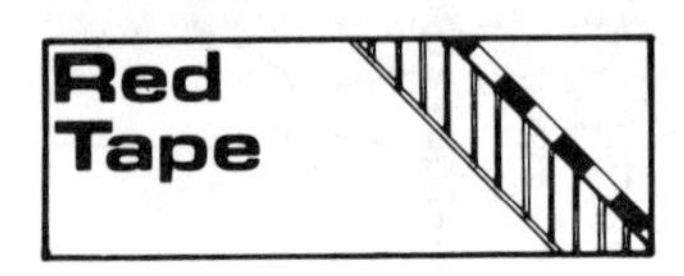

Visas
UK and Commonwealth tourists need no visa to enter Pakistan. If you stay longer than 30 days you must register with the local foreigners' registration office. American tourists need a visa only if they intend to stay longer than 30 days (but less than three months). These are free of charge and can be valid for up to six entries. Visas are valid for up to six months after the date of issue.

Customs
Travellers may import personal possessions only, including up to 200 cigarettes or 225 grams of tobacco. Importation of alcohol is forbidden, but luggage is not searched as assiduously as it is in Iran. If a bottle of spirits were found it would be confiscated and could be reclaimed upon exiting the country.

Currency Regulations
Pakistan has the expected regulations concerning currency importation and exchange, though they appear not to enforce them very rigorously. Officially you may import only Rs100 and must enter all currency transactions on a declaration form (FM). However, form FM is not always given to incoming travellers and most banks don't even issue receipts. It is probably not worth insisting unless you anticipate having to reconvert a significant quantity of rupees back into a hard currency (which is always best avoided). The maximum amount accepted for reconversion is Rs500.

Drugs
Many dealers are reported to moonlight as police informers, so be very careful about buying on the street, particularly in Lahore. Under the influence of the US government who are trying to curtail the trade in hard drugs, penalties for smuggling have become very severe, as much as life imprisonment. But in the Northwest Frontier Province, many of the locals indulge (especially bus drivers before long mountain journeys) and it should be safe to join them. The fact that policemen join in corroborates the view that dope smoking is legal in that part of the world.

Liquor Permits
Liquor can be bought only by non-Moslem foreigners, and the regulations make this very difficult. Don't get excited when you see shops labelled "Bottle Shop" with rows and rows of whisky and rum bottles: they are all empty. First you

must get a Tourist Certificate (just as for the railway reduction) and take it to the Excise Tax office where you pay a fee of Rs12 for a one month permit allowing six bottles of liquor and 60 bottles of beer. There are no bars and so you must drink it in your hotel room.

Fancy hotels will sell you the decent beer bottled in the hill resort of Murree at a very inflated price (Rs50 per bottle). It is more economical to make friends with expatriates who have access to local beer and whisky at reasonable prices. There is even a weekly disco with subsidized bar in Quetta; ask any Red Cross or United Nations worker.

Motoring Documents

If you are driving your own vehicle, you will need a *carnet de passages,* registration book, third party insurance and an International Driver's Permit (1924 Convention). The maximum period of validity for your *carnet* is three months. If you are transiting Pakistan in less than 15 days, you do not need a *carnet.*

£1 = Rs20   Rs10 = £0.50
$1 = Rs16   Rs10 = $0.63

Currency: 100 paisa = 1 rupee (R)

Coins

5, 10, 25, 50 paisa; 1 rupee (uncommon). Surprisingly few transactions involve coins; only the odd city bus trip or a plastic carrier bag costs less than one rupee.

Notes

There is not the same reluctance to give change as in India nor do Pakistani traders baulk at battered notes as noticeably. The notes are as follows: Re1 (mauve, or very occasionally blue, which is also legal tender), Rs5 (brown), Rs10 (green), Rs50 (purple), Rs100 (red).

Changing Money

The five Pakistani banks which deal in foreign exchange are the Allied Bank of Pakistan, the Muslim Commercial Bank, the National Bank of Pakistan, the United Bank and the Habib Bank. You will probably be directed to the main branch in any particular town. There is little to choose among them since banks in Pakistan do not charge any commission (or at least it's built into the exchange rate); if the rate quoted for sterling is Rs20.54 you will be given Rs205.40 for a £10 travellers' cheque. Do not try to do your banking first thing in the morning since most banks wait until they are advised of that day's rates, usually by 11.00. There are American Express offices in Karachi, Lahore, Rawalpindi and Islamabad (addresses below), which are preferable to local banks.

The black market rate for dollars is only marginally above the official rate, and is therefore not worthwhile.

Before striking off to remote areas make sure that you have enough local currency. For example there are no exchange facilities in Hunza, so get your money changed in Gilgit.

Emergency Cash

Most Western gadgets can be sold in Pakistan, though you should choose only cliché brands and then bargain hard to obtain a good price. There is also a demand for whisky which can fetch as much as £25 a bottle though it requires considerable tact to find a buyer. Most Moslems would be shocked by such a suggestion and, unlike in India, rickshaw drivers and hotel employees are not constantly asking for things to buy. If you're coming from India stock up on pan leaves and (if you have room) coconuts which can be sold at four times what you paid at Lahore bus station.

Opening Hours

Banks observe a 6-day week with Friday as a rest day. Hours are from 09.00 to 13.15 Monday to Thursday and 09.00 to 11.30 on Saturday and Sunday. These hours are altered during the month of Ramazan: 08.30 to 11.30 and to 10.30 on weekends. Government offices have recently decided to work a 5-day week Sunday to Thursday 08.00 to 15.00. Shops are usually open 09.00 to 20.00 with a few hours of closure in the middle of the day. During Ramazan many shops and businesses are shut up tight by 13.00 and do not reopen until sunset, when they stay open later than usual to compensate for their daytime loss of business.

Public Holidays

23rd March	Pakistan Day
1st May	Labour Day
14th August	Independence Day
6th September	Defence of Pakistan Day
11th December	Death Anniversary of the Quaid-i-Azam (Jinnah)
25th December	Quaid-i-Azam's Birthday

There are also two bank holidays on 1st July and 3rd December. For information about Moslem holidays, which change from year to year, see the introductory section on Islam.

Arrival and Departure

There is only one land frontier post between Iran and Pakistan (Mirjaveh/Taftan) and another with India at Atari (rail) and nearby Wagah (road). For more details about the Iran-Pakistan crossing see the chapter on Iran. Since the Sikh troubles in the Punjab in 1984, the Indo-Pak border posts (which are only about 20 miles from Amritsar) have not been consistently open. Many travellers have found themselves stranded or forced to fly from Lahore to Delhi (at a cost of about Rs1100). Whenever troubles flare up, the border closes. Indian representatives in Karachi and Islamabad may have up-to-date information about the border openings, but you won't be sure of getting across until you're actually there. It is open to people travelling in their own vehicles or other foreign vehicles only on a couple of specified days of the month, when compulsory convoys are organized. (The first few convoys apparently lost the way, but this problem has been ironed out.) Convoy dates are usually notified in advance to tourist offices in Pakistan; in late 1985 these were the 2nd, 12th and 22nd of the month between 09.00 and 13.00. if you want to meet up with vehicles going on to India, go to the Hotel International on the Mall in Lahore or the Tourist Camp in Islamabad. If the border is open, there may be a through train Amritsar-Lahore and vice versa. The first class fare is Rs22 for the 46km trip which takes at least three hours to allow for a lengthy customs inspection at Atari. The train departs from Lahore at 09.30 and from Amritsar at 13.35.

Most international flights use Karachi airport though there are several direct flights per week between London and Islamabad which are useful if you are interested in heading straight for the mountains. Karachi International Airport is located ten miles east of the city centre. When leaving the airport turn sharp right and walk over some heaps of rubble to the next building, where you can get a minibus (D-3) to the city centre and Cantonment Railway Station for Rs1.75. The service starts at about 6 a.m. Alternatively ask an airport policeman for a "taxi control" form which forces taxi drivers to use their meters. The trip shouldn't cost more than Rs25. If you must catch an awkwardly timed flight, the last D-3 minibus leaves the Saddar market for the airport at about 22.30. If you miss this, take a bus to Malir or Landhi which are suburbs past the airport, get off at Star Gate and walk the one mile into the airport. There is a Rs100 departure tax for international flights.

There is a very limited boat service between Karachi and the Middle East (via the Pan-Islamic Steamship Co., P.O. Box 4855, Writer's Chambers, Dunolly Road, Chundrigar Road), but no passenger service to Bombay.

Flights

The distances in Pakistan are so great that you may want to consider taking one of P.I.A.'s domestic flights. Flights are daily from Karachi to Lahore and Islamabad but only four times a week to Quetta.

Fares are:		
	Karachi-Quetta	Rs960
	Karachi-Lahore	Rs1,530
	Karachi-Islamabad	Rs1,860
	Karachi-Peshawar	Rs1,860
	Peshawar-Quetta	Rs875

Flights between Islamabad and Gilgit or Skardu and between Peshawar and Swat or Chitral are particularly worthwhile. The main drawback with these is not expense but seat availability. The government subsidizes these mountain flights to such an extent that they are often not much more expensive than the 24 hour bus trip. For example the flight to Gilgit costs Rs150 and Gilgit to Skardu (a spectacular flight over very high peaks) costs just Rs85. During the high season (which corresponds to the hot season) many Pakistani tourists book up these flights months in advance. But on each flight there are at least two seats reserved for foreign tourists and these are not in nearly as much demand. Enquire at the P.I.A. office in any of the big cities. There is usually a Rs15 tax on domestic departures.

Motoring

The style of motoring in Pakistan is similar to that in India; drivers stick to the middle of the road until another vehicle looms into view. The large cities are connected by paved roads, though the overland route west from Quetta to the Iranian border can be hair-raising at times. This highway (Karachi to Ankara) is sometimes known as the R.C.D. Highway. The road map of the country published by the Survey of Pakistan in Rawalpindi (cost Rs10) was revised in 1981 and shows the location of petrol stations.

The A.A. of Pakistan (175/3 Shah Jamal, P.O. Box 76, Lahore; tel: 414854) and the Karachi A.A. (Standard Insurance House, Chundrigar Road, Karachi) can provide information about road conditions and other motoring matters to members of the A.A. or the R.A.C. The Lahore office can also provide some (antique) brochures on places of interest.

Bus

If the flights are full or you are not short of time, buses are the best way to get into the valleys of Northern Pakistan. Timid travellers will be relieved to learn that the beautifully graded and paved Karakoram Highway is much easier on the nerves than the old precarious jeep tracks which can be marvelled at from across the River Indus. There are buses departing for Gilgit frequently from the Pir Wadhai bus station in Rawalpindi, all in competition with one another. If N.A.T.C.O. (the Northern Area Transport Company) is not leaving at a convenient time, ask around. N.A.T.C.O. operates two levels of service; deluxe simply means that the bus will be less crowded. Students are eligible for a 50% discount (Rs45 instead of Rs86) on the ordinary fares offered by N.A.T.C.O. and other companies which may help to reconcile them to the prospect of a 16 to 20 hour journey. It is very difficult to sleep since you must grip the seat in front to remain upright.

Bus services are more frequent and therefore more popular than trains on the Peshawar-Rawalpindi-Lahore route. The trip Rawalpindi-Lahore costs Rs25 or Rs60 for an air-conditioned coach. The Pakistan Development Corporation (P.T.D.C.) operate luxury air-conditioned buses between Karachi and Quetta and possibly between Rawalpindi and Gilgit. The journey to Quetta takes 12 instead of nearly 24 hours but costs Rs150, three times as much as the second class rail fare. The time of departure is 06.00 from the tourist offices in both cities. The Baluchistan Road Transport Board run fairly comfortable buses several times a day from Quetta to the Iranian border. The trip takes 24 hours and costs about Rs80.

In addition to plain-coloured government buses operating on all the major routes, there is a host of private minibuses (called "wagons") and light vans (called "Suzukis" or "Datsuns" irrespective of their make). Every square inch of these vehicles is brightly adorned. Women travellers are normally ushered to the front seat. Driving in the front of a Suzuki across a mountain pass is just as comfortable and scenic as being a passenger in a private car.

Train

Except for one short railway line, the Pakistan railway system was built by the British prior to 1947, and the network continues to flourish. Inevitably steam is being replaced by diesel, though there are still plenty of steam engines left, especially on local routes. As in India, the trains are a cheap but not necessarily very fast way of getting around. A journey scheduled to take 20 hours can easily take 28. The classification of trains is the same as in India, with air-conditioned, first class and second class reserved or unreserved. On long distance trains there are also first and second class ladies' carriages.

With a reservation, second class is fairly comfortable, with fans and lights. Unfortunately it is not possible to reserve a second class berth on certain trains, for example you can reserve a berth Peshawar to Quetta but not Rwalpindi to Quetta (both on the *Quetta Express*), nor is it possible to book on the *Bolan Mail* Quetta-Karachi. This has the advantage of saving you the Rs20 fee for a berth, but the disadvantage that you will have to push and shove as you attempt to claim a seat. It is possible to tip a porter (say Rs10) to do the work for you. Even on bookable routes, you can't normally make a reservation more than 15 days in advance.

The concessions available on Pakistani Railways are very worthwhile: 25% for tourists and 50% for students, journalists and boy scouts. The first step is to get a letter from any tourist office vouching for your genuine tourist/student status. (An I.S.I.C. number may suffice.) The tourist office in Karachi recommends getting several photocopies made if you plan to take more than one rail journey, however this is unnecessary since the letter is always returned to you. Next you go to the office of the District Superintendent of Railways, Commercial Branch, in the station from which you intend to travel. Here you fill out a form (or write out your particulars longhand). The information is transferred to another form, which must be signed by yet another official who is invariably elsewhere. In other words the procedure can take some time, but usually no more than an hour. You then return to the reservation office with your concession letter and buy your ticket.

Even on express trains, there are frequent stops, which are of indeterminate length. Follow the example of the natives, and keep your eye on the train as you are filling your water bottle or eating your curried chickpeas on the platform. Trains pull out of stations so gradually that it is always possible to hop aboard. Doors between carriages are frequently kept locked, presumably to protect first class passengers from the ravening hordes. This makes life difficult for the liveried stewards whose job it is to deliver meals from the dining car to the rest of the train. They must perform astonishing gymnastic feats to stretch between carriages while balancing trays of food. It is much more economical to eat food and drink tea from the platform than from the dining car.

Railway stations are not quite as full of chaos and commotion in Pakistan as in India; in fact the station in Peshawar seems nearly deserted, since bus is the favoured mode of transport from Peshawar. The impressive fort-like station in Lahore (so designed to keep out belligerent tribesmen in the last century) should be admired. In Peshawar and Karachi there are both City and Cantonment stations, so be sure to go to the right one. For instance, you must get your tourist concession at the Karachi City Station on Chundrigar Road, but most long journeys begin at the Cantonment Station.

Here are a few sample prices (before discounts and berths) and timings:

Karachi-Lahore: At least six trains per day, taking 16-22 hours. The *Shalimar Express* is the quickest but it doesn't run every day. Only four continue on to Rawalpindi, a further 6½ hour journey (cost Rs105 second class).

Peshawar-Quetta: One departure per day at 17.00. Journey takes 48 hours. Price Rs125 second class.

Quetta-Karachi: One departure per day at 15.30. Journey takes 21 hours. Price Rs70 second class.

Quetta-Taftan (near the Iranian border): Saturday only, departs 09.50. Scheduled to take about 26 hours, often takes 36. Price Rs65 second class, Rs150 first class.

City Transport

Taxis and auto rickshaws seldom use meters, so you must always fix on a price before embarking. If you have plenty of patience, you can flag down a series of rickshaws until you find one willing to use the meter. Meter prices are always less than you can get by bargaining. Sometimes it can be difficult to communicate your destination to the drivers, few of whom know English. Even a simple destination like Post Office or GPO can leave them staring blankly or (worse) nodding uncomprehendingly. Horse drawn tongas are more fun but no cheaper than auto rickshaws, unless you can find one which is already going in your direction rather than "chartered" just for you. Old-fashioned carriages with folding hoods called "Victorias" are used in Karachi and congregate around tourist destinations like the Inter-Continental and the National Museum.

If possible master the routes favoured by municipal buses (plain coloured), private wagons and Suzukis. Once you have established the main route, e.g. in Peshawar between the General Bus Stand on G.T. Road and the Cantonment Railway Station, it is easy to flag one down. The standing charge on most private city bus routes is Re1, and a few paisa less on public buses.

As on long distance trips, women are expected to sit at the front of a wagon, Suzuki or bus.

Trekking

There are many excellent treks amidst the dauntingly high mountains of the Northern Territory. Expeditions to famous mountains like K2 and Nanga Parbat cannot be undertaken by the inexperienced, but there are plenty of other snow-capped peaks and glaciers to tempt the adventurous. These treks are far less frequented than those of Nepal, and consequently there are few facilities for trekkers. It is essential to carry a tent and food unless you confine yourself to jeep tracks between villages.

One problem is the shortage of detailed maps and guides to the area. The Tourist Corporation is hoping to publish a guide to trekking and mountaineering in due course. *Pakistan — A Travel Survival Kit* by Jose Roleo Santiago (1984) contains over 50 pages of information on trekking, including a number of sketch maps of trekking areas, and details as to whether a permit or hired guide is necessary. If you choose to do a trek in a restricted zone (i.e. in sensitive border areas over 6,000 metres), you must apply for a permit from the Ministry of Culture and Tourism in Islamabad (Shalimar F 7/2; tel: 827017) at least one month in advance. You will be required to hire a guide in Islamabad, and so most trekkers go through an approved trekking agency. If you want to arrange this before leaving home, allow three to four months.

Post

The postal service in Pakistan may be slower than that in the rest of the subcontinent but no less reliable. Not every town in remote areas has a post office (such as Kalam in Swat or Yakmach in Baluchistan) but the ones that do exist in rural areas seem to process mail to Europe more quickly than in the big cities. As in India, try to see your stamps franked. This often involves taking your stamped mail to a separate building (as in Peshawar) or around the back to the sorting office.

The GPOs in the major cities are located as follows:

Karachi — Chundrigar Road
Peshawar — Shahrah-e-Pehlavi
Lahore — the western end of Shahrah-e-Quaid-e-Azam (The Mall)
Rawalpindi — just off the Mall on Kashmir Road
Quetta — Shara-e-Zarghum (also known as the Mall) about a mile beyond the railway station.

The following postal rates should be checked before buying stamps: Rs.2.65 for a post card to the UK/Europe; Rs2.90 for a post card to USA/Australia. Unlike aerogrammes in other countries, prices vary according to destination, so that an aerogramme to the UK costs Rs3 and to the USA Rs3.50.

Telephone
Local and foreign telephone calls can be made from public telegraph offices which are usually next door to the Head Post Office. Local calls generally cost Re1, and a 3 minute call to Britain is about Rs90. You can send telegrams at any hour of the day or night from the Central Telegraph Offices in Karachi, Lahore and Rawalpindi.

Newspapers
There are six English language papers in Pakistan. The most important are the *Karachi Morning News,* the pro-government *Pakistan Times,* the *Dawn* (which has the reputation for being the most liberal and independent) and *The Muslim.*

Broadcasting
There are many programmes transmitted in English by the government-owned Radio Pakistan, as well as World Service news broadcasts throughout the day. For frequencies used by the BBC World Service, see the Introduction.

Malaria is endemic throughout the country, below 2,000 m. year round. Because Pakistan is much drier than India and Sri Lanka, the mosquito population seems to be less . There is no evidence to indicate that mosquitoes in Pakistan are resistant to chloroquine, so a regular course of Maloprim (weekly) will suffice.

There is no free medical treatment in Pakistan, so it is essential to have adequate insurance.

Karachi
Jinnah Post-Graduate Medical Centre, Malir Road. Tel: 512551.
Karachi Adventist Hospital, M.A. Jinnah Road. Tel: 78086. I.A.M.A.T. member.

Lahore
Mayo Hospital, Allama Iqbal Road. Tel: 60822.
Lady Aitchison Hospital, Anarali, Lawrence Road. Tel: 53616.
United Christian Hospital, Gulberg. Tel: 881962. I.A.M.A.T. member.
Lady Willingdon Hospital, Ravi Road. Tel: 58051.

Rawalpindi
General Hospital, Murree Road. Tel: 40381.
District Hospital, Ganjmandi Road. Tel: 72932.

Islamabad
Central Government Polyclinic, off Nazimuddin Road. Tel: 24545. I.A.M.A.T. member.

Peshawar
Lady Reading Hospital, corner of Hospital Road and Khyber Bazaar. Tel: 75281.

Water
All tap water must be considered contaminated, even in mountainous areas where the tap water is reputed to come straight from a glacier.

Pakistani food derives from Mogul cuisine and overlaps significantly with the cuisine of North India. Chillis are used sparingly, and occasionally the food is quite bland especially in the Northern Areas where it is said that garlic encourages unbridled passions and so should be avoided. If you have just come from a Hindu or Buddhist area where the diet is exclusively vegetarian, you'll be in for a shock in Pakistan. Meat (usually mutton) and chicken curries abound while vegetable and pulse dishes are less common. Pakistani shoppers are not too particular about their cuts of meat: the price of meat in Quetta, for example, is Rs16 per kilo, whether fillet steak or hoof. *Tikka* (spicy barbecued meat) is tasty and the Pathan version at feast times consisting of freshly slaughtered wide-backed lamb cooked on metre long skewers is superb.

The staple is wheat, mostly served as chappatis, nan or parathas. Rice is sometimes available, usually in combination with meat and spices in biriyanis. The quality of the fruit is outstanding, especially mangoes, melons, apricots (fresh and dried) and dates. Watermelons cost a mere Rs2 per kilo; find some friends with whom to share a large one. Street and railway platform snacks (samosas, chickpea salad, fried fish, etc.) are normally delicious and economical.

Tea (the strongest drink you will find — see the section on Liquor Permits) is served as in India, sweet and milky. The *lassi* is universally delicious, assuming you are not being absolutely conscientious about avoiding ice cubes. Occasionally you see sugar cane presses on the street but be warned that they sometimes add salt instead of ginger and lime and the results are disappointing. During hot weather it is essential that you have your own method of purifying water since bottled soda water is not available, and sweet soft drinks do not quench your thirst over a long period. During Ramazan, it can be difficult to find cold drinks of any kind prior to sunset. Since, according to Islamic law, travellers are permitted to break their fast, you can usually buy food and drink at railway stations, but you'll have to step behind a canvas curtain to avoid giving offence. If you are in the Northern Areas in winter and become friendly with the locals you may be offered "Hunza Water", a local equivalent of brandy made from mulberries or grapes.

KARACHI
Within 200 years Karachi has grown from a tiny fishing village on the shores of the Arabian Sea into the largest city in Pakistan with a population of over

5 million, dominating industry, commerce and communications. This means that the architecture is neither of particular antiquity nor of interest and the bazaars lack the character of older cities. For a glimpse of Pakistanis at play, visit Clifton Beach where children and camels frolic. A popular pastime for groups of visitors is to charter a small crab-fishing vessel. No matter how ricketty the boat, it will usually have a brazier on which the fresh crabs can be cooked for instant consumption.

What to See

National Museum — houses the best collection in Pakistan of the art and archaeology of the country's past. Well ordered and uncrowded. Rs2 entrance fee.

Mausoleum of Jinnah — east on the Jinnah Road. M. Ali Jinnah, honoured by the people with the name Quaid-i-Azam, "Supreme Leader", united the Moslem population in the subcontinent and helped to create the new nation of Pakistan after Partition in 1947.

Tropical Aquarium — located at Clifton Beach. Has some amazing and colourful aquatic fauna. Between August and October, turtles lay their eggs on the sandy beach at night.

Thatta — former capital of Sind, 60 miles east of Karachi, and site of one of Shah Jahan's great mosques. Nearby are the Makli Hills where you can see the world's largest necropolis (literally "city of the dead") covering six square miles. There may be as many as a million graves, some of which are beautifully carved or tiled. Thatta can be visited in one day from Karachi by taking an early morning bus from Lee Market. If you want to stay overnight, try the Aga Mohd Hotel on the National Highway (Rs12 single, Rs25 double).

Accommodation

Y.M.C.A. — Aiwan-e-Saddar Road, across from PIA office. Tel: 516927. Rs30 single (men only), Rs60 double, plus Rs25 temporary membership fee (valid one month).

Amin House — Boy Scouts headquarters on Molvi Tammizzuddin Khan Road. Dormitory bed for Rs15, Rs25 single, Rs50 double. Cheap but cheerless.

Y.W.C.A. — Jinnah Road. Tel: 71662.

New Kashmir Hotel — 4 Hasrat Mohani Road, near Habib Plaza. 40 Rs single, Rs45 double.

Estate Hotel — Ragagazanfar Ali Road in the Saddar. Rs35 single, Rs45 double. Spartan but honest. One of many hotels south of Empress Market.

Shalimar Hotel — around the corner from the Estate. Rs45 single, Rs55 double. Recommended.

Salvation Army Hostel — Frere Road near Empress Market. Rs20.

Abaseen Hotel — next to the Cantonment Railway Station. Rs40 single, Rs50 double. Smart-looking hotel.

Useful Addresses

Tourist Information Centre — corner of Abdullah Haroon Road and Club Road. Tel: 510234. Very helpful, with brochures on all parts of the country. Ask for Syed Nazim Ud-din.

American Express — Shaheen Commercial Complex, Dr. Ziauddin Ahmed Road (corner of Chundrigar Road). Tel: 520261/65.

Thomas Cook — 14 Service Club, Merewether Road. Tel: 516698.
British Consulate — York Place, Runnymede Lane, Port Trust Estate, Clifton. Tel: 532041.
British Council Library — 20 Bleak House Road. Tel: 512036.
City Railway Station — Chundrigar Road. Tel: 232200.
Cantonment Railway Station — south end of Dr. Daud Pota Street. Tel: 513965.

MOHENJO-DARO

Mohenjo-daro means "The Mound of the Dead" and is a representative city of the Indus Civilization which flourished c. 2500-1500 B.C. It was not discovered until 1922, 350 miles north-east of Karachi. The scattered remains are mostly of baked brick houses and shops in which staircases, bathrooms and drains can be identified. There is also an interesting archaeological museum.

There is a dak bungalow which provides meals, though advance permission to stay must be obtained from the Archaeological Department in Karachi. There is no other cheap accommodation.

QUETTA

Although the capital of Baluchistan, Quetta (like Peshawar) is predominantly a Pathan not a Baluchi city. At 5,500ft it has a pleasant climate in the summer which attracts many visitors from the lowlands, just as it did during the Raj. There were no cities in Baluchistan (which was populated mostly by nomadic tribesmen) until the British built them in the nineteenth century. Today, Quetta's population has been more than doubled by the arrival of about 200,000 Afghan refugees, who have set up shops and restaurants in the bazaar. But it remains a more spacious, restful city than the others in the country. You can hire a bicycle on Prince Road for a few rupees to explore the city.

The train ride to Quetta through the Bolan Pass is spectacular, and nomads and camel caravans can be seen. Excursions may be made to nearby scenic places such as Hanna Lake, the Pichin Valley (halfway to the Afghan border) and Ziarat, 76 miles east of Quetta, from which you can go for pleasant walks.

Accommodation

Tourist Hotel — railway station end of Jinnah Road, Rs15 single, Rs25 double. Built round a pleasant garden.
Muslim Hotel — even closer to the station (i.e. 5 minutes' walk) Rs25 single, Rs45 double. Attached restaurant.
Al Shams Hotel — Jinnah Road in the bazaar area. Rs35 single, Rs45 double.
Chilton — Jinnah Road. Rs85 single, Rs120 double.

Useful Addresses

Tourist Information Centre — Al-Shams Buildings, Jinnah Road. Tel: 74653.
Iranian Consulate — Hali Road. Tel: 75054.
Railway Station Enquiries — Tel: 71200.
PIA — Jinnah Road (corner of Hali Road). Tel: 72011.
Grindlay's Bank — Jinnah Road. Tel: 75188.
Archaeological Museum of Baluchistan — off the Jinnah Road near the Tourist Office. Tel: 75142.

PESHAWAR

Peshawar has some of the most picturesque bazaars in Central Asia as a result of its long history as a major halting place on important trade routes. The bazaars, particularly the Qissa Khawani ("Street of Storytellers"), are as interesting for the shoppers and storekeepers as for the merchandise such as carpets and jewellery, embroidery, leatherwork, copperwork, cartridge belts, soap, lentils, almonds, dates and melons. Peshawar is the great city of the Pathans (pronounced P'tans), hence the picturesqueness of the locals: the men are striking looking and often strikingly armed and beturbaned. At the base of the Khyber Pass (now off-limits to travellers) and only a day's travel from Kabul, Peshawar has always had a strong Afghan influence. With over two million Afghan refugees in the Northwest Frontier Province (of which Peshawar is the capital) there are even more Afghani handicrafts available.

The Peshawar Museum (entrance Re1), housed in the gracious Victoria Memorial building half a mile east of the Cantonment Railway station, is full of interesting collections including a series of lovely detailed sculptures of the Buddha's life, and an original letter written by Shah Jahan. They also have a good selection of post cards.

Accommodation

Khyber Hotel — Saddar Bazaar. Rs15 per person. Free laundry delivery.
Kamran — Khyber Bazaar. Rs20 single, Rs40 double.
Hotel New Mehran — Sunehri Masjid Road (extension of Grand Trunk Road and therefore easy to reach from bus or train station). Rs20 single, Rs30 double.
Shahzad — Saddar Bazaar. Rs27 single, Rs37 double.
Youth Hostel — Peshawar University Campus, Jamrud Road. Rs10 per bed. A long way from the centre of town.
City Hotel — Sarki Gate. Tel: 74162. Rs30 single, Rs50 double, attached bath.

Useful Addresses

Tourist Office — Dean's Hotel (corner of Islamia Road and Shahrah-e-Pehlavi). Tel: 724238.
General Post Office — Shahrah-e-Pehlavi. Tel: 74425.
Iranian Consulate — Sahibzada A. Qayum Road. Tel: 73061. May or may not be issuing visas.
Railway Station Enquiries — Tel: 74437.
British Council Library — corner of the Mall and Khadim Shaheed Road. Tel: 73278.
Grindlay's Bank — The Mall (opposite Arbab Road). Tel: 72246.

LAHORE

There is a saying current among Pakistanis, that if you haven't been to Lahore you haven't lived. Lahore has (by far) the most beautiful buildings in Pakistan and is the cultural capital of the country. Lahore was the intermittent home of the great Mogul rulers (Akbar, Shah Jahan and Aurangzeb), all of whom left palaces, mosques, tombs and gardens.

Unfortunately Lahore also has a persistent reputation for being full of cheats and robbers, especially in the budget hotels along Macleod Road (now called Shahrah-e-Liaquat Ali Khan). See the introductory section on Thieves and Con-Men for advice on how to avoid problems.

What to See

Central Museum — traces the history of Pakistan through prehistoric times; the Indus and Gandhara, Buddhist and Mogul periods, etc. Contains a collection of coins, sculptures and Mogul paintings, as well as present-day examples of arts and crafts. Rudyard Kipling's father was the curator for a time. Closed Fridays.

Lahore Fort — the present structure dates back to 1556, though extensive restoration has taken place to eradicate the vandalism which the fort suffered at the hands of both the British and the locals.

Badshahi Mosque — built in 1674 by Aurangzeb. The central courtyard is capable of holding 70,000 worshippers. A panoramic view can be enjoyed from the top of the minarets, which are 175 feet high. Women should dress modestly.

Mosque of Wazir Khan — beautiful Persian-influenced mosque in the old city, built in 1634. Exquisite tiles, incorporating verses from the Koran.

Shalimar Gardens — 5 miles east of the railway station. 80 walled acres of fountains, canals, gazebos and flowers. En route to the Shalimar is the Gulabi Bagh (Rose Garden) laid out by a sultan in the mid-seventeenth century.

Accommodation

Al-Farooq — 10 Shah Alam Market. Rs25 single, Rs50 double.

Y.M.C.A. — Rashid Masih, 16 Shahrah-e-Quaid-e-Azam (Upper Mall). Tel: 54433. Rs15. Popular.

Y.W.C.A. — 15 Fatimah Jinnah Road. Rs20 dorm.

Youth Hostel — 110B3 Gulberg III, near Firdaus Market. Tel: 883145. Rs8 under 18; Rs15 otherwise. 1½ miles from Cantonment Station.

De Plaza Hotel — Data Darbar Market. Rs18 single, Rs36 double. Also nearby Yaqoob Hotel.

Chamman Hotel — 93 General Bus Stand, Badami Bagh. Tel: 200787. Rs25 single, Rs40 double.

Clifton Hotel — 23 Nicholson Road. Clean with English-speaking manager.

Useful Addresses

Tourist Information — Faletti's Hotel, Egerton Road. Tel: 303660.

British Council — 65 Mozang Road. Tel: 52755/6.

American Express — 112 Rafi Mansion, Shahrah-e-Quaid-e-Azam (Mall). Tel: 312435.

Thomas Cook — 3 Transport House. Tel: 306208.

Bus Station — Allama Iqbal Road.

RAWALPINDI/ISLAMABAD

Whereas Rawalpindi is an ancient settlement on the old Silk Trade Route between Persia and the Indian subcontinent, and Islamabad is a totally planned city started in 1961, neither is very interesting to the sightseer. However you may have occasion to go to the capital Islamabad for visas or permits or to catch an airplane, and you may want to stop over in Rawalpindi en route to the northern areas. The Rajah Bazaar area of Rawalpindi (sometimes abbreviated to "Pindi") is bustling and pleasant, and the bus station at Pir Wadhai (tonga to Rajah Bazaar, Suzuki to Pir Wadhai) is colourful and full of activity. There is a very frequent bus service (both private and government vehicles) between Rawalpindi and Islamabad (Rs1.25-Rs.2.50).

A very worthwhile excursion (by bus or train) can be made to Taxila (21 miles away) which was an important centre for many centuries before and after Christ, a place where Greek, Zoroastrian and Buddhist cultures held sway and, to some extent, intermingled. Buddhist stupas (domes to hold relics) and Ionic pillars can be seen side by side. It was the most famous seat of learning in ancient India for a time. The ruins are spread over an area of 25 square miles and so some time will be needed to see Taxila. There is an excellent archaeological museum.

Accommodation

There is virtually no budget accommodation in Islamabad, so it is advisable to stay in Rawalpindi.

Bolan Hotel — Railway Road (5 or 10 minute walk left out of station). Tel: 63416. Rs35 single, Rs45 double.

Al Shams Hotel — just around the corner from the Bolan. Tel: 68487. Rs22 single, Rs34 double.

New Kamran Hotel — Kashmir Road. Rs24 single, Rs48 double.

Nadir Hotel — Pir Wadhai. Rs25 single, Rs40 double.

There are also several cheap hotels on Jinnah Road (singles from Rs20) including the Magrib, Sweet Delux and the National.

Taxila Youth Hostel — opposite the Taxila Museum, a quarter mile from the railway station. Rs10 per bed.

Useful Addresses

Tourist Information Rawalpindi — Flashman's Hotel, The Mall. Tel: 64811.

Tourist Information Islamabad — Islamabad Hotel, Municipal Road, Ramna 6.

American Express Rawalpindi — Rahim Plaza, Murree Road. Tel: 65766.

American Express Islamabad — Elahi Chambers, I & T Centre, Ramna 6/1. Tel: 29422.

Thomas Cook Islamabad — 10 Khyaban-e- Suhrawardy, P.O. Box 1088. Tel: 28324.

Post Office Rawalpindi — Kashmir Road (off the Mall).

PIA Office Rawalpindi — top end of the Mall. Tel: 67011.

British Embassy — Diplomatic Enclave, Ramna 5 (PO Box 1122), Islamabad. Tel: 822131.

British Council — 23 Street 87, G-6/3 (PO Box 1135), Islamabad. Tel: 820153/4.

GILGIT

Although its setting is not particularly picturesque, surrounded as it is by dry stony slopes, Gilgit is a pleasant place in which to recuperate from the heat of the plains (altitude 4,770ft) and to plan further forays. The town itself is centred on two bazaars which are interesting to explore. There is an excellent bookshop called G. M. Baig's in the Jamaat Khana bazaar, which stocks a full range of books on this part of the world, plus local handicrafts.

What to See

Rock Buddha — located about 3 miles from Gilgit just past the village of Nowpur Nala. The carving is about 10 yards up on the cliff face, which rises above a lush meadow beside the river.

Polo Stadium — off the Saddar Bazaar. It is used less often than it once was. Tournaments are held in early November.

Rakaposhi Inn — too expensive to stay in but affords great views of the peaks from its balcony, especially in the early evening.

Accommodation

Tourist Cottage — near airport. Rs20 single, Rs30 double. Very pleasant with a garden. Excellent dinners are served, out-of-doors in summer, which can turn into sociable and informative occasions. The owner (Mr. Karim) is full of useful advice.

Golden Peak Inn — Rs50 single, Rs70 double. Centrally located and pleasant.

Jubilee Hotel — near PIA office. Rs15-30 single.

HUNZA

The interesting anthropology and the sublime scenery combine to make the Hunza Valley a wonderful place in which to spend some time. The main town of the area — there is no village by the name of Hunza — is Karimabad, which is located a few hundred feet directly above the village of Ganesh on the Karakoram Highway. The people of Hunza are renowned for their longevity, believed to be because of their diet consisting almost solely of apricots, which flourish locally. But since the opening of the Karakoram Highway in 1971, the diet is changing along with many other aspects of their traditional lifestyle. The people are remarkably Caucasian-looking and speak a variety of languages. They are welcoming without being effusive. Although women are not in purdah, they do not approve of scantily clad tourists.

The Karakoram Highway was built in order to facilitate trade with China. Unfortunately it is possible for tourists only to get as close as 35 miles to the Khunjerab Pass on the border. The locals are optimistic that this border may be open to foreigners in the near future (though it is probable that visas for China would still have to be obtained in Hong Kong). Passu, a nondescript town in a magnificent setting, is as far as you can go.

If you want to organize a trek or hire a jeep in Hunza, contact Ibrahim Baig through the Hunza Inn in Karimabad.

What to See

Baltit Fort — 2-storey wooden structure 10 minute walk from Karimabad bazaar. Tibetan type tower on roof. Rs5 fee to chowkidar.

Ultit Fort — 16th century fort with carved wooden doorposts. Bird's eye view of village life from the roof and of the Hunza River far below on one side. Rs5 fee to chowkidar.

Duikar — a pleasant morning's stroll along a jeep road which is not always open. Good views over the Hunza Valley.

Ultar Glacier — 2 or 4 day trek from Karimabad, during which it is possible to camp at a shepherd's hut at 16,400ft. A local guide (daily fee approximately Rs80) is essential if you want to go a further 3,000ft to the top of the glacier.

Accommodation

Hunza Inn, Karimabad — delightful place with shaded verandah overlooking the high peaks (Rakaposhi, Diran, etc.). Rs10 for cell-like single, Rs10-15 for wholesome vegetarian dinners.

Mountain World Tent Village — this was just in the planning stages in 1985. Planned as a somewhat upmarket tented camp in a scenic location outside Duikar.

Plenty of other hotels in Karimabad (e.g. New Hunza Tourist Hotel, Hilltop Hotel) which are all more pricey than the Hunza Inn.

Batura Inn, Passu — Rs20 single, Rs25-30 double. Commodious rooms and friendly landlord who can advise on walks up to the Batura Glacier.

BALTISTAN

Once accessible only by air or by mule, there is now a road from Gilgit to Skardu, the principal town in this ancient land (8-10 hours by bus). The flight (daily from Islamabad weather permitting, and Wednesdays only from Gilgit) is very scenic and, with luck, you will see Nanga Parbat (26,660ft). If you have travelled by road from Rawalpindi, you will not be unaware of the existence of Skardu, since rocks all along the highway are emblazoned with advertisements for the ambitious Shangri-la Tourist Resort on Katchura Lake. Many jeep or walking excursions can be made in the area, and the 16th century castle of Queen Mindok can be admired in Skardu town.

CHITRAL

Chitral, 18 hours by bus from Peshawar (via Dir), lies in a high valley very close to the Afghan border. Situated in the Hindu Kush, it is possible to see Tirich Mir, a perfect conical peak which, at 25,230ft, is the highest in the range. Chitral is more often visited for the nearby valleys of the Kalash people than for its scenery which is arid and desolate.

The villages of Bumboret, Rumbur and Birir comprise Kafiristan, the home of the "Kafirs", an Arabic word meaning "unbeliever". Kafiristan extends over the Afghan border, which was artificially drawn by the British when they realized they could not master the Afghans. For some reason the people of the Kalash Valleys resisted the sweep of Islam and retain many of their ancient and pagan traditions. The women wear elaborate shell and bead headdresses on their characteristically plaited hair. If you are in the area in late September/early October try to attend the Phoo Festival held at harvest time. Each year more and more Kalash people are converted to Islam, so the sooner you can visit, the better.

SWAT

The Swat Valley lies between Chitral and Hunza and is accessible from both. The ride over the Shangla Pass between Besham on the Karakoram Highway and Mingora (principal town of Swat) is very scenic (Rs20 for a 2 hours Suzuki ride). Although the scenery is somewhat tamer in Swat, the people are wilder. Swat is a favourite destination for affluent Pakistani tourists who come for the cool air and the fishing. There are hotels in Mingora/Saidu Sharif, Madyan, Bahrain and Kalam in Upper Swat which is reached after a rugged wagon ride (over 2 hours to go 26km at a cost of Rs5 from Bahrain). In late spring and autumn, you might see groups of wild nomadic looking people; these are Gujjar nomads who bring their animals and all their possessions down to the Peshawar Valley for the winter.

Bibliography

Dervla Murphy, *Where the Indus is Young* (Century, 1983).
Salman Rushdie, *Shame* (Picador, 1984).
Jose Roleo Santiago, *Pakistan – A Travel Survival Kit* (Lonely Planet, 1984).
Bapsi Sidhwa, *The Crow Eaters* (Fontana, 1978). A Pakistani novel about the Parsee community in Lahore.
Hugh Swift, *Trekker's Guide to the Karakoram* (Hodder, 1982).

India

THE FIVE RATHAS, MAHABALIPURAM

Capital: Delhi

Government: Federal Republic (within the Commonwealth)

India encompasses many races, languages, customs and religions, from the well-educated Roman Catholics of Kerala state in the south to the wild Naga warriors on the Burmese border. The country acquired its independence from the British in 1947 and since then there have been vast improvements in the economy, agriculture, health and industry. India's greatest problem remains its enormous population.

Most people tend to think of disease, flood, famine, squalor and poverty when they think of India. However, upon arrival, these charity-organization images give way before the vitality, colour and cheerfulness displayed by the majority. The first-time visitor to India is likely to be astonished by the vast rangeof Indian-manufactured products, from heavy vehicles, e.g. TATA, to soft drinks, e.g. Thums Up (sic). After all, India is the tenth largest industrial producer and is currently engaged in a space satellite programme and Antarctic exploration.

The pace of life in India is undeniably slower than the one we are used to and the bureaucracy in India causes some visitors frustration. A relatively simple operation such as buying a rail ticket or changing a travellers' cheque can take a considerable length of time. It is no good becoming impatient since anger accomplishes nothing. Take a copy of thc *Raj Quartet* or *War and Peace* if you are worried about getting bored while waiting.

Westerners can often be heard exclaiming with outrage at the discrepancy between the rich and the poor in India (as if inequality didn't exist in Europe and North America). Certainly seeing lepers outside the luxury hotels of Calcutta or pavement dwellers near the banking complexes of Bombay is a shocking experience and one which will recur in various forms throughout your travels. This fear of exposure to extreme poverty, the continuing troubles in the Punjab and the Bhopal gas leak disaster have perhaps discouraged some would-be travellers. But on the whole, the level of interest in India is increasing, prompted partly by films like *Gandhi, Heat and Dust* and *A Passage to India,* and by the television series *A Jewel in the Crown* and *Far Pavilions*. In 1984 150,000 British people visited India. The famous tourist destinations such as Agra (the Taj Mahal), Jaipur the Pink City and Kashmir are now overflowing with Western as well as Indian tourists. But India is an enormous place, stretching 2,000 miles from the Himalayas to the beaches of the Arabian Sea, and is capable of absorbing a great many more tourists without adverse effects. A civilization as ancient and as complex as that of the Indian subcontinent is in many ways incorruptible, and infinitely rewarding.

Climate

India has three main seasons: the hot season, lasting from April to June, followed by the monsoon, which continues until September and accounts for most of India's rainfall and winter which lasts from November until March. South of Bombay, light clothing can be worn all year round, but in the hillier regions something warmer will be needed. The best time of year to visit India is between October and March, when mid-day temperatures on the plains range from 21°C-32°C (70°F-90°F).

Language

The Constitution of India is written in 15 languages, and there are a staggering 1,652 other languages and dialects. The adoption of Hindi to replace English as the official language sparked riots in the south where Tamil, Telagu and other Dravidian languages predominate. Speakers of Bengali, Gujarati and other northern languages have less trouble learning Hindi since these languages all derive from classical Sanskrit in much the same way that French and Italian derive from Latin.

Just as the railway system which the British set up during the Raj unites this unwieldy country so does the English language. English is widely spoken and understood, and you would be unlucky to find yourself in a situation in which no English speaker was available. Even in a crowded second class railway carriage in which the majority of travellers will be poor and illiterate, you are quite likely to be asked by someone to describe the book you are reading or to comment on (i.e. condemn) Pakistan's expansion of its nuclear arsenal. And if you are travelling first class, you will no doubt fall into conversation with educated Indians, many of whom speak a delightfully old-fashioned English.

Useful Hindi Words

The Department of Tourism publishes an amusing phrase book for tourists which begins with the useful phrase "India welcomes YOU" *(Bharat apka swagat karta hai).*

hello	— namaste	tea	— chai
good-bye	— phir milenge	water	— pani
please	— putchiyeh/meharbani	milk	— doodh

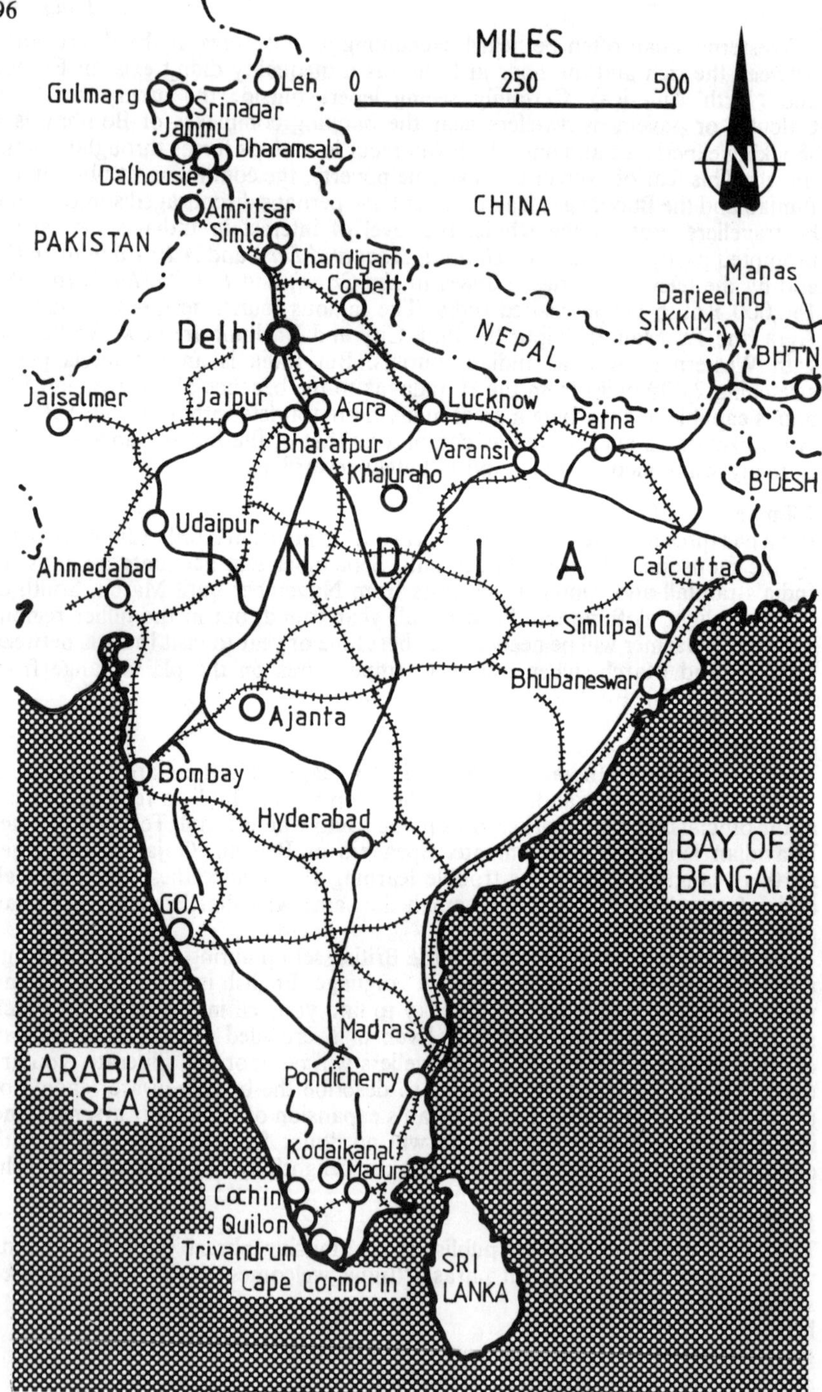
MILES
0
250
500
N
Leh
Gulmarg
Srinagar
Jammu
Dharamsala
Dalhousie
Amritsar
Simla
PAKISTAN
CHINA
Chandigarh
Corbett
Manas
Darjeeling
SIKKIM
Delhi
NEPAL
BHT'N
Jaisalmer
Jaipur
Agra
Lucknow
Patna
Bharatpur
Varansi
Khajuraho
B'DESH
Udaipur
INDIA
Ahmedabad
Calcutta
Simlipal
Bhubaneswar
Ajanta
Bombay
Hyderabad
BAY OF BENGAL
GOA
Madras
ARABIAN SEA
Pondicherry
Kodaikanal
Madurai
Cochin
Quilon
Trivandrum
Cape Cormorin
SRI LANKA

thank you — dhanyavaad/choukria
how are you? — kya haal hai?
how much? — kidna paisa?
good, okay — acha
yes — han
no — nahe
garden — bagh
bread — roti/chappati
egg — anda
meat — gosht
meal — thali, khana
maybe — shayad
caretaker — chowkidar
launderer — dhobi

1 — ek
2 — do
3 — teen
4 — char
5 — panch
6 — tchay
7 — saat
8 — aat
9 — naw
10 — das

The word lakh, which you will often see used in newspapers, refers to 100,000; 3 lakhs would be written 3,00,000. A crore is equivalent to 100 lakhs or 10 million, and written 1,00,00,000. You will often be asked how many lakhs of rupees your home income is. (An annual salary of £6,500 is just over one lakh of rupees.)

Visas

Shortly after the Sikh uprising in June 1984, the Government of India began to demand visas from all visitors. It is highly recommended that you apply for the visa in your country of residence since people applying in foreign capitals (Athens, Singapore, etc.) have had to wait for six or eight weeks while the Indian consulate sends your passport to your home country. Other capitals such as Colombo, Bangkok and Ankara are processing them more quickly at present after you obtain a letter of approval from your consulate, but there is no guarantee that this will continue. The cost in London (High Commission, India House, Aldwych, London WC2B 4NA; 01-240 2084) is a very steep £10. If you drop off your application in person (between 09.00 and 13.00) you can pick up your passport the next day between 16.30 and 17.30; postal applications are processed in about three weeks.

Tourist visas are valid for 3 months from the day of entry. Extensions of a further 3 months can be obtained by applying in person to one of the Foreigners' Regional Registration Offices or to a District Headquarters office of a Superintendent of Police. There you will be issued with the necessary income tax clearance certificate for which you will have to prove you have been self-supporting. The addresses of the registration offices are:

Delhi — 1st Floor, Hans Bhawan, Nr. Tilak Bridge, I.P. Estate, Bahadur Shah Zafar Marg, New Delhi. Tel: 272790.
Bombay — S.B. II, C.I.D., Office of the Commissioner of Police, Annexe 2, Dadabhoy Naroji Road. Tel: 268111.
Calcutta — 237 Acharya Jagdish Bose Road. Tel: 443301.
Madras — Bureau of Immigration, 9 Village Road, Nungambakkam.

Internal Travel Restrictions

Certain areas of India are open only to visitors with permits. These areas are usually politically sensitive, especially those on the border with China. For the purposes of issuing travel permits, these areas are classified into two groups, known as "restricted areas" and "protected areas". The main restricted areas are Sikkim, Darjeeling, parts of Assam and other areas east of Bangladesh. Permission for 7 to 15 day stays (renewable) in Darjeeling may be endorsed by Indian Consulates abroad or by the Foreigners' Regional Registration Offices (addresses above); this is unnecessary for people who fly in and out of Bagdogra Airport near Darjeeling (Calcutta-Bagdogra return costs $120). Permits to visit Sikkim are granted by the Deputy Secretary, Ministry of Home Affairs, North Block, New Delhi; applications must be made at least six weeks — preferably eight — in advance of the proposed visit either to an Indian High Commission abroad, to the Home Political Department (Writer's Building, Calcutta) or to the Ministry of Home Affairs. Your permit will probably be for only a few days, but you can renew at the Foreigners' Registration Office in Gangkok, capital of Sikkim, unless there has been recent trouble in the area. Permits for a few approved tourist destinations in Assam including the Manas and Kaziranga Wildlife Sanctuaries and the capital Gauhati are issued by the Trade Advisor and Director of Movements, Assam House, 8 Russell Street, Calcutta.

At the same time that India introduced the necessity of getting a tourist visa, it began to prohibit travellers from crossing the Punjab unless they had a permit. Again you must go to the Ministry of Home Affairs in New Delhi. Apparently they do not issue permits to people in transit to Kashmir so you might be discreet if that is your intention. Otherwise just board the train for Jammu and trust that they won't ask to see a permit on the train.

Permits for all other restricted zones such as the north-eastern tribal areas of Nagaland, etc. are issued through the Ministry of Home Affairs, North Block, New Delhi. Apply well in advance, be prepared for a long wait before being refused. The frontier regions have been plagued by violence and discontent and it is unlikely that a permit will be granted.

Bhutan is not under the jurisdiction of the Indian government. See the next chapter for more information about Bhutan.

Customs

Customs reserves the right to search the luggage of arriving foreigners. Any personal effects of high value (e.g. camera, stereo, binoculars) should be entered on an official form which you sign, promising to re-export the named items. After you have been asked by your first rickshaw driver or hotel clerk "Something to sell?" you will understand the point of the formality. But if your oral statement that you have nothing of value convinces the Customs Official and if you look like an average relatively clean-cut traveller, they don't tend to go through with the search.

All visitors (except those from Pakistan, Nepal and Sri Lanka) are allowed to bring in 200 cigarettes, and up to .95 litres of alcohol (wine or spirits), as well as a reasonable quantity of medicines and perfume.

Currency Regulations

There is no restriction on the amount of foreign currency that can be brought into India, but if you have over $1,000 or equivalent, you must enter the exact sum on a currency declaration form. Indian rupees are not allowed in or out of the country.

A store of foreign cash may be useful. Indian Airlines for example, offer a 25% discount on certain internal flights, if payment is made in a hard currency. Also if you're staying in upmarket accommodation, you may be required to pay for hotels in foreign currency.

Visitors who have been in India longer than 90 days must get a tax clearance form before departure (though there is a strong chance you won't be asked to show it at the airport). Take your currency exchange slips to the Income Tax Office (Foreign Section) and make sure they tally with the amount you claim to have brought in.

Health Certificates
There are no health formalities for travellers arriving from Britain or the U.S. Cholera and typhoid shots are merely recommended.

A vaccination certificate for yellow fever is required for travellers from an infected area, i.e. most of Africa and Latin America.

Drugs
There are sporadic checks of Westerners, especially on trains coming from Nepal, as well as on trains going in and out of Delhi, Varanasi, Goa, Patna, Calcutta and Bombay. Imprisonment is rare for any drug offence, unless you really can't pay the fine. It is wiser to proffer some discreet baksheesh than face the time-consuming processes of law.

Liquor Permits
Strict Hindus do not drink alcohol, and there is an important government lobby to make India completely teetotal, like its Islamic neighbours. However in 1981, prohibition was lifted from hotels, even for Indian guests and there is a sprinkling of so-called "wine shops" (which sell only beer and spirits) in most Indian states. Tamil Nadu, which once practised strict prohibition, has relaxed the regulations and it is now possible to buy arrack (the local spirit) or beer, though the bottle may bear the message "Drinking liquor is injurious to health". The two other traditionally dry states are Gujarat and Bihar.

Tourists are exempted from any prohibition through the issuance of an "All India Liquor Permit". Apply to a Government of India Tourist Office abroad or in New Delhi, Calcutta or Madras. The permit is valid for the length of your stay, and an extension will be granted if you extend your visa. A permit is not valid for more than 30 days in any one state, and there are limits to the amount of liquor you may buy.

Motoring Documents
If you are taking your own vehicle into India, then a *carnet de passages* or tryptique is needed. This allows duty free importation of the vehicle for up to 6 months. The regulations insist that the vehicle be re-exported; it cannot be sold or even donated. Third party insurance (available from the New India Assurance Company or National Insurance), an I.D.P. and a registration book are also required for all motor vehicles.

£1 = Rs16 Rs10 = £0.62
$1 = Rs12 Rs10 = $0.83

Currency: 100 paisa = 1 rupee (R)

Notes
Re1 (mauve), Rs2 (red/brown), Rs5 (green/multicoloured), Rs10 (brown/

orange), Rs20 (red), Rs50 (mauve, green and brown), Rs100 (slate grey; multicoloured reverse).

Be very careful about accepting torn or even worn notes. Most merchants will not accept them. There is a complicated procedure for changing damaged notes at the Reserve Bank of India, but many people saddled with such bills resort to "Damaged Note" dealers who offer 80%-90% of the face value. It is a better policy to use them in posh settings (Indian Airways bus, cold drink at a luxury hotel) where the staff are less liable to make a fuss. If all else fails, save it for your departure tax.

Another problem is a chronic shortage of change. Soon you will be hoarding small notes with the best of them. The shortage of small denomination bills is reputed to be worst in Bombay where sweets are proffered in lieu of cash.

Changing Money

As usual, it is simplest to change money at the airport; the major ones are open 24 hours a day. The service will be much quicker than at a bank and the commission less than at a hotel *bureau de change*. Banks outside the big cities will often refuse to cash travellers' cheques which they don't recognize. American Express cheques have been causing problems since the company stopped honouring stolen cheques leaving the banks out of pocket, so it might be an idea to carry more than one brand. Even when you find a bank willing to change your money, the operation can take an entire morning.

Grindlay's Bank is fairly widespread on the subcontinent and is linked to Lloyds Bank. With a Lloyds cheque book and cheque guarantee card, you should be able to cash a personal cheque at Grindlay's up to the rupee equivalent of £50. Similarly the Andra Bank will advance cash on your Barclaycard (though interest will begin to accrue from the moment of the transaction).

Emergency Cash

Many Indians, especially in the cities, are interested in the latest gadgets of the West such as pocket calculators or expensive watches, and there is usually a preference for a well known brand of goods. Indians will often pay more for a known brand than for a better quality of unknown brand. Cameras are expensive in India, especially Canon and Yashika, and fetch high prices. Assuming your gadgets have not been listed on a form at immigration, you are at liberty to sell them. You can make a very good profit on Kodak 35mm film.

If you are going to sell (or buy) anything on the street, always be very wary of your "business" contact. It is probably better to do any trading with a shop-keeper or hotel employee rather than auto-rickshaw drivers. Some of them have been known to cheat or even rob Westerners and then flee in their vehicle. If you do bring in something from Hong Kong or Singapore to sell, your budget hotel should be able to put you in touch with potential buyers. Near famous tourist sights such as the Meenakshi Temple in Madurai, you will find traders in foreign goods.

There is a continuing demand for namebrand imported whisky and cigarettes. For example Red Label Johnny Walker whisky sells in Calcutta (around Sudder Street) or in Kovalam Beach for up to Rs200 a bottle, over twice what you pay in a duty-free airport. The vogue cigarette is "555".

If you're forced to have money sent from home, Thomas Cook in both Bombay and Delhi have been recommended as being efficient enough to get the money to you in 24 hours, an astonishing statistic for India. If for some reason you find yourself temporarily stranded in Delhi you might donate your time to the Joint Assistance Centre (H-65 South Extension-1 New Delhi 110049; tel: 697986) in exchange for humble board and lodging. This voluntary organization tries to cope with small scale famine, poverty and basic social problems. If in Calcutta, try Mother Teresa's home at 54a Lower Circular Road.

Opening Hours

Banks are open from 10.00-14.00 Monday to Friday and from 10.00 to noon on Saturdays. (For some reason opening hours in Bombay are later: 11.00-15.00 on weekdays and till 13.00 on Saturdays.) Office hours for government and businesses normally begin at 10.00 and end at 17.00 with a period of closing for lunch. The working week usually includes Saturday morning. Most shops are open until 18.30 or 19.30; many close in the early afternoon during the hottest part of the day.

Public Holidays

There are numerous local holidays in India, many of a religious nature. The national holidays are:

1st January	New Year's Day
26th January	Republic Day
1st May	Labour Day
30th June	Bank Holiday
15th August	Independence Day
2nd October	Mahatma Gandhi's Birthday
25th December	Christmas

In addition to these fixed holidays there are many moveable feasts. In many areas the Moslem festivals of Id-ul-Fitr, Idu'z Zuha (equivalent to Eid-ul-Azha), Muharram and Id-e-Milud are celebrated (see Introduction for dates). There are also the Hindu holidays of Pongal (mid-January), Holi or the Festival of Colour (February/March), Diwali (October/November) and Shivarati (February/March). Sikhs and Jains, Buddhists and Christians also have their own holidays. Ask the government tourist office for a complete list. Many of the festivals are very colourful and are worth seeking out.

Arrival and Departure

With the Indo-Pakistan border crossing uncertain (see page 80), the ferry service between Sri Lanka and India curtailed (see page 162) and the (temporary?) demise of the Madras-Penang ship (see page 12), most travellers will arrive at one of India's international airports. There is generally a choice of transport into the city centre. For example, assuming you have ignored all the taxi drivers at Delhi Airport, you can take the ex-servicemen's bus to Connaught Circle (Rs8), the airport bus to either Old or New Delhi Railway Station (Rs5) or the public bus which costs a mere 75 paise to cover the 9 mile distance. For this service turn right out of the airport and then left into a dusty row of houses where the bus will probably be parked.

Arriving at Bombay's International Terminal (called Terminal 2) you can either take the Rs15 Air India bus into central Bombay or the Rs5 bus to the domestic terminal (Terminal 1) from which it is possible to take a local bus (or more reliably a rickshaw) to the Palace Railway Station and then proceed on the train (Rs2) to Churchgate Station.

There is an Indian Airlines bus from the memorably named Dum Dum Airport in Calcutta to the Indian Airways office. If you are worried about your first night's accommodation it is possible to enlist the help of the tourist desk at the airport though they will place you only in upmarket establishments. Do not believe for a moment the young men who will flock round you as you emerge from the airport warning you that a convention of Buddhist beauticians has occupied all the downtown hotel rooms and so you really must stay at the concrete block next to the airport. If your flight arrives or departs at an awkward time which will make it difficult to sleep in accommodation downtown, ask about the airport retiring rooms. For example there is a dorm at Delhi Airport with beds for Rs85. Enquire at the airport manager's office.

Well before leaving India, make sure that you have a confirmed seat reservation, and try to do this in person. Travel agents may be willing to make the necessary phone calls, but they will charge Rs100-Rs200 for the service. It is best to have a return ticket when you arrive, since it is a complicated and risky business buying a discounted ticket in India. (Indian residents with friends or contacts in London often arrange for their tickets to be bought in London.) If you happen to be proceeding via the Bangladesh Biman flight to Rangoon which claims to include a free night's accommodation during the compulsory stop-over in Dhaka, insist that this be clearly marked on your ticket at the time of purchase.

Just before leaving the country spend all your rupees except the Rs100 you need for your departure tax (Rs50 for the neighbouring countries of Bangladesh, Bhutan, Burma, Nepal, Pakistan and Sri Lanka). Only hard currencies are accepted in the airport duty free shops. When paying your departure tax, specify your airline.

Although Bombay and Delhi both have new terminals, nothing seems able to solve the inefficiency and inevitable delays encountered when departing. The Asian inability to queue means that the security guards at the doors of the departure lounge are often forced to lock the doors until passengers consent to move through in an orderly file rather than a seething mass. Since not all airlines allocate seats you cannot always afford to withdraw with dignity from the fray.

Unfortunately there is no passenger service between Bombay and Karachi, though there is plenty of shipping traffic. It is possible (though only remotely possible) to work a passage on a cargo ship leaving Bombay. Simply offer your services to all captains in harbour. There is even the occasional yachtsman looking for crew for a trip across the Indian Ocean.

Flights

If your time is limited and your itinerary is ambitious, you'll have to consider taking one or more domestic flights. The Indian Airlines reservation system is not computerized, and can cause almost as much anxiety as making railway reservations. Often you will be told that your name will be added to a waiting list and you won't be sure of getting a seat until the last minute at the airport. If you have an itinerary planned in advance, book several flights at once. There is a 21 day "Discover India" air pass which is really intended for affluent tourists since it costs Rs4413 (£275).

The airline advertises a 25% discount for youthful travellers (under 30) who pay in hard currency. But sometimes the advertised schemes and the reality do not coincide.

Motoring

Traffic circulates on the left. Indian measurements are at least partially metric, so that distances are in kilometres, and petrol is sold in litres. The highway code does not exist in India. The official speed limit varies from town to town and even in the same city; speed in the country is governed by the state of the road and wandering cows. When driving, do not feel inhibited over the use of the horn as it is common practice to hoot before overtaking. The roads are dusty towards the end of winter and during the summer, but can be murderous during the monsoon. National and state highways are motorable throughout the year but minor roads may close down.

The motoring organizations should be able to give up-to-date information on road conditions, route planning, etc. Their addresses are:

Automobile Association of Upper India — 6 Pratap Building, 14 F Connaught Place, New Delhi. Tel: 42063.

Automobile Association of S. India — 38A Mount Road, PB 729, Madras 6.

Western India Automobile Association — 76 Vir Nariman Road, Churchgate Reclamation, Bombay 400020. Tel: 291085.

Automobile Association of Eastern India — 13 Promothesh Barua Sarani, Calcutta. Tel: 479012.

There are no self-drive hire facilities in India; the compulsory chauffeur represents a small proportion of the fee which is usually about Rs400 per day. If this is divided among a group, it isn't outrageous.

Bus

Although buses are not necessarily cheaper than trains, they do enable access to more remote regions and often they are quicker than the trains. Bus journeys along winding Himalayan roads can be very exciting as well as breathtakingly scenic. Whereas everyone in northern India seems to travel by train, most people in the south travel by bus. Bus travel seldom involves an elaborate process of making a reservation, though you can reserve a seat on so called "deluxe" buses which may or may not offer any deluxe features. Typically you will pay a fee of one rupee to make a reservation (after having paid 10 paise for a reservation request form).

On major routes, there are genuine deluxe services which feature videos, fans, etc. and will cost a little more. (Some travellers have recommended carrying a pair of earplugs to cope with the non-stop Hindi videos.) A very rough guide to short bus journeys would be to expect a 50 mile journey to take 2½-3 hours and cost about Rs10, i.e. you travel about 5 miles for one rupee.

Many long distance coaches leave from the Inter-State Bus Terminus (I.S.B.T.) at the Kashmiri Gate (just north of the Red Fort) in Old Delhi, bound for popular Himalayan destinations such as Srinagar in Kashmir (24 hours), Kulu (15 hours) and Dharamsala (12/13 hours). Before setting off sample the excellent food at the station workers' canteen.

Try to sit as close to the front of the bus as possible since the suspension favoured in Indian buses means that if sitting near the back you will have to find some fixed object with which to steady yourself. Windows on ordinary buses often lack glass and so you may be afflicted by swirling dust in the dry season (locals cover the mouth and eyes with a shawl) and buckets of water in the monsoon. Buses in the south are equipped with accordion blinds which can be used to keep out the suffocating hot winds as well as the monsoon rains.

Train

The railways of India are a wonderful institution and it doesn't take long before you grow fond of them. There are 37,500 miles of track covering all but the most mountainous parts of the country. There are still 7,245 steam locomotives in service and several mountain railways such as the Darjeeling Toy Train and the Ootacamund cog railway. Indian Railways convey a staggering 10 million people every day. It is no wonder that stations are hives of activity. If you are interested in the railways, you might look at a book by Michael Satow called *Railways of the Raj* (Scolar Press, 1980) or at Paul Theroux's *The Imperial Way* (Hamish Hamilton, 1985).

You may at first be overwhelmed by the great number of ticket and reservation wickets, administrative offices and waiting rooms, not to mention the Indian families who seem to be camped on the station platforms. But the often-exaggerated frustration associated with the railway bureaucracy soon disappears once you become familiar with the procedures.

First you have to choose where on the spectrum of comfort you wish to travel. There is an air-conditioned class (which includes free sleeping accommodation on overnight journeys), first class, air-conditioned chair, second class reserved and second class unreserved. There is even a substantial difference (30%) between travelling second class on a local train and on an express train. Apart from that, the formula seems to be to double the price for every jump in class, so for example a 48 mile journey second class costs Rs55, chair class Rs115, first class Rs210 and air-conditioned class Rs418. Second class reserved is comfortable enough for most hardy travellers, especially if they can improvise a cushion to place between their hip and the wooden berth. The Government Tourist Office isn't so sanguine about the hardiness of tourists: "Second class is rather uncomfortable for a foreign tourist who is therefore advised to purchase either air-conditioned or first class tickets." But the savings made by travellers willing to travel second class are gratifying.

In view of the long distances, nearly all compartments have seats designed to convert into bunks. On a busy line (such as Delhi to Agra) or on a journey involving a night on the train, advance booking is essential, since a wait of a week or 10 days can be common before a seat or berth becomes vacant. If you are told there are no berths, always enquire about the tourist quota and emergency quota. In the headquarters of the four railway regions, there is a special office which administers the tourist quota. The addresses are as follows:

Eastern Railway: Central Reservation Office, 6 Fairlie Place, Calcutta 1. Tel: 22 27 89. This is inconveniently located across the River Hooghly from Howrah Station.

Central Railway: New Administrative Building, 2nd Floor, Dadabhoy Naroji Road, Bombay 1. Tel: 26 80 41.

Western Railway: Reservation Office, Churchgate, Bombay 20. Tel: 29 80 16.

Northern Railway: Baroda House, Kasturba Gandhi Marg (near India Gate), New Delhi. Tel: 38 78 89. Even if your reservation here takes several hours to arrange, it will be a pleasant experience in the air-conditioned surroundings. You must take the form you are given at Baroda House to the station to purchase the ticket. If Baroda House is closed for a holiday, go to counter 43 in New Delhi Station.

Rules vary from station to station (and from class to class) concerning how far in advance you can reserve. You will pay a small reservation charge of Re1 or Rs2.

Travelling unreserved on trains is definitely a memorable experience. Women can sometimes travel on a special unreserved ladies' coach, which is usually less crowded. In order to obtain a seat on an unreserved coach, leap on through a door or window before it stops, grab the nearest seat or corridor space and establish yourself. This works best with two people: one can board, and the other can get on with the luggage when the train stops. You may be able to hire a porter (identifiable by their red jackets) to do the pushing and scrambling for you; this won't cost more than a couple of rupees.

When buying a ticket, first locate the ticket office. Enquire about reservations; there is usually a board indicating which trains are full. An 'A' indicates seats are available; 'F' indicates that a train is fully booked. If seats are available, obtain a reservation slip from the enquiries counter, fill it in and hand it in at the counter which takes the booking for that train. Make sure you are queuing at the right counter or you will waste a lot of time. Women travellers should look for a ladies' queue since these are often shorter.

Arrive at the station at least an hour (preferably several) before departure and locate your train's platform. Your seat and sleeper number will either be posted on a board or displayed on the window of your compartment, possibly misspelled out of recognition. Waiting rooms are usually pleasant, though segregrated; some have free showers. Railway stations are copiously staffed and you may sometimes be tempted to believe that all 1.6 million employees of Indian Railways must be consulted before a ticket and reservation can be issued.

There is an "Indrail Pass", which is available to all foreign nationals who must pay in dollars or pounds, and is valid on all trains including the high speed express trains. The prices in dollars for the passes are as follows:

	Air-Conditioned Class	First Class	Second Class
7 days	$160	$80	$35
15 days	$200	$100	$45
21 days	$240	$120	$55
30 days	$300	$150	$65
60 days	$450	$225	$100
90 days	$600	$300	$130

These passes are available in India from the "Railway Tourist Guides" or Central Reservation Offices in Delhi, Bombay, Calcutta, Madras (addresses above), and in Agra, Jaipur, Trivandrum and several other cities. The Indrail Pass is not as convenient as a Eurail pass because you will still have to queue in advance to reserve a berth or seat. Although the prices seem very cheap, you have to travel many miles to make it worthwhile. An overnight journey of 380 miles (second class sleeper), for example, will only cost about Rs45 and second class prices are usually in the region of 8 miles per rupee. The first class fare for a journey of 325 miles will be approximately Rs157 (about 2-2½ miles to the rupee). Unless you are sure you will be travelling more than 6,250 miles in second class or 28,000 miles in air-conditioned class in 30 days, for example, it is not worthwhile to buy the 30-day pass.

The Ministry of Railways in conjunction with the department of Tourism issue a handy (and free) tourist railway timetable setting out not only the times of the principal services, but explaining the fare structure, giving details of additional facilities (e.g. how to hire a bedroll for Rs5, how to reclaim a portion of an air-conditioned class ticket if the air conditioning breaks down, etc.) and also provides a list of railway retiring rooms. Large railway stations have guest rooms (single, double or dorm) for the use of ticket-bearing passengers. Prices vary from Rs125 for an air-conditioned double in Bombay Central to Rs3.50 for a dorm bed in Dwarka (admittedly a place of little interest) but average about Rs20 per person.

Boat

The most picturesque way of travelling between Bombay and Goa is by the ferry which leaves daily (except Tuesdays) from the New Ferry Wharf in Bombay. The trip takes just less than 24 hours, but is suspended during rough weather (principally during the monsoon). A lower deck fare is about Rs50; a cabin (which must be booked several weeks in advance) Rs250. For advance bookings enquire at the state tourist office. Without an advance booking, try to get down to the docks before 07.00 when boarding begins.

A unique boat trip run by the Kerala State Navigation Company takes you through the inland waterways of Kerala. The 8 hour trip between Quilon and Alleppey can be done by day or night, though most of the pleasure derives from observing the local life. The cost is Rs5. Boats also travel inland from Alleppey to Kottayam, from which you can travel on to the Periyar Wildlife Sanctuary.

Hitch-hiking

It is possible to hitch-hike in India, but with the time it takes and the amount of money spent whilst travelling, it is probably just as cheap to use the rail or bus service, and a lot faster.

Camping is best in the protected gardens of the government rest houses, dak bungalows, circuit houses, tourist bungalows, etc. which are found throughout the country. A small tip (of about Rs2) should be given to the chowkidar. For information on camping, contact the Indian Camping Association, c/o National Councils of Y.M.C.A.s of India, Bharat Yuvak Bhavan, Jai Singh Road, New Delhi 110001.

City Transport

Buses in the centres of cities tend to be intimidatingly crowded, though easier to use in the suburbs. The fare will probably be less than one rupee. The other forms of city transport are three-wheeled taxis, bicycle rickshaws, horse-drawn tongas and taxi-cabs. Taxi charges will be about Rs2 per mile. Always remember to agree a price before embarking since functioning meters are rare, and even when you do find a driver willing to use the meter, it will be "meter and card"; the card shows official surcharges. An average tri-car taxi ride in Delhi will cost Rs5-Rs7 for two people, so there isn't much incentive to master the municipal bus system. Tongas are not found everywhere but are a highly enjoyable mode of transport — far better than the cycle rickshaws which are depressingly hard work for the pedaller. It might be better for your conscience to hire a bicycle to pedal yourself, though this is not advisable in the traffic-filled big cities.

Post

Indian towns are well-provided with post offices and the postal service is generally good, a relic of colonization. Post offices are usually open from 10.00-17.00, Saturdays until 13.00, though most major ones keep longer hours. You can usually find a post office in railway stations. Although most stamps are now pre-gummed, there is a glue pot in all post offices. You should wait to see your stamps franked — which will often be done without your having to ask — to prevent postal workers from steaming them off. Aerogrammes (costing Rs3.75) are the most convenient way of sending letters. Post cards can be found in most places of tourist interest, though the quality is often very poor. Pictures of the Taj are cheaper in Bombay than they are in Agra. The cost of sending a post card to Europe is Rs2.70.

A poste restante service is available at city post offices, but not from the New Delhi G.P.O.; in Delhi visit the Pahar Ganj post office for poste restante pick-ups. You should try to time your mail collection carefully since some post offices (e.g. Bombay and Madras) hold mail for only 15 days. American Express might be preferable if you are in Delhi; Bombay, Calcutta, Madras or Srinagar (addresses in relevant sections below).

If you want to send a parcel overseas from a post office you will have to have it sewn up in cloth (tailors positioned outside major post offices will readily oblige) and sealed with wax. They may ask to see your passport at the postal desk. Alternatively you can pay a private parcel packer to do it for you, but you should use only ones which have been personally recommended.

Telephone

There can often be delays of several hours when trying to make an international call, and even then there is no guarantee of success. It is possible in some telephone offices to book a long distance call well in advance, and arrive back just 15 minutes before the arranged time. The rate is Rs84 for 3 minutes. Phone calls between major cities in India cost Rs45. For urgent phone calls within India ask for an express call; the price for 3 minutes will be about Rs175.

If using a public call box wait for the connection to be made before dropping in the money. Indians tend to shout down the phone which may seen to you at first as though they have not quite grasped the point of the technology; in fact many of the connections are so poor that shouting is essential.

Urgent telegrams cost Rs2 per word to Britain. Letter telegrams cost Re1 per word but with a stipulated minimum of 22 words. You may see in some post offices a sign board suggesting popular telegraphic greetings such as "Hearty congratulation on success in election" or "Many thanks for your Good Wishes which I/we reciprocate most heartily", but not "Congratulations on the birth of your daughter". It is a rule of the post office that you must supply the name of the recipient as well as the address.

Newspapers

It is possible in large towns to obtain British newspapers (usually the *Times* or *Telegraph*) though they are expensive. The best way to find out what is going on is to locate the British or American Consulate in a large city, and read the newspapers they have on display. There is an excellent American Library near Baroda House in New Delhi.

The Indians also publish some good English language newspapers, e.g. the *Times of India,* the *Indian Express,* the *Statesman* and the *Hindustan Times.* These include little international news, but are full of domestic matters.

Cinemas

There is at least one cinema in every town, the larger ones in the cities being air-conditioned or fan-cooled (try to sit directly under a fan). The Indian film industry is claimed to be the largest in the world, and specializes in musical melodramas of the rags to riches variety. Most cinemas also show Western films. Do not expect to see anything very racy; the chaste kiss in *Siddhartha* elicited cat calls and giggles.

Broadcasting

The news is frequently broadcast in English on regional radio stations throughout the country. For the B.B.C. World Service frequencies and times, see the Introduction. Although there is just one television per 700 people, the government is expanding the network. Even remote villages have access to American movies and improving educational programmes in Hindi.

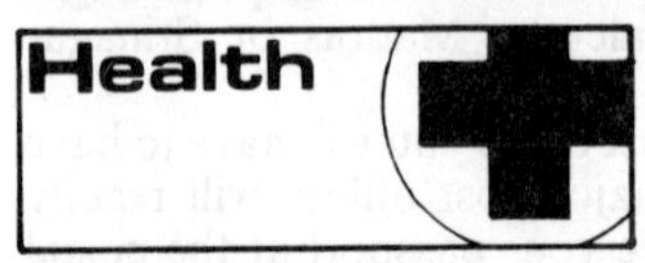

Malaria risk exists throughout the year in all parts of the country. Resistance to chloroquine has been widely reported particularly in areas which border Bangladesh, in Orissa, and in certain areas of Gujarat and Rajasthan, including around Bharatpur. Visitors to these areas should take both chloroquine and paludrine.

Medical care is free in India, though it is a very over-subscribed service. Private treatment is always available, but if you do become seriously ill, it may be wise to fly home. Nevertheless, India has many fine hospitals and clinics, often religious in foundation, which employ medical staff trained in Europe and America. These include the Breach Candy Hospital in Bombay (tel: 363651), the Belle Vue Clinic in Calcutta (tel: 442321), the S.D.M. Hospital in Jaipur (tel: 74149), the Holy Family Hospital in New Delhi (tel: 632355), the Jaggi Home in Agra (tel: 73315) and the Lady Willingdon Nursing Home in Madras (tel: 85868).

Vaccinations are available for a small fee from the New Delhi Medical Centre on Parliament Street. You can also have a gamma globulin shot but you have to buy your own vaccine. The N.D.M.C. is open 10.00-12.30 and 13.30-16.30.

Local Indian medicine relies more heavily on home remedies and herbal medicine than on drugs. For example fleaseed husk is used as a natural version of Lomotil and is very effective for diarrhoea. It is sold in chemist shops throughout India under the name Isabgol. Lomotil is available over the counter in India. If your skin is burnt by the sun or irritated by the strong soaps employed by a dhobi on your laundry buy "Caladryl" which is the Indian equivalent of Calamine.

Try not to become too paranoid about illness in India. Despite popular belief, few travellers contract anything very serious.

Food and Water

Water, unless boiled or treated, is definitely not safe to drink. You will often find yourself tempted to ignore this knowledge, especially if you see other Westerners drinking tap water. This may be because they have been in India long enough to build up at least a partial immunity. An even harder temptation to resist is the ice. A few city chemists in India sell a liquid called "Steriliq", which doesn't alter the taste much and can easily be added to fruit juices, etc. Avoid any food which looks unwashed or may have been washed in untreated water. On the whole street food which has been freshly cooked is safe.

India is predominantly vegetarian. Although meat is available, especially in the Mogul-influenced north, it is relatively expensive and more likely than vegetables to lead to digestive problems. In the north, wheat is the staple, and various breads (*roti*)

are served with spicy sauces: a *chappati* is a thin pancake-like bread, *poori* is deep fried, *paratha* is fried in ghee and *nan* is baked. The south is where most of the rice is consumed and meals are almost exclusively vegetarian.

The food eaten from street stalls or in bazaar restaurants is as tasty as it is cheap and is on the whole safe to eat. If you're feeling homesick you might want to try the new "Wimpy" bar in Connaught Place, New Delhi where a burger costs Rs7 and is served amidst sterile American-style surroundings. In South India, a *masala dosa* (fried rice or lentil dough stuffed with potato and onion curry) or *idli* (rice dumpling with spicy lentils or vegetables) will cost no more than Rs2. (South Indian food is probably the cheapest in Asia.) Few meals in India, apart from the occasional splurge in an upmarket restaurant, will cost more than Rs5. A day chosen at random from a traveller's budget might show a total of Rs5 spent on food: curd for breakfast, *pakoras* (savoury fritters) and bananas for lunch and *poori* for dinner. The liquid intake in the hot season would be much more expensive: 3 coffees (Rs2.40), 2 bottles of mango juice (Rs5), 3 soda waters (Rs4.20), 2 sugar cane juice (Re1) and 1 beer (Rs13.50).

Food is much hotter in the south, though not as fiery as in Sri Lanka. Goan cuisine is among the hottest in India and unusual because of the strong Christian (i.e. beef- and pork-eating) influence and the availability of fresh fish. This is probably the only place in India where you can eat sausage.

Wherever there is a community of Tibetan refugees, you will be able to get Tibetan food which is not nearly as spicy as Indian cuisine and uses a lot of noodles. *Thukpa* is a noodle and vegetable soup, and *mo-mos* are boiled, fried or steamed dumplings surrounding meat or vegetables.

If you are feeling frail or homesick, you can always order English food at railway stations — omelettes, toast, sometimes even cornflakes.

dal	— lentils or any pulse, stewed
aloo	— potatoes
dahi	— yoghurt (curd)
anda	— egg
khichhari	— lentils and rice cooked together (the origin of the word kedgeree)
sambhar	— chilli flavoured lentils and vegetables often served with idlis
sabzi	— vegetables
biriyani	— spiced fried rice and meat dish
samosa	— like a Cornish pasty, filled with vegetables
panir	— cheese
ghulab jamun	— small flour and almond sweet balls soaked in syrup
jalebi	— deep-fried pretzels soaked in syrup
barfi	— boiled condensed milk sweet, with pistachios and silver leaf (which is edible)
pani	— water

The heat forces you to drink a great deal. You cannot rely on soft drinks such as Thums Up and Campa Cola which are too sweet and too expensive (Rs2.50) to be enjoyed frequently. Soda water with lime is a pleasant (and cheaper) alternative. Bottled mango juice is good, as is apple juice made in Kashmir. Always return the bottle to the vendor.

Lassi is a delicious thick yoghurt drink with ice and salt or sugar, sometimes with rose water. Also try sugar cane juice if you notice a machine on the street resembling a wringer. The sugar canes are repeatedly fed through the mangle and the resulting liquid is flavoured with ginger and lime juice. This pleasure will cost less than 1 rupee (no discount for refusing the ice).

Tea is sweet and milky. If you would like to try some good quality Indian tea instead of tea dust, visit the tea-tasting centre in Old Delhi (Aap Ki Pas, Sterling House, 15 Netaji Subhash Marg). Coffee plantations abound in the south and excellent coffee is readily available (50 paise per cup).

Indian beer is passable. Kingfisher beer brewed in Bangalore is now imported to British off-licences, but is far from the best. Rosy Pelican and Golden Eagle are both much better. A 625ml bottle will cost between Rs11 and Rs20. Government bottle shops are substantially cheaper than hotels. Indian wine is not easy to find, and when you do it costs £6 and tastes rough. Like Sri Lanka, South India has arrack and toddy. A spirit distilled in Goa is made from cashews and is called *fenny*.

The following information covers just 25 places of interest in India. There are dozens of others which could have been included. The first group is in the north, and the second south of the Bombay-Calcutta line. The places are arranged roughly in a clockwise route from Delhi. For a list of Servas members in India, with whom you can stay if you are a member (see page 39), contact Harivallabh Parikh, Anand Niketan Ashram, P.O. Rangpur (Kavant), Via Kosindra, Dist. Baroda 391140.

DELHI

Delhi has intermittently been the capital of the subcontinent throughout its history and was the seat of government for the Moguls, the British and now for independent India. The architecture reflects the succession of ruling peoples. New Delhi, the spacious sprawling area south of the old city, was largely planned by the British architect Edwin Lutyens between 1920 and 1930. The architecture combines European with oriental style, the most noted building constructed during this period being the Secretariat and Viceroy's House (now the Presidential Palace). The centre around which most visitors' activities revolve is Connaught Circus. It has everything from a Wimpy bar to a Russian bookshop.

Old Delhi has a great deal of character. Visit Chandni Chowk, where all manner of exotic foodstuffs and handicrafts can be bought. A more sanitized place to shop is the Cottage Emporium on Janpath, New Delhi.

What to See

National Museum — on corner of Janpath and Raj Path. Contains collections of art, archaeological and anthropological finds, decorative arts and textiles. Closed Mondays.

Red Fort — in Old Delhi. Built of red sandstone in 1648 by the Moguls in honour of the great Shah Jahan. Well worth a visit for its splendid interior, museum of Mogul paintings, etc. and tiny, graceful Pearl Mosque. The Indian Tourist Board arranges entertaining son-et-lumiére exhibitions (Rs5).

Jami Masjid — also in Old Delhi. Huge mosque built by the Mogul emperor Shah Jahan in 1658. Made of marble and sandstone.

Delhi Zoo — Mathura Road, New Delhi. Contains twice as many cages as animals, but still exciting to see white tigers.

Qutb Minar — 9 miles south of the city. Huge and ancient tower surrounded by gates, pillars and the oldest mosque in India.

Accommodation

The two areas to look are Pahar Ganj, on the road stretching away from New Delhi Railway Station and, slightly more upmarket, along and near Janpath.

Vivek Hotel — 42 Pahar Ganj (Main Bazaar). Rs50 double with shared bath. Honest management.

Hotel Navrang — 644 C Mohalla Baoli, 6 Tooti Chowk, Pahar Ganj. Tel: 521965. Rs15 single. Friendly.

White House Tourist Lodge — 8177 Arakashan Road, Pahar Ganj. Rs70 double.

Tana Home — behind Regal Cinema on outer circle of Connaught Circus near Parliament Street. Rs35 double.

Roshan Villa — 7 Babar Lane, near Indian Airlines office. Rs30 dorm, Rs60 for a room. Guard your belongings.

Ashok Yatri Niwas — Ashok Road off Janpath. Rs80 double. Good views from top storey.

Y.M.C.A. Tourist Hotel — Jai Singh Road. Open to both sexes. Only for those seeking luxury. $6.50-$21.50.

Y.W.C.A. — International Guest House, Parliament Street. Accepts men. Very luxurious. Rs150 double.

Youth Hostel — 5 Nyaya Marg, Chanakyapuri. 4 miles from New Delhi Station. Rs15 per bed.

Tourist Camp — opposite Irwin Hospital, near the Delhi Gate. Tel: 27 89 29. Rs22 single, Rs35 double. Rs10 extra for deluxe rooms.

Useful Addresses

Government of India Tourist Office — 88 Janpath, near Connaught Place. Tel: 320005. Free city maps; open 08.00-19.30.

British High Commission — 8 Shantipath, Chanakyapuri. Tel: 690371.

British Council Library — AIFACS Building, Rafi Marg. Tel: 381401.

American Embassy — Shantipath, Chanakyapuri. Tel: 690351.

American Express — Wenger House, Connaught Place (near Radial Road 2). Tel: 344119. Open 10.00-14.00.

Thomas Cook — Imperial Hotel, Janpath (opposite Tourist Office). Tel: 312171.

Nepalese Embassy — Barakhamba Road. Tel: 381484.

General Post & Telephone Office — Janpath (not far from Tourist Office).

Poste Restante New Delhi — Post Office, Gole Dak Khana (corner of Baba Kharak Singh Marg and Ashoka Road). Open 08.00-18.00.

Central Telegraph Office — Bangla Sahib Road. Open 24 hours a day.

AGRA

The first mention of Agra occurs in the ancient Hindu epic (the *Mahabharata*), when the town was called Agrabana, meaning "Paradise" in Sanskrit. Agra became the capital of the Mogul Emperor Shah Jahan under whom a number of splendid buildings were constructed such as the famous Taj Mahal and the Fort.

What to See

The Taj Mahal, India's quintessential tourist attraction, was begun in 1630 by Shah Jahan as a tomb for his favourite queen, Mumtaz-i-Mahal, who had died in childbirth. Like many Islamic tombs throughout northern India, its serenity celebrates love rather than death. It took a large number of local and imported artisans twenty-two years to build. Maintenance is still necessary; in October 1985 a tourist noticed a leak in the dome roof. The details of ornamentation as well as the general effect are exquisite. Around the times of the full moon, the gardens remain open until midnight. Entrance fee Rs2.

Although the Taj Mahal has absorbed most tourists' attention the Tomb of I'timud-ud-daula across the River Jamuna is also a beautiful symmetrical building of white marble.

An interesting excursion can be made from Agra to the ruined city of Fatehpur Sikri, 23 miles away. This was the capital of the great Emperor Akbar (Shah Jahan's grandfather) for just 15 years during the 16th century, before it was abandoned in quest of a more reliable water source. The buildings are mostly of red sandstone except for the magnificent marble tomb of Salim Chishti, Akbar's private prophet. The bus leaves the Idgah Bus Station regularly and the cost is Rs9 return.

Accommodation

Tourist Bungalow — opposite Raja Ki Mandi Railway Station. Rs40double. Not very central (Rs8 rickshaw ride to Taj).
The Jaggi — 183 Taj Road. Singles from Rs20. Good food.
Hotel Akbar Inn — 21 Mall Road. Camping available. Competitive prices.
Laurie's Hotel — Gandhi Road. Camping can be negotiated. Swimming pool filled with mineral water.
Hotel Blue Star — Rs15 single.
Shanti Hotel — near south gate of Taj. Clean and friendly. Good views of Taj from the balconies. Rs30 double, Rs15 single.
Mrs Framjee's Guest House — 16 Mansfield Road. Tel: 72205. Rs25 single, Rs40 double. Quiet location. Homely atmosphere. Unfortunately guest house closes whenever proprietress visits her children.

Useful Addresses

Tourist Information — 191 The Mall. Tel: 72377.
Head Post Office — The Mall (across from the Tourist Office). Tel: 76914.
Indian Airlines — Hotel Clarks Shiraz, Taj Road. Tel: 73434. Hotel has a swimming pool which you can use for a fee.

JAIPUR

Jaipur is named after its founder, Maharaja Jai Singh II, who built the "pink city" at the beginning of the 18th century. The pinkness derives from the red sandstone which the Maharaja used to build his City Palace and next door Palace of the Winds, so called because of its large number of latticed windows which admit the breeze. Jai Singh was not only a ruler but an astronomer, and his observatory (or Jantar Mantar) is worth visiting.

Accommodation

Government Tourist Bungalow — opposite the railway station. From Rs40. Private bathrooms.

Jaipur Inn — Shiva Marg. Tel: 66057. Cheap dorm and camping available.
Hotel Chandra Lok — Sansar Chandra Marg (behind GPO). Rs50 double.
Hotel Rose — B6 Shopping Centre (near Subhash Nagar Bani Park). Rs25 double.
Youth Hostel — SMS Stadium Grounds (near Ram Bagh Palace Hotel, where evening folk dance performances take place). Tel: 67576.

Useful Addresses
Tourist Office — State Hotel. Tel: 72200.
Post Office — Mirza Ismail Road.
Indian Airlines — Ajmer Road. Tel: 72940.

JAISALMER

Although remote, this mediaeval desert city is visited by many tourists who consider the 24 hour journey from Jaipur across the Great Indian Desert to be worthwhile. They come to ride the camels (Rs75 per day on a camel safari) and to admire the yellow sandstone architecture. (As in Cotswold villages, new buildings must use a matching building material.) Unfortunately Jaisalmer has several military establishments built to defend India against Pakistan. The border is just 75 miles away.

Accommodation
It is easy to find a room for less than Rs20. The Rama Guest House will let you sleep on the roof for considerably less. Also try the Hotel Pleasure (near the bus stop) for Rs20 double or the Tourist Hotel near the railway station.

UDAIPUR

The setting of Udaipur is more beautiful than that of Jaipur or Agra. The island palace, now a luxury hotel, appears to be floating on the untroubled waters of Lake Pichola. The larger City Palace which overlooks the lake contains some wonderful Rajput mosaic and mirror decorations. The busy bazaars are in marked contrast with the otherwordly serenity of the lake.

Accommodation
Lal Ghat Guest House — behind Jagdith Temple (a carved temple in honour of Vishnu). From Rs25 (prices vary according to view). Quiet atmosphere.
Hotel Chandra Prakash — Lake Palace Road. From Rs35. Own restaurant.
Hotel Badi Haveli — Rs15-Rs25. Good location.
Royal Hotel — near bus station. Rs60 double.

Useful Addresses
Tourist Office — Railway Station. Tel: 3605.
Indian Airlines — Delhi Gate. Tel: 3952.
Post Office — Hospital Road.

MOUNT ABU

This hill station in southern Rajasthan is nearly 4000 ft. above sea level and therefore provides some welcome coolness after the heat of the western deserts. The place abounds with exotic birds and plants, and it also has many interesting Jain temples. The sight-seeing tour (6 hours for Rs15-Rs18) is recommended since it is difficult to see all the places of interest independently. A fascinating phenomenon takes place every day at sunset: all the visitors and many local people walk out to a place called Sunset Point, which is a natural amphitheatre on a cliffside, to watch the sunset as if it were a piece of theatre.

There are many suitable hotels and a youth hostel. The Government Tourist Bungalow is excellent and costs about Rs30 double.

AHMEDABAD

Ahmedabad is a prosperous city with some impressive modern architecture (e.g. the Centre for Management Studies) as well as exquisite 14th and 15th century mosques. In 1985 it was sadly afflicted with violence sparked by an increase in the quota of "untouchables" in education and employment.

What to See

Ahmad Shah's Mosque, Rani Sipri's Mosque and the *Jami Masjid* all have ornate and delicate decorations.

Gandhi's Ashram — across the Sabarmati River, and 4 miles from the city centre. Founded by Mahatma Gandhi in 1915. Has a handicrafts centre and a spinning wheel factory. A small museum contains Gandhi's few possessions and an account of his life and achievements.

Calico Museum of Textiles — "Retreat", Shahibag. Wonderful selection of handmade textiles, some ancient, from all parts of India. Clear descriptions of the techniques used. Set in group of buildings designed by Le Corbusier.

Accommodation

Hotel Capital — Chandanwadi, Mirzapur. Tel: 24633. Comfortable. Rs60 double. Large pleasant garden. Own restaurant.
Apna Ghar Guest House — Relief Road. Rs30.
Gandhi Ashram Guest House — Ashram Road. Run by state government. From Rs75.

Useful Addresses

Gujarat Tourist Information — H.K. House, Ashram Road (near Jivabhai Chambers). Tel: 449683.
Indian Airlines — Lal Darwaja. Tel: 391737.
Post & Telegraph Office — 8 Salapus Cross Road.

BOMBAY

The site of Bombay was originally a cluster of seven fishing villages. Then it became a Portuguese settlement and was officially founded in 1534. In 1661 the territory was ceded to Britain as part of the dowry settlement of Catherine of Braganza. At that time Bombay consisted of seven islands separated by the sea at high tide. The major development of Bombay took place in the second half of the 19th century with the construction of the docks, development of cotton mills and erection of many impressive public buildings. It is a wealthy centre of commerce, and compared to the rest of India, expensive. Bombay is now the capital of the state of Maharashtra, and one of the biggest problems facing the city is the rapidly increasing population, which at the 1981 census stood at 8,200,000.

Bombay is also a good jumping-off point for a visit to the caves of Ajanta and Ellora, an impressive complex of Buddhist temples, some of which are painted.

What to See

Prince of Wales Museum — Fort Bombay, which has two collections of art, archaeology and natural history. The galleries contain some good examples of early Indian art and Mogul miniatures. Closed Monday.

Elephanta Caves — little island, about 6 miles from Bombay harbour. On the hill are temples carved from rock, dating back to the 4th and 8th centuries. To go there, enquire about boats from Apollo Bunder at the Gateway of India.

Hanging Gardens — contain the famous "Towers of Silence" where bodies are left to be eaten by vultures rather than buried or cremated. This ritual is practised by those of the Parsi faith, who were originally Zoroastrian refugees from Persia during the 8th century A.D. Although the Towers are off limits (too much human activity frightens off the birds), you can admire the topiary in the gardens.

Chowpatty Beach — magicians and holy men make evening visits bizarre and amusing.

Accommodation

Salvation Army Hostel — "Red Shield House", 30 Merewether Road, Fort. Tel: 241824. Rs40 for dorm bed and three meals. Rs150 double with board. If full, try Whalley's Guest House or the Carlton Hotel on the same road (from Rs60).
Y.W.C.A. — 18 Madame Cama Road, Fort. Men and women accepted. Advance booking essential.
Y.M.C.A. — 18 YMCA Road. Tel: 891262. $9-$13.
Lawrence Hotel — Ashok Kumar Lane (behind Prince of Wales Museum). Tel: 243618. Rs100 double.
Wadia House — 120 Wodehouse Road.
Suba Guest House — near Gateway of India. Rs75 double.

Useful Addresses

Tourist Information — 123 Karve Road, Churchgate. Tel: 293144. Also at Santa Cruz Airport.
U.K. High Commission — Hong Kong Bank Building, Mahatma Gandhi Road. Tel: 274874.
British Council Library — Mittal Tower "C" Wing, Nariman Point. Tel: 223480.
American Consulate — Lincoln House, 78 Bjhulabhai Desai Road. Tel: 823611.
American Express — Majithia Chambers, 3rd Floor, 276 Dadabhoy Naroji Road. Tel: 266361.
Thomas Cook — Dadabhoy Naroji Road (P.O. Box 46). Tel: 239640.
Main Post Office — Bori Bunder near Victoria Terminus.
Central Telegraph Office — Flora Fountain, Veer Nariman Road.

GOA

Goa is a former Portuguese colony, which has a large Christian population and many churches, cathedrals and monasteries. Portugal established its rule in 1510 and abandoned it only in 1961 when India reclaimed the territory. As a result, Goan people have many unique customs, for example the women rarely wear saris. As the writers of purple prose employed by the Department of Tourism say "Goa is an exhilarating distillation of the Latin and Indian temper brought to a brilliant culmination under a tropical sun."

The area is famous not only for its beautiful beaches but for its semi-permanent community of Western "freaks". They say that coach tours used to be organized for Indians from Bombay to come and watch the antics of the hippies in Goa. Some reports make the crowded beach life sound very depressing. However there are villages all along the coast, and you can choose between the disco music and hamburger joints of Calangute, Anjuna and Chapora, and more unspoiled and humble places such as Benaulam Beach. When you tire of lazing on a beach, visit the Friday market at Mapuca, 18 miles north of Panaji. You can also hire a bicycle to explore the coastal villages.

Useful Addresses

Government Tourist Office — Communidada Building, Church Square, Panaji. Tel: 3412 (Panaji is the capital of Goa).

Mogul Lines — V.S. Dempo & Co., Panaji. Tel: 3842. For booking steamer to Bombay.

COCHIN

In addition to the Portuguese influence on Cochin, there are also Dutch, Chinese and ancient Jewish influences. Scattered over several islands connected by a very cheap ferry service, Cochin is both geographically and culturally a fascinating city.

What to See

The Dutch Palace — in Mattancherry south of Fort Cochin. The Mattancherry Palace was built by the Portuguese in 1557 but renovated by the Dutch a century later. Wonderful murals.

The Jewish Synagogue — in the Mattancherry spice bazaar and near interesting junk shops. The Jewish community in India is 2,000 years old but has now almost disappeared. Lovely Chinese tiled floor. Entrance fee 25 paise.

Chinese fishing nets — stretch along the western part of Fort Cochin. These spindly wooden structures work like see-saws and are operated by about four men. The fishermen are very friendly and may invite you up onto the platform.

Accommodation

Hotel Elite — near St. Francis Church in the Fort. Rs7 single.
Princess Lodge — across the road from the Elite. Same price range.
Sheetal Tourist Home — near Idgah bus station in Ernakulam. Rs25 double.

Useful Addresses

Tourist Office — Shanmughan Road, Ernakulam. Tel: 33234. (Ernakulum is the name of the mainland part of Cochin, where the bus and railway stations are located).

TRIVANDRUM

Trivandrum in the deep south is the state capital of Kerala and is the favoured destination for people coming from Sri Lanka by air. There is a good museum of art with works from China, Tibet and Bali, as well as examples of work by modern Indian artists. The aquarium and zoo are also worth visiting. Ten miles away from the 7 hills on which Trivandrum is built are the beaches of Kovalam, probably some of the best in India, but not undiscovered by young Westerners.

Away from the beach on the road up to the road junction and post office, is an untouristy cafe which serves toddy, arrack and good food.

Accommodation

International Tourist Home — Press Road. Doubles from Rs25.
Hotel Shalimar. — near station. From Rs30.
Y.W.C.A. — Main Road.
Youth Hostel — Nr. Boat Club, Veli. Rs6.
Moon Cottage — Kovalam Beach. Standard budget accommodation. Rs10 single. Should shop around for accommodation and bargain in Kovalam.

KANYAKUMARI (Cape Comorin)

This is the southernmost tip of India where the Arabian Sea, Bay of Bengal and the Indian Ocean converge. It is an important Hindu pilgrimage place and has a festive seaside resort atmosphere. It is famous for its sunsets and sunrises, especially December to March. There is a helpful information centre at the bus station with maps, leaflets and boards displaying bus and train times and prices.

Accommodation

Tamil Nadu Hotel — next to lighthouse (visible from information office). Youth hostel annexe of former government tourist bungalow. Dorm beds Rs7.50.
Township Lodge — at bus stand. Accommodation for Indian tourists mainly. Rs8 single, Rs10 double.
Ariya Bhavan — opposite Tri-Sea Lodge in main street. Rs30 double.

MADURAI

Madurai means "City of Festivals" and has one of the most splendid Hindu temples in South India. The Meenakshi Temple was built in the mid-17th century and is dedicated to Shiva and Parvati. Ten thousand devotees visit daily and it is endlessly interesting to watch them carry out their devotions (*pujas*) such as crossing their arms and touching their ears three times in front of Ganesh or throwing butter pats at the angry second son of Shiva to cool him down. Best of all are the trained elephants who take rupee offerings in their trunks and bless (and at the same time terrify) small children. It is worth climbing the south gopuram or tower (entrance Re1) early in the morning since it is cooler than most places and affords a good view over the temple complex. An excellent guided tour can be provided by Mr. Pandidurai (telephone 27064 before 10.30) for Rs10.

Accommodation

Ravi Lodge — Mandayan Asaril Street, just off Town Hall Road (5 minutes walk from bus and train stations). Rs15 single with attached bath.
Ruby Lodge — 92 West Perumal Maistry Street, close to Town Hall Road. Tel: 25458. Rs15 single, Rs20 double.
Hotel Tamil Nadu (formerly Government Tourist Bungalow) — West Veli Street. Single Rs35, double Rs60.
Hotel Subham — Rs35 double.

KODAIKANAL

Known as Kodai, this hill station is beautifully situated looking over the steaming plains to the south. Your time may be pleasantly spent walking around the lake (about four miles), past flower bedecked bungalows with names like "Sleepy Hollow" and "Orchard Cottage", past locals (and resident hippies) fishing and watching the Indian tourists out boating (Rs15 per hour).

The best place to stay by far is the new Greenlands Youth Hostel on Coaker's Walk. Magnificent views, especially at night. Rs7 plus Re1 hire of blanket for chilly nights.

MADRAS

Madras is the fourth largest city in India (1981 population of 4.3 million), sprawling over an area of 50 square miles on the ocean front. But despite its size, it is a relaxing city, especially compared to Bombay and Delhi. The city is also the site of the oldest European settlement in India, first Portuguese and then British. Under the British, Madras became the first major town of the East India Company. The present day city is very industrialized and, along with Calcutta, is a centre of the prolific Indian film industry. It is a good centre from which to visit some of the ancient temples of South India, especially Mahabalipuram, 36 miles south along the coast. The 7th century Dravidian architecture of the Rathas (temples) is quite remarkable.

Accommodation

Broadlands Hotel — 16 Vallabha Agraharan Street, near the Star Cinema. Tel: 845573. Excellent establishment offering many services: bicycle hire, poste restante, doctor, etc. Rs20/30 single; Rs 40/55 double. Dorm beds available.
Godavasi Hotel — Anna Salai.
Y.W.C.A. — 1086 Poonamallee High Road. Open to all. Rs30 single. Bathrooms, fans and linen provided. Camping Rs3 each.
Gokula Hotel — 1089 Poonamallee High Road. Tel: 39081. From Rs125 double. Near station.
Youth Hostel — Indira Nagar, 5 miles from city centre. Rs6.

Useful Addresses

Tourist Information — 154 Anna Salai (formerly Mount Road). Tel: 88520.
British High Commission — 24 Anderson Road. Tel: 83136.
British Council Library — 150A Anna Salai. Tel: 82857/9.
General Post Office — North Beach Road.
American Express — Binny Ltd., 65 Armenian Street. Tel: 30181.
Thomas Cook — 20 Rajaji Road. Tel: 24976.

BHUBANESWAR

The new city, capital of Orissa State, is impressive but it is the old Bhubaneswar which you will find more interesting. Old Bhubaneswar once rivalled Varanasi as a centre of Jainism and at one time there were over 7,000 shrines encircling the lake in the centre of the town. Today there are only 500 left, but they do illustrate the different phases of Orissan art.

The finest carving and architecture are found in the Great Temple or Lingaraja (closed to non-Hindus), the Raja Rani and the Parashuramesvara. The tourist office, located in the Panthanivas government hotel, can provide more information on historic details of these temples.

34 miles away is the seaside resort of Puri, popular with Hindus who come on pilgrimage, and with foreign visitors.

What to See

Tribal Research Centre and State Museum — tribal ornaments, weapons and dress, palm leaf manuscripts and ancient sculptures.

Accommodation

Jolly Lodge — Cuttack Road. Rs20.
Panthanivas — formerly state tourist bungalow. Tel: 54515. Rs100 double.

KHAJURAHO

The thousand year old Hindu and Jain temples are completely covered with carvings of gods, demons and women. Khajuraho is most famous for its erotic carvings, but there are many other subjects, including every day activities such as applying makeup or emerging from the bath.

Accommodation

Hotel Sunset View — Main Road (near bus station). Rs40 double.
Rahil — Government tourist hotel not far from temples. Rs40 single. Dorm beds for Rs10.

Useful Addresses

Tourist Office — near Western Temple Group. Tel: 47.
Indian Airlines — Khajuraho Hotel. Tel: 35.

VARANASI (Benares)

This is the foremost place of pilgrimage in India and is sacred both to Hindus and Buddhists. The city is said to be among the oldest in the world, although much of it was destroyed by Moslem invaders in the 13th century. Worship of Shiva, Lord of the Universe, predominates.

The banks of the holy River Ganges are lined with temples and *ghats,* flights of stone steps descending to the water where pilgrims bathe. For a Hindu, Varanasi is the preferred place to die because this guarantees salvation. The best time to see the various rituals is just after dawn, but photography is forbidden.

Six miles away is Sarnath where Buddha preached his first sermon. Several centuries later the great Buddhist convert, the Emperor Ashoka, built numerous stupas and monasteries, and Buddhism flourished from this centre.

Accommodation

Tourist Bungalow — near station. Tel: 63186. Rs30 double.
Tandon Guest House — Gai Ghat near Machodari Park. Tel: 55485. Rs10/15 single, Rs15/25 double some with private bath. Good view of the Ganges.
Trimurti Guest House — near Golden Temple. Rs10.
Sri Venkateswar Lodge — D 5/64 Dashawamedh, near Golden Temple. Rs10 single, Rs20 double.
Maharaja Hotel — Jangambari Road. Tel: 55089. Rs30/40 double. Meals available.

Useful Addresses

Tourist Information Office — 15B The Mall. Tel: 64189. Also an information desk in the railway station.
Post & Telegraph Office — Bisheswarganj (near Panchganga Ghat).

CALCUTTA

Calcutta is one of the most heavily industrialized cities of India. Along with Bombay, the city is the commercial capital of India, with many factories and sweat shops, and a population exceeding 9 million. There is extreme poverty and extreme wealth and people often find Calcutta an upsetting place.

Until 1911, Calcutta was the capital of India, and as a result was endowed with many splendid Victorian buildings, such as the Victoria Memorial Building (which now houses the museum) and the New Gothic St. Paul's Cathedral. There is also an open park area beside the river, where you can watch the polo or the setting sun.

The bazaar area is worth visiting, and shirts, shoes, etc. can be bought here at very cheap prices provided you're willing to bargain.

What to See

The Indian Museum — corner of Sudder Street and Jawaharlal Nehru Road. The oldest museum in India, opened in 1878. It has a good collection of art, archaeology, geology, history, etc. Closed on Mondays.

The Victoria Memorial Museum — not far from the Tourist Office. Built to commemorate Queen Victoria's jubilee. It is an impressive building set in a spectacular garden. The contents mainly deal with British India, but there are some good water-colours of old India.

Accommodation

Red Shield Guest House (Salvation Army) — 2 Sudder Street. Tel: 242895. Dorm beds only Rs10. Very clean and pleasant.

Paragon — 2 Stuart Lane (off Sudder Street). Rs10 dorm, Rs15 single, Rs25/40 double.

Astoria — 6/2 & 6/3 Sudder Street. Tel: 241359. Rs45 single, Rs90 double.

Y.W.C.A. — 1 Middleton Road. Tel: 240260. Rs50 double.

Y.M.C.A. — 25 Jawaharlal Nehru Road (Chowringhee). Tel: 233504. $8.

A very good place to eat is the Kalsa Sikh Restaurant, opposite the Red Shield. Also try Moghul Durbar on Free School Street.

Useful Addresses

Tourist Information — 4 Shakespeare Sarani. Tel: 441402.

U.K. Consulate — 1 Ho-Chi-Minh Sarani. Tel: 445171.

British Council Library — 5 Shakespeare Sarani. Tel: 445378.

U.S.A. Consulate — 5/1 Ho-Chi-Minh Sarani. Tel: 443611.

American Express — 21 Old Court House Street. Tel: 232133.

Thomas Cook — Everett Travel Service, 4 Government Place North. Tel: 239640.

Nepalese Consulate — 19 Sterndale Road (near the Zoological Gardens). Tel: 454293.

Bhutanese Consulate — 48 Tivoli Court, Pramothesh Barua Sarani. Tel: 441301.

General Post Office — BBD Bagh (Dalhousie Square).

DARJEELING

You will need a permit to visit this area of India unless you fly to Bagdogra Airport 50 miles away (see section above on Internal Travel Restrictions).

The name in Tibetan means "place of the thunderbolt", but it is a hospitable place, not as posh as other Indian hill resorts. At 7,000 feet, it offers cool temperatures and wonderful views of the Himalayas, (especially, Kanchenjunga, third highest in the world). The high season is April to June and October/ November. Outside these times hotel prices drop.

Darjeeling is built on a series of terraces up a hill. The "ground floor" is probably the best as this is where most of the working population lives, and so is less developed for tourism. The centre of the town boasts Observatory Hill, which is the site of Mahakala Cave, sacred to Shiva. Another interesting excursion is to the Happy Valley Tea Estate. Many people go on short or long treks from Darjeeling; a popular one is the 6 day trek to Sandakphur, from which you can see Everest.

Accommodation

Timber Lodge — Laden La Road. Rs15 single, Rs25 double, including linen.

Youth Hostel — Dr. Zakir Hussain Road. Rs6 a bed. Advance booking recommended. Trekking equipment and information available.

Shamrock Hotel — Upper Beechwood Road. Rs10-20 single, Rs25-30 double in off-season. Rs75 double in high season; extra charged if you're accompanied by a tout. Nice wooden rooms upstairs with beautiful views.

Useful Addresses

Tourist Information — Bellevue Hotel, Chowrasta. Tel: 2050.

Foreigners' Registration Office — Laden La Road, where you extend your permit.

Post Office — Laden La Road (next to Sikkim bus stand).

SIKKIM

Sikkim is a Himalayan state which merged with India in 1975 and is now a restricted area. The capital is Gangtok (5,800 feet). The best seasons to visit are mid-February to late May, and October to mid-December which avoid the heavy monsoons. Permits are essential; see section on Internal Travel Restrictions above.

A regular bus service runs between Darjeeling and Gangtok operated by Sikkim Nationalized Transport, which is often booked up in advance (cost Rs40) and is a beautiful ride. Sikkim is another trekking centre, though you must have a permit.

What to See

Research Institute of Tibetology — famous collection of Tibetan books and Buddhist icons. Closed Sunday.

Orchid Sanctuary — best seasons to visit orchid collection are April to August and October to November.

Tsuk-La-Khang — royal chapel with beautiful wood carvings, rich mural paintings and lavishly decorated altars. Not always open.

Institute of Cottage Industries — outlet for traditional handicrafts including woven woollen carpets, blankets, shawls, choktses (carved tables), etc.

Enchey Monastery — 2 miles from Gangtok. The monastery is over 200 years old. Religious dances are performed every December.

Rhumtek Monastery — 15 miles from Gangtok. The headquarters of a Buddhist sect. The building has Tibetan architecture.

Accommodation

Tourist Lodge — Tel: 292. Government run. Rs35 single, Rs50 double.
Green Hotel — Tel: 2254. Hotel motto: "Come as a tourist, go as a friend" Rs40/55 single, Rs50/80 double.
Orchid Hotel — Tel: 381. Seasonal fluctuations in price. Good food.
Deeki Hotel — Tel: 301.
Hotel Mayur — Tel: 2752. Singles Rs40, doubles Rs60.

Useful Addresses

Tourist Office — National Highway at junction with Main Bazaar.
Foreigners' Registration Office — National Highway near bus station.

DHARAMSALA

Dharamsala is a bustling Indian town situated on a spur of the Dhauladhar range of perennially snow-capped mountains. 3 miles beyond Dharamsala at an altitude of 7,185ft (bus connections every ½ hour) lies the settlement of MacLeod Ganj. It is here that the 14th Dalai Lama, religious and political head of 100,000 Tibetan refugees in India, resides. Nearby his residence where he gives public and private audiences to foreigners, is Namgyal monastery where he may often be seen officiating at rituals. The offices of the Tibetan government in exile as well as the Library of Tibetan Works and Archives are 20 minutes downhill from the monastery. The Library houses many books in Western languages about Tibet and the neighbouring countries of Ladakh, Nepal, Sikkim and Bhutan. It also runs courses for foreigners in the Tibetan language and Buddhist philosophy (find out in advance about these courses from Tibet House in Delhi). Other places of interest in MacLeod Ganj are the Tibetan Medical Centre where herbal medicines are prepared according to the ancient Tibetan tradition. Ama Lobsang, a famous female medical practitioner, has her clinic in the main bazar. She specializes in women's ailments and prescribes herbal contraceptive pills. Another Tibetan organization housed nearby is the Tibetan Music, Dance and Drama Society. Tibetan operas are regularly staged at least once a year in spring and/or autumn.

Accommodation

Cheap accommodation (Rs5) and food are available at the Library of Tibetan Works. There are many Tibetan hotels in and around the bus station in MacLeod Ganj. Prices vary between Rs12 and Rs20 for a single room. Try the Rainbow Hotel and Himalaya Hotel. For greater comfort try the Tibet Hotel (Rs60 double) or Hotel Bhagsu (Rs65 double). There are many Tibetan restaurants in MacLeod Ganj used regularly by Tibetans as well as foreigners.

DALHOUSIE

This is a charming mountain village with a large Tibetan refugee population. About 2 miles from town there is a Tibetan carpet weaving centre where it is possible to see all stages of the process from the spinning and dying of wool by hand to the clipping of the finished carpet.

You can make an interesting expedition by foot to Chamba, the chief town of the district, 20 miles away, via Kalatope and Khajiar. In the spring the semi-nomadic water buffalo herders gather in Chamba on their way to summer pastures. Also you might see some Gaddi shepherds, identified by the 20 metres of rope they wear around their waists, to rescue sheep in distress.

Accommodation

Tourist Bungalow Dalhousie — large rooms with verandahs. Rs45 double.
Tibetan Hotel — wonderfully humble place. No plumbing. Rs4 per person. Also good dinners for Rs4. (Avoid eating at the Metro Hotel.)
Kalatope Forest Bungalow — 6 miles from Dalhousie. Beautiful isolated setting. Permission must be obtained in Dalhousie. Rs15 double.
Tourist Lodge Bungalow — Rs20 single. Dorm beds available.

SRINAGAR (Kashmir)

The Vale of Kashmir in the Himalayas has more in common with Pakistan than India because of the Moslem majority. Lingering shots of Kashmir near the end of the film *A Passage to India* have made it an even more popular destination for tourists. Srinagar, capital of Kashmir, has been called the Venice of the East, but a Venice at 5,227 feet above sea level and surrounded by the Himalayas. The city with its canals was largely built during the 6th century A.D. The best view of the city with its many gardens can be obtained from the hill Takht-i-Sulaiman (Throne of Solomon) which is crowned by an 8th-century Hindu temple.

The most famous aspect of Srinagar is the large number of houseboats on the lakes which visitors may rent. Nagin Lake is cleaner and more beautiful than Dal Lake. During the British Raj many colonial families spent the hot summers on these houseboats because land was difficult to obtain in the area. The Tourist Office, located in the Residency Palace, can advise on the category of houseboats (luxury to D-class) and will help you to find a suitable one. Student discounts are available. You must hire a *shikara* or water taxi (about one rupee) to transport you between your boat and the shore. Unfortunately it is difficult to avoid touts and high pressure salesmen, urging you to buy all manner of services and souvenirs.

The surrounding area is excellent for trekking and other sports. 20 miles away is the resort of Gulmarg at 8,500 feet which is a "meadow of flowers" in the spring and summer and a good place in winter for novice skiers. Five days of skiing, including the hire of equipment, will cost a fraction of what it would in the Alps, say Rs800 for seven days all included.

Accommodation

Loloma Houseboat — Dal Lake, Gate 2.
Export Houseboat — next door to the Loloma and under the same management. Rs40 single, Rs80 double including breakfast and good dinners. Free Kashmiri tea.
King Suliman — 90 Zero Bridge, Bund Side. Reasonable prices. Proprietor's son is a mountain guide.
Shah Palace — opposite the Boulevard, Dalgate. Reasonable prices with good service and excellent food.
Snow Goose — as above. Trekking and fishing expeditions can be arranged.
Chaco Palace Hotel — Dal Lake, Gate 1. Rs15-20.

Useful Addresses

Tourist Office — off Sherwani Road. Tel: 72449.
American Express — Kai Travels, Tara Bhavan Place, Boulevard 2. Tel: 4180.
Medical Clinic — Dr Turki, c/o J.R. Smith & Co., Chemists, Lalchowk.

LADAKH

Until about a decade ago, Ladakh and Zanskar were the preserve of the local Buddhists, whose culture is similar to Tibetan culture, and the odd explorer or mountaineer. Now with the completion of the road from Srinagar to Leh (capital of Ladakh) more and more travellers are discovering this barren but beautiful region. Buddhist monasteries (called *gompas)* are perched on peaks and clifftops and most can be visited by bus, jeep or on foot. The trekking is magnificent; information on routes and guides is available from the tourist office in the Dak Bungalow.

Accommodation

Shalimar Guest House — Rs30 double.
Hotel Omasila — 15 minutes walk from Indian Airlines office. Quiet and out of the way.
Himalaya Hotel — good food. Camping for Rs10.
Bimla Guest House — Pharka Leh. Tel: 194101. Near Tourist Reception Centre.

WILDLIFE SANCTUARIES

The age of the maharajas who conducted wholesale slaughters of elephants, tigers, etc. is long over, and nowadays India's government is as conservation-conscious as the West. Most national parks cater to the budget traveller who is willing to sleep on a bench in an observation tower as well as to the luxury-loving tourists. Although admission is charged, it is usually very modest; for example Periyar Wildlife Sanctuary in South India charges Rs4 for a 1½ hour boat trip from which almost every one sees elephants, Rs2 Kerala state surcharge, Rs5 to sleep overnight in an observation tower and Rs10 for the boat transport and guide to take you to the tower. Some parks are more regimented than others, but it is often possible to wander in the jungle or to rent a bicycle to explore independently.

Keoladeo Bird Sanctuary near Bharatpur is just 35 miles west of Agra and so is included on many tourist itineraries. Thousands of migratory birds, including the rare Siberian crane, come between October and March, the best season for a visit (though during the monsoon it is possible to see the birds nesting). Bicycles may be rented for Rs5-Rs8 per day.

Parks famous for their tigers are Corbett National Park in the foothills of Uttar Pradesh, Sunderbans which mostly consists of mangrove swamp on the Bangladesh border, Similipal Tiger Reserve in Orissa and the Periyar Wildlife Sanctuary in Kerala. Partly due to their scarcity (a single tiger's territory will be about 28 square miles) and partly because they emerge only at night, it is exceedingly rare for a passing visitor to see a tiger. Still, it is worth going for the excitement of hearing the noises of the jungle, among them the growl or roar of a tiger.

Bibliography

J. G. Farrell, *The Siege of Krishnapur* (Penguin 1975).
Trevor Fishlock, *The India File: Inside the Subcontinent* (John Murray, 1983).
E. M. Forster, *The Hill of Devi* (1953, Penguin Travel Library, 1983).
Gita Mehta , *Karma Cola* (Fontana, 1981). About the exploitation of Eastern religions by the West.

Dervla Murphy, *On a Shoestring to Coorg: An Experience of Southern India* (John Murray, 1976).

V. S. Naipaul, *An Area of Darkness* (Penguin, 1970).

Paul Scott, *The Raj Quartet* (Panther, 1979). A set of 4 novels which traces the complex relationship between Indians and Englishmen in the 20th century.

Tony Wheeler, *India – A Travel Survival Kit* (Lonely Planet, 1984).

Heather Wood, *Third Class Ticket* (Penguin Travel Library, 1980). A moving account of Bengali villagers who get the chance to travel around India by train.

The novels of Salman Rushdie, Ruth Prawer Jhabwala and R. K. Narayan are also recommended.

Bhutan

Capital: Thimphu **Government:** Constitutional Monarchy

Unlike so many other Asian governments, the King of Bhutan and his ministers place a higher value on the preservation of their culture than on the material benefits to be gained by opening their frontiers to the West. It is only since 1974 that foreign tourists have been permitted to visit Bhutan and the number allowed in per year has been held to 2,000. However there is some indication that they are willing to double that figure by the end of 1987.

To get a visa you must apply 2½ to 3 months in advance, and be willing to join a tour for which you pay (a large sum) in American dollars in advance (see below). But some travellers think that the rewards of visiting a largely mediaeval Buddhist community outweighs the difficulties and expense, so we have included a short section on the country. There are many monasteries and Tibetan style forts called *dzongs* to see, as well as spectacular Himalayan scenery and the wonderfully untainted culture.

Bhutan is an independent country which has had its own seat in the United Nations since 1971. Although heavily dependent on India for its foreign policy and for material assistance, it follows a strict policy of accepting no aid from the U.S. nor the U.S.S.R. Its people are almost entirely subsistence farmers and yak herders. The only industry listed for Bhutan in the *World Almanac* is "Handicrafts". It is the world's largest producer of cardamom.

Climate

At 8000 ft. summer temperatures vary from 8°C (46°F) to 20°C (68°F). In the mountainous north, winter lasts from December to February and is extremely cold. Many villages are snowed in completely for months at a time. The southern part of the country, bordering Assam, has a tropical climate with monsoon rains.

Language

The national language is Dzongkha, a dialect of Tibetan, though only about 60% of Bhutanese people speak it. As in primitive isolated communities around the world, eccentricities of dialect develop through the centuries so that people in different mountain valleys cannot understand one another.

English is now taught in schools but very few people can converse fluently.

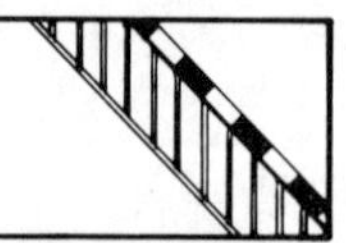

Visas

Your best chance of getting a visa is through a travel agent who organizes package tours to Bhutan and who has experience of the lengthy processes involved. You can also try it on your own, or rather in a group of at least six. Applications should be sent to the Bhutan Tourism Corporation (Royal Government of Bhutan, Tashichhodzong, P.O. Box 159, Thimphu, Bhutan) or to one of their representatives abroad, in New York (120 East 56th Street, New York, NY 10022; tel: 212-838-6382), Delhi (Chandragupta Marg;

tel: 699277) or Dhaka. Don't confess to being a mountaineer or a writer/journalist.

The cost of the organized tours which all visitors must join varies according to the season and the age of the visitors. In the popular tourist season (March-June and September-December) the cost is \$130 per day for a maximum of 12 days. Out of season the cost is \$90. Students under 25 are charged \$55 in all seasons. The cost of a trekking tour is a flat \$90 a day. There are surcharges of \$20 for attending the famous festival in Paro.

It is now possible for individuals to join sightseeing or trekking tours in Calcutta or Darjeeling, which range in price from \$808 for a 5-day tour off-season to a 30-day trek costing \$2,700 plus hotel surcharges. There is a further \$20 visa fee at the frontier.

Nul = 1 Indian rupee
For exchange rate, see chapter on India.

Currency: 100 chertums = 1 ngultrum (Nu)

Coins
5, 10, 25, 50 chertums; 1 ngultrum

Notes
1, 2, 5, 10, 20, 50, 100.
Many transactions among the locals still take place by bartering goods.

Changing Money
There are exchange facilities at the Bank of Bhutan in Thimphu, Phuntsholing (the border town in south-west Bhutan) and in other towns. Banks are open 09.00-1300 but close at 11.00 on Saturday. However since you pay for your inclusive tour in American dollars, you will not have to change much money.

Public Holidays

2nd May	Birth of King Jigme Dorji Wangchuk, father of the present monarch
2nd June	Coronation
21st July	Anniversary of the late King's Death
11th November	King's Birthday (lasts several days)
17th December	National Day

There are of course a large number of fluctuating Buddhist holidays and festivals.

Until 1960 there were no roads (they had hardly discovered the wheel). Now there is a paved highway which stretches from Phuntsholing at the border with India to the capital Thimphu and beyond. Public buses do run, but you will be limited to the Department of Tourism's own fleet of vehicles. Tour groups are usually met at Bagdogra Airport in Darjeeling and proceed by road (two days) to Thimphu.

Bhutan has had its own airline called Druk Air Corporation (not a misprint for Drunk but a word meaning Thunder Dragon) only since 1983. There are three flights between Calcutta and Paro per week (more in peak tourist season).

The return cost is $240 (as opposed to Nu1,800 or about $150 for locals). Druk's Indian office is at 48 Tivoli Court, 1A Ballygunj Circular Road, Calcutta. One advantage of flying to Bhutan directly is that you don't have to get a restricted area permit for Darjeeling. But if you're patient enough to get a Bhutanese visa, you probably won't mind the Indian form-filling.

Trekking

There are many unclimbed and unnamed peaks in the remote mountainous north of Bhutan, and many mountaineers are itching to have a crack at them. But at the moment the Government gives permission for one peak only, with the prospect of a new peak every other year. You needn't be a peak-bagger to want to walk in the utterly unspoiled mountains of Bhutan where the flora and fauna are far less disturbed than in neighbouring Nepal. The number and variety of trekking tours are increasing, so that the hitherto closed central part of Bhutan is now being opened to a handful of trekkers. Yaks and horses usually accompany trekking parties to carry the baggage.

Post and Telephone

With an increasing number of roads, more mail is being transported by vehicle rather than by runner. Stamps are one of Bhutan's main sources of foreign exchange. The G.P.O. in Thimphu is open from 09.00-15.00, though the philatelic department is in Phuntsholing.

The main districts are now connected by a reasonable phone network. It is even possible to make an international phone call making use of an Indian satellite. But normally the line is so poor as to render the exercise pointless.

Newspapers and Radio

There is a single journal published at irregular intervals in Thimphu. It is called *Kuensel* and is in Dzongkha, Nepali and English. The radio station broadcasts for nine hours a week.

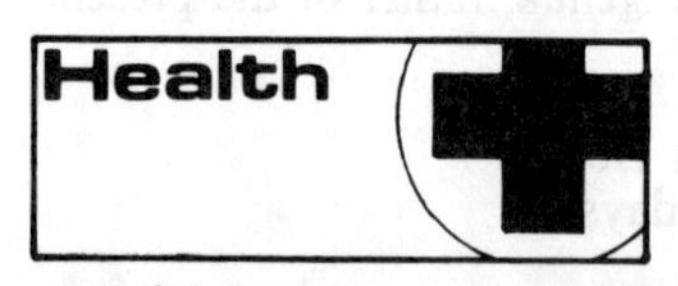

Malaria risk exists all year in the southern five districts (Chrang, Gaylegphug, Samchi, Samdrupjongkhar and Shemgang). The lowland plains of Bhutan were once so malarial that they were almost unpopulated. There are 13 hospitals in Bhutan. Naturally the water can't be trusted, and your cholera shot should still be valid.

Bhutanese food is more Tibetan than Indian. A large quantity of rice is eaten and meat is well liked, which is surprising in a country of Buddhists. (It is said that farmers graze their yaks near cliffs, so that the animals will die of "natural" causes.) The curries are fairly hot. Bhutan is the world's largest producer of the world's second most expensive spice after saffron, cardamon. Dried yak cheese called *churpi* is a popular snack.

As in Tibet tea is made with butter and salt, and called *souza.* You may find it easier to acquire a taste for *chang* the local wheat-based beer or *tomba* the millet beer. Indian lager-style beer is imported and is no more expensive than in India. The local spirit made from rice, barley or maize is called *arra.* A bottle costs about Nu80.

A Bhutanese guide will accompany your group to the Buddhist monasteries and other places of interest. *Dzongs* or fortress-monasteries are found throughout the country. Some date back to the 17th century; others are in spectacular cliff-side locations. Another highlight is browsing in the Government Handicrafts Emporium or attending the Saturday and Sunday markets. Sunday is also the day on which you are most likely to see an archery contest (the national sport).

You may also have a chance to visit the huge Manas Wildlife Sanctuary which straddles the border with Assam and contains a great variety of big game, tropical birds, etc.

Visitors are accommodated in government hostels of recent construction which are located near all the important sites.

Bibliography

Far Eastern Economic Review, *All-Asia Guide* (Hong Kong, 1985).
Bob Gibbons & Bob Ashford, *The Himalayan Kingdoms: Nepal, Bhutan and Sikkim* (Batsford, 1983).
Michael Peissel, *Lords and Lamas: A Solitary Expedition across the Secret Himalayan Kingdom of Bhutan* (Heinemann, 1970).
Peter Steele, *Two and Two Halves to Bhutan: A Family Journey in the Himalayas* (Hodder & Stoughton, 1970).

Nepal

Capital: Kathmandu **Government:** Constitutional Monarchy

Access to Nepal for Westerners was only granted in the late 1950's. Until then a policy of isolationism had been maintained, and a white face in Nepal was extremely rare. Since then, there has been a great deal of tourist development and the process continues. Some concrete monstrosities with air-conditioning have gone up in Kathmandu, many villagers are learning to charge for any services rendered and young people are wearing Levis for which they have paid an outrageous price. Despite all this, most tourists confine themselves to the Kathmandu Valley or the most popular treks, and there are many other places which remain unspoiled.

Nepal is like another world after the heat, hustle and bustle of the Indian plains. For one thing, a quarter of the land surface is under ice and snow, and fields and villages can be found up to an altitude of 14,500 feet. The people are friendly but more reserved than on the lowlands.

The country is roughly rectangular in shape, being 525 miles long and 110 miles wide. It is the only country in the world to be ruled by a Hindu monarch. Many of the village people believe King Bihendra to be a reincarnated Hindu god, making it very difficult to institute fair democratic procedures. Nepal held its first election in May of 1981 and the people voted overwhelmingly for the King.

The population is about 16½ million, over 90% of whom live in small villages.

There are only 7 towns with a population exceeding 10,000 and 3 of these are in the Kathmandu Valley. About half the people are of Mongolian (Tibetan) descent and the other half of Indian descent. The famous Gurkhas continue to play an important part in the British army, and many return to their villages after retirement to run hotels.

Trekking is one of the chief attractions of a visit to Nepal. The scenery is as spectacular as everyone says and though the walking can be hard, the rewards are worth it.

Climate

In January the average temperature of Kathmandu varies from 22°C (72°F) at noon to −5°C (23°F) at night; in July the temperature reaches an average of 31°C (88°F) by day, 19°C (65°F) at night. Most of Kathmandu's rain falls during the monsoon season, i.e. in June, July and August.

The best time of the year to visit Nepal is during the winter months from mid-October through to March though both warm and light clothing will be needed. After March, it is too hot to travel comfortably, and fogs often obscure the mountains.

The most popular months for trekking are October and November which means that the most popular routes become clogged. Winter is fine for trekking provided you have a good quality sleeping bag for the very cold nights, and provided you don't plan to cross any high passes, i.e. above 14,000 or 15,000 feet. Summer trekking, i.e. during the monsoon, is possible though there are disadvantages: paths in river valleys become flooded so alternative routes must be found, leeches are abundant and thirdly the overcast sky obscures the mountain views.

Language

Nepali, which is related to Hindi, is the official language, with over 30 local dialects. It is written in the Devnagari script. Dialects of Tibetan are spoken near the Tibetan border. English is often understood in the larger towns but little is spoken or understood in the rural areas, except by ex-Gurkhas and the local teacher.

Useful Nepali Words

hello, good day — namaste
thank you — danyi vaad
yes — ho
no — oyno
how much money? — kati paisa?
how far? — coti tara?
go away — ja ja
good — o shall ramru
bad — palno
milk — dood
water — pani
bread — kapin
today — aaja
yesterday — hijo
tomorrow — bholi

1 — eke
2 — dui
3 — din
4 — char
5 — panch
6 — chaa
7 — saat
8 — aath
9 — nau
10 — das
100 — ek soy

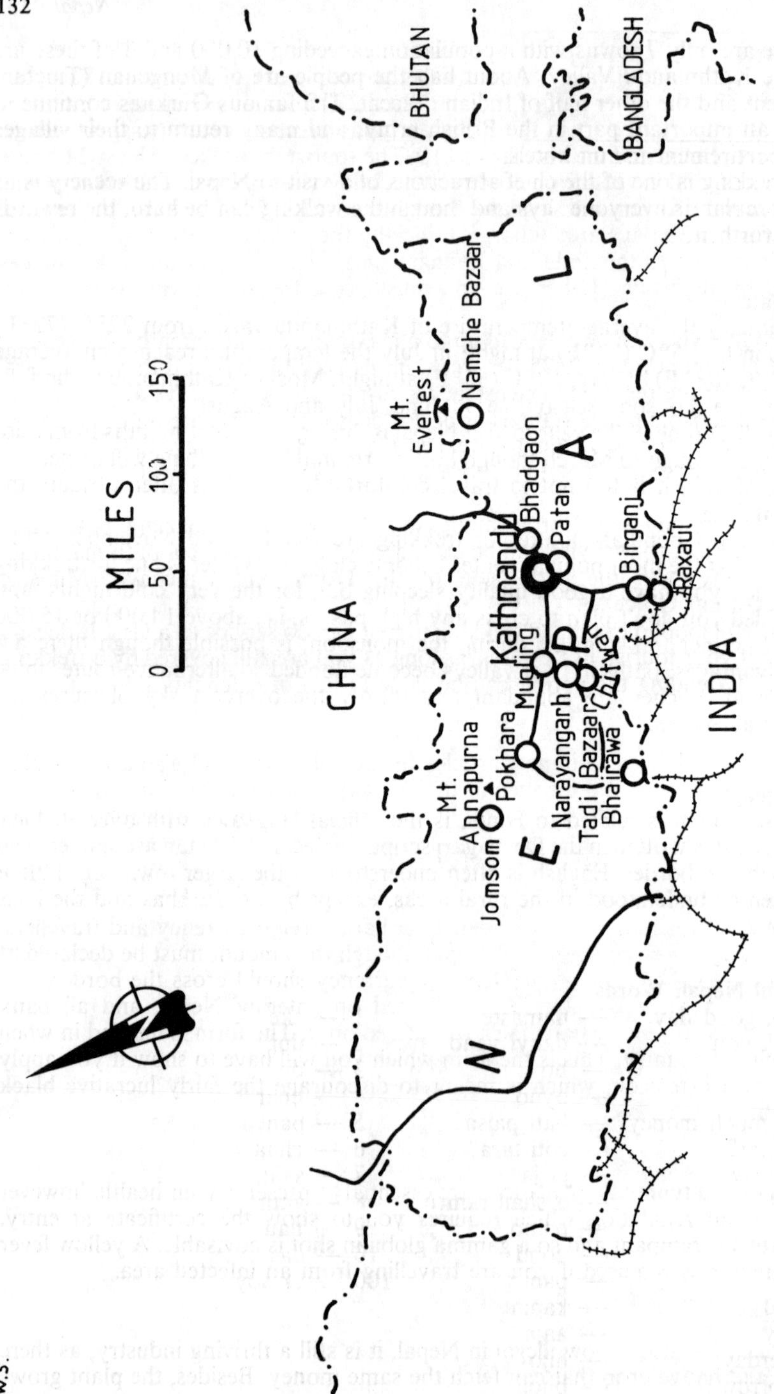
CHINA
BHUTAN
BANGLADESH
INDIA
N E P A L
MILES
0 50 100 150
Mt. Everest
Namche Bazaar
Bhadgaon
Patan
Kathmandu
Birganj
Raxaul
Mugling
Chitwan
Narayangarh
Tadi Bazaar
Bhairawa
Pokhara
Mt. Annapurna
Jomsom
W.S.

Visas
Visas are required by all visitors. They can be obtained from any Nepalese Embassy after you present your passport, three passport photos and the visa fee of £10. The tourist visa takes at least 24 hours to process, and is valid for a 30-day stay. 7-day visas are issued at entry points (Kathmandu Airport and land borders) and cost Rs175. These can be renewed for a further 30 days at no charge. Officially the ordinary visa is valid only for the Valleys of Kathmandu and Pokhara plus Chitwan Park and other places linked by highways. Otherwise you must get a trekking permit (see section below).

A tourist visa can be extended up to a maximum of three months. Extensions in the first month cost Rs75 per week; in the second and third they cost Rs50 per week of the requested extension. Extensions of up to 7 days at a time may be obtained from police stations or post offices where there are no Immigration Offices. Extensions work out to be expensive since you also have to show official exchange slips to prove that you have converted $5 for each day of the proposed extension.

In Kathmandu, the Central Immigration Office is at Dillibazar, Ghatte Kulo (tel: 12336). A tourist visa can be extended beyond the three month maximum period only with the permission of the Home and Panchayat Ministry (Immigration Office).

A useful loophole is that a trekking permit can do service as a visa. It doesn't matter if your tourist visa expires, as long as you are still covered by a trekking permit. Extending the permit can be done in lieu of extending the visa.

Customs
Visitors are allowed to import articles for personal use, and also a reasonable amount of alcohol and tobacco at the custom official's discretion. An average allowance would be 200 cigarettes or 20 cigars, two bottles of alcohol and six bottles of beer.

Currency Regulations
There is no restriction on the amount of hard foreign currency and travellers' cheques that may be taken into Nepal, though the amount must be declared at customs. Neither Indian nor Nepalese currency should cross the border.

A currency declaration form is issued on entering Nepal, and all bank transactions or conversions must be entered on it. The form is handed in when leaving the country. This is the form which you will have to show if you apply for a visa extension, which is meant to discourage the fairly lucrative black market for hard currency.

Health Certificates
Cholera and typhoid inoculations are essential to preserve your health, however there is no regulation which requires you to show the certificate at entry. Hepatitis is rampant and so a gamma globulin shot is advisable. A yellow fever vaccination is required if you are travelling from an infected area.

Drugs
Although hashish is now illegal in Nepal, it is still a thriving industry, as there is no alternative crop that can fetch the same money. Besides, the plant grows

very easily in the wild, and it would be rather like declaring hedges illegal in England. Searches of travellers do sometimes take place, especially when leaving the country. In theory the maximum penalty for drug offences is two years, although it seems extremely unlikely that such a drastic sentence would ever be passed.

Motoring Documents

If you are taking your own vehicle into Nepal, you will need a *carnet de passages,* registration book, third party insurance and an International Driver's Permit which is valid for 15 days. The *carnet* exempts you from customs duty for three months. If you do want to sell your vehicle in Nepal, the duty is high: 80% on a vehicle up to 1,000 cc and 195% on a vehicle 1,300-2,000 cc for example.

Trekking Permits

If you are intending to trek outside the Kathmandu Valley or areas linked by highway, then a permit is required from the Central Immigration Office in Kathmandu or from the Immigration Office, Pardi (near the bus station), Pokhara. This process usually takes much less time in Pokhara (half an hour) than in Kathmandu (half a day). Two photos are required plus a fee of Rs60 for each week of the first month of your proposed trek, and Rs75 per week thereafter. As with visa extensions you must show that you have exchanged $5 a day into rupees for each day of your trek.

The permit is valid for only one route at a time. Permits are spot-checked on routes, though it is possible to trek without a permit by avoiding the checkpoints. The inspection of permits is a very haphazard affair; the penalty is Rs10 per day. Mountaineering parties must apply well in advance for permission to climb certain peaks. There may be a queue several years long. The fee for climbing Everest at present is $3,000.

£1 = Rs24 | Rs10 = £0.41
$1 = Rs17 | Rs10 = $0.59

Currency: 100 paise = 1 rupee (R).

Notes

Re1 (brown or multicoloured): Rs5 (red or green/pink with brown reverse); Rs10 (brown/green or multicoloured reverse or multicoloured); Rs50 (mauve; blue reverse); Rs100 (green); Rs1000 (multicoloured).

Changing Money

Banks will sometimes take an infuriatingly long time to change travellers' cheques. When you are changing money take your currency declaration form and passport. Exchange facilities are available at the Nepal Rastra Bank and at both the Banijya Ratriya Bank and Nepal Bank; there are branches in the main administrative towns as well as Kathmandu. Hotels will also change money, as will authorized dealers who are much quicker, and give the same rate. The black market fluctuates but is generally fairly lively.

You should dispose of your Nepalese currency before moving on to India, since the Nepalese rupee is not readily acceptable (not to mention the illegality of exporting Nepalese rupees).

The inefficiency of the banking system may work in your favour. A few of the posh restaurants in Kathmandu (such as the Sunkosi) accept Barclaycard and there is a good chance a debt incurred in Kathmandu will never make it onto your bill.

Emergency Cash

Tents, sleeping bags, hiking boots and any camping equipment can be sold in Kathmandu, where visitors often arrive without the necessary trekking gear. Shop prices for these things are very high in Kathmandu, especially now that expeditions no longer dump their equipment but take it away with them, so you will have some scope for profit and still be competitive. You might even find a local who wants to buy your boots as a status symbol. The smaller your shoe size the better your chance.

Cameras and film are also expensive, so they too can be sold easily. There is also a market for electronic devices, such as calculators and digital watches. The second hand book trade is flourishing. The author sold the previous edition of this guide to a bookshop in Thamel for not much less than the retail price.

To obtain the best price arrange the sale yourself by contacting other travellers in the restaurants where they tend to congregate. Many of these establishments have notice boards for this purpose. Whoever your prospective buyer is you will have to haggle over the price; the assumption will be that you are selling because you need the money.

Opening Hours

The shops open about 09.00 and close at 20.00 or 21.00. The closing day is Saturday, though most shops seem to stay open seven days a week. Banks open 10.00-15.00 Sunday to Thursday, and till 12.00 on Friday. The general business hours are 10.00-17.00 Monday to Friday, with early closing on Fridays.

Government offices close on Saturdays, but open on Sundays; Western embassies do the reverse. Government offices all close on Christmas Day and New Year's Day in addition to the Nepalese holidays outlined below.

Public Holidays

Most of the festivals and holidays celebrated in Nepal do not have fixed dates because they are based on a calendar which dates from 57 B.C. Therefore the following are only approximate:

11th January	Day to honour King Prithivi Narayan Shah, maker of modern Nepal
19th February	Anniversary of the late King Tribhuvan
February/March	Shivaratri (the night of Lord Shiva)
12th/13th April	Nepalese New Year
late October/early November	Festival of Lights (5 days)
16th December	Constitution Day
28th December	King Birendra Bir Bikram Shah Dev's birthday

Arrival and Departure

The cheapest way to get to Nepal is to buy a bucket shop ticket to Delhi and then go by public transport, for example train to Lucknow, bus to Gorakhpur and the border crossing at Nautanwa/Bhairawa for Pokhara. This exhausting but inexpensive trip can be done in about 32 hours. There are private express bus services from Delhi to Kathmandu; enquire in the Pahar Ganj area of New Delhi. There are several other crossings. One of the most interesting is from Darjeeling at the eastern end of Nepal to Kathmandu, a 385 mile trip which takes 14 hours and costs Rs125. A flight from Delhi to Kathmandu when added on to a cheap ticket to Delhi would probably work out to be more than a direct flight London to Kathmandu (£470 return on Bangladesh Biman at the time of going to print). It is cheaper to piece together two flights such as Delhi-Varanasi/Varanasi-Kathmandu or Delhi-Patna/Patna-Kathmandu than to fly directly. One disadvantage of passing through India (even if transiting through the airport) is that you have to get a £10 Indian visa.

If entering Nepal by land be sure to exchange some money at the border. Snack sellers during the 8 hour bus trips Bhairawa to Pokhara or Birganj to Kathmandu do not accept Indian rupees. There is a departure tax of Rs100.

Flights

The Royal Nepal Airlines Corporation operate scheduled flights between Kathmandu and 28 airfields throughout the country. Many of these operate only between October and June, and there can be delays during the monsoon and in cloudy conditions. Foreign tourists pay more for domestic flights than the locals do, plus there is a domestic airport tax of Rs15-Rs25. Although very touristy, the scenic flight to Everest (which has to be paid for in a hard currency) can be thrilling on a clear day.

Motoring

Spare parts tend to be difficult to obtain in Nepal, so it is advisable to have a good supply for emergencies; petrol also is expensive. Roads are narrow with sharp bends, and drivers are potentially lethal. Most roads are very rough and hard on vehicles and many roads disappear during the monsoon. The Automobile Association of Nepal (Ram Shah Path, opposite Sinadnar, H.M. Government Secretariat Building, Kathmandu; tel: 11093) will advise on the local road conditions, spare parts and any other difficulties. Driving is on the left.

Car Hire

Hertz are represented in Kathmandu by Gorkha Travels, Durbar Marg; tel: 414895. The prices begin at $20 per day. Avis (Yeti Travels, Durbar Marg) also offer a chauffeur-driven service only.

Bus

Since there are no trains in Nepal, you will probably make use of the bus services which connect the main towns whenever road conditions permit; mountain passes are often blocked by snow in winter and many roads are flooded in the summer monsoon.

Birganj to Kathmandu — private buses depart at 04.30, 06.30 and 07.30 arriving 8 or 9 hours later. Book a seat as soon as you arrive.

Bhairawa to Pokhara — takes 8 hours.

Pokhara to Kathmandu — several competing companies. Just go to the bus station very early (05.30 or 06.00) and you'll get a seat for the pleasant 6 hour trip. Cost Rs40.

On privately-owned long distance buses, insist on a confirmed seat and definite departure time before handing over money. For local buses, it is advisable to book tickets a day or two before departure, but do not take any notice of the seat allocation, as no one else will. The booking office in Kathmandu is near the main post office near Ratna Park. Buses are comfortable though there is little leg room to spare. Luggage is stowed on the roof; make sure your baggage is held down (even better, climb up and secure it yourself) as things have been known to fly off on hairpin bends. Don't make any valuables too easily accessible though, on the whole, your luggage should be safe on the roof. On long journeys the buses set off early in the morning and stop for innumerable tea breaks.

There is an all-weather highway heading north-east from the capital which links Kathmandu with Tibet. It is possible to travel to the border, and as of spring 1985, the possibility of crossing into Tibet was introduced. It is not clear whether the independent traveller who has acquired his Chinese visa in Hong Kong can cross here yet since at the moment the border is open only to tour groups. Enquire in Kathmandu when you arrive.

City Transport

There are taxis in the main cities, but they are much more expensive than buses or rickshaws. Always agree on the price first, except in the orange-striped taxis which are metered. Taxis, jeeps and cars can be rented for journeys outside Kathmandu, at fixed charges.

Rickshaws are the most enjoyable form of transport, and cheap. If you walk around Kathmandu late at night, you will see the drivers sleeping in them. The drivers are usually helpful, and have a lot of local knowledge. They can be very useful if you are looking for a bed for the night. The main rickshaw stand is at the junction of Kanti Path and Kamaladi.

Bicycles can be hired in Kathmandu for the day. Your passport number is all that is required to be noted at the time of hiring. The rental is between Rs5 and Rs10 per day. They can be hired at the top end of Freak Street or from some hotels. Arrive early to pick out the better cycles.

Trekking

Trekking in the Himalaya of Nepal has become almost as popular as cruising in the Mediterranean or skiing in the Alps. The way that Yuppies (Young Urban Professionals, for whom Nepal has become a favourite holiday destination) arrange it is normally to book through a trekking agency which charges several hundred pounds for making the arrangements (say £400 for 10 days). This is fine if your ambition is to scale wild and remote heights. But if you simply want to see some wonderful scenery and observe the Nepali way of life which revolves around walking between villages, then one of the standard treks is perfectly suitable and manageable unaccompanied.

A useful trekking guide is distributed free of charge by the Kathmandu Tourist Office in Durbar Square. It advises how to hire guides and porters locally if you decide that you do not want to carry your belongings. If you hire a porter/guide independently, you should be able to find one for about Rs100 per day including food and hired equipment. The most popular trekking season is October/

November. Trekking during the monsoon is possible, though alternative routes are sometimes necessary to avoid submerged tracks, and leeches must be guarded against. Trekking in mid-winter is highly enjoyable except at very high altitudes, which is usually impossible in any case since high passes close in the winter. You will have to carry a good quality sleeping bag for very cold night-time temperatures. But the days are warm and sunny. If your visit to Asia is solely for trekking, then it is preferable to bring the necessary equipment from home. But if you are on a grand tour of Asia, you won't be lugging around a down sleeping bag, and you will have to rent one in Kathmandu or Pokhara. Beware of fleas in a rented bag. You can get a down jacket for about Rs6 per day. Ambitious trekkers will require a tent and dehydrated foods which are expensive in Nepal. If you are interested in buying second-hand equipment, of which there is seldom a shortage in Kathmandu, check the adverts on the café notice boards on Freak Street.

The fitter you are, the more you will enjoy your trek, and the less chance of finding yourself humiliated by barefoot whistling octagenarian locals who pass you. Be very watchful above about 12,000 ft for symptoms of altitude sickness, i.e. severe headaches and nausea. If you feel really unwell, descend a couple of thousand feet and rest for a day or so. Your body will soon adjust to the reduced oxygen intake.

The two most accessible treks from Kathmandu are Helambu and Langtang. Both involve about 9 days of trekking an average of 7 hours per day. If you simply want to take a stroll from Kathmandu which affords good views, head for Nagarkot, 15 miles away. You can trek here easily in 4 days. A much more ambitious trek of about three weeks is to Namche Bazaar and on to Everest Base Camp at 17,400 ft. There are several detailed guidebooks available, describing the treks of Nepal (see Bibliography).

A popular and yet thoroughly enjoyable trek is the two-week trek from Pokhara to Jomsom covering 75 miles round trip. This trail, which follows the Kali Gandaki Valley for some of its length, is an ancient Tibetan trade route, and traders still bring their wares to sell in the cities. The trail is dotted with small villages and there are plenty of tea shops and lodges at which you can stay. It is easily possible to get away with a pack weighing no more than 15lbs. The trail is well used by the Nepalese people and their donkey trains and is easy to follow. Throughout the walk there are breathtaking views of the Annapurna Range and Machhapuchare (Fish Tail Peak). More adventurous trekkers may attempt the 19-day circuit of Annapurna which crosses the 16,700 ft Thorong La Pass. But most people are content to go to Jomson and then on to Muktinath, a Hindu and Buddhist pilgrimage place, at about 12,000 ft. The sketch map shows an alternative route back to Pokhara.

Here is a very basic itinerary:

Day 1. *Pokhara to Naudanda* (6 hours). Follow the path round the lake and along the valley; the village of Naudanda is on the range of hills to the right.

Day 2. *Naudanda to Hille* (7 hours). This is the actual Jomsom Trail. The track keeps to the ridge until it comes to the end of the range. The path then steeply descends to Birethanti. The walk on to Hille is a 4-hour walk alongside the river.

Day 3. *Hille to Ghorepani* (6 hours). The first 2 hours of walking is up the steep track to Tirkhedhunge. This part of the walk is best done early in the morning while it is still cool. From Tirkhedhunge to Ghorepani the walk is very shaded and passes through jasmine-scented woodland. The trail follows the river with waterfalls and ice cold pools. The heavily shaded gorge eventually opens up into the village of Ghorepani at 9,000 ft (where some people experience slight sensations of mountain sickness). The village has 5 lodges and all have large open fires, as nights are cold at this altitude. A further hour (optional) brings you to the top of Poon Hill where there is a raised platform with uninterrupted views of Annapurna.

Day 4. *Ghorepani to Tatopani* (5 hours). Most trekkers have a rest day here in order to wash their clothes and themselves in the hot springs (Tatopani literally means "hot water").

Day 5. *Tatopani to Ghasa* (5½ hours).

Day 6. *Ghasa to Marpha* (6½ hours). The Buddhist influence begins to predominate. A very strong wind blows up the valley.

Day 7. *Marpha to Kagbeni* (4 hours) from which you can make a one-day return excursion to the pilgrimage place of Muktinath. Kagbeni is as far north as you are permitted in this direction. (Tibet is only 3 days walk away.)

You can vary the return route to Pokhara by branching west at Tatopani to Beni, which is much lusher and more like India than the barren north of the Kali Gandaki Valley.

All of the towns and villages along the route have lodges and tea houses; some even provide blankets. Accommodation varies from Rs5 to Rs15 per night. Food is basic (mostly rice and lentils) but good; soft drinks and beer are available, though the higher the altitude the higher the price.

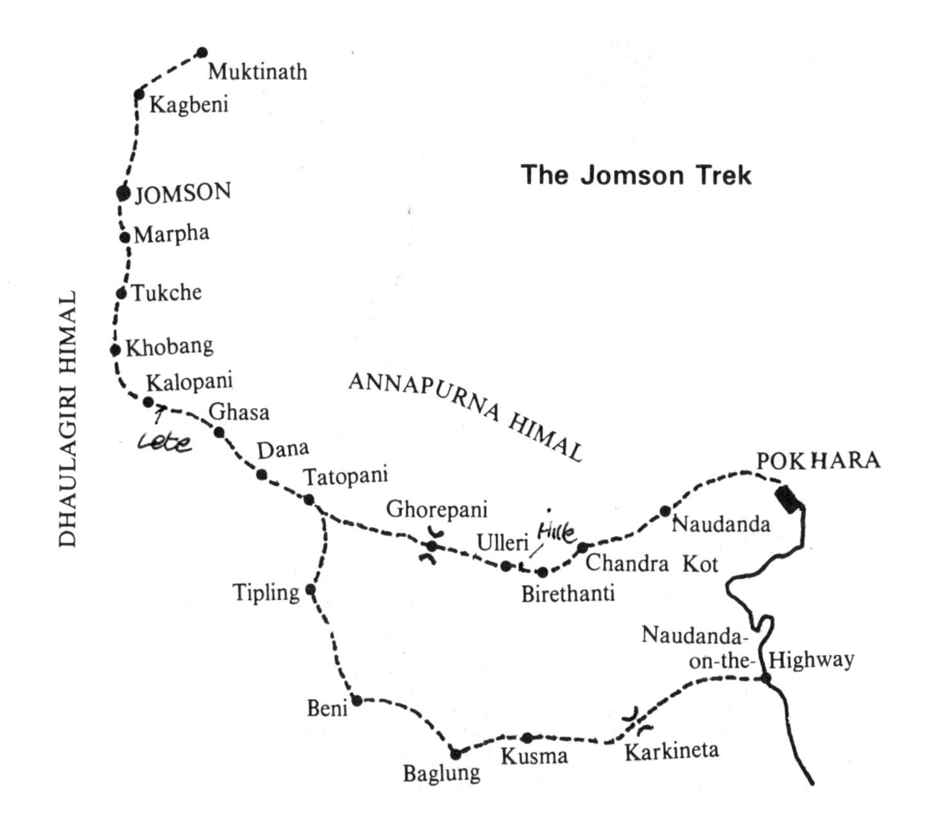

Post

Nepal's postal system operates throughout the Kathmandu Valley, and postal facilities are available at district administrative towns; in outlying regions deliveries are slow and stamps are not always available. Post cards cost Rs3 and aerogrammes Rs4.50.

There is a poste restante service at the main post office in Kathmandu which does not inspire confidence. You may prefer to use American Express in Kathmandu or nominate a hotel such as the Kathmandu Guest House or the Inn of Serenity who will hold any mail.

Telephone

In the Kathmandu Valley there is a telephone service linking the main towns, and a trunk and telegraph line linking Nepal with India, Pakistan and Bangladesh. Overseas calls are chancy. The telegram rate is Rs9.50 per word.

Newspapers

The British Council in Kathmandu has a splendid library, with English newspapers, books and magazines. The English language newspapers are not quite as nationalistic as they sound, e.g. *The Rising Nepal* and *The Motherland*.

Malaria is prevalent throughout the country except in the cities, but especially in the Terai Plains where a double dose of proguanil is recommended. Chloroquine resistance has been reported.

There are hospitals in various parts of the country, though it is perhaps best to seek treatment in Kathmandu in the Shanta Bhawan United Mission Hospital (tel: 21034). Another recommended hospital is the Shining Hospital, Kasbi Jilla, Gandhaki, Pokhara. A local practitioner of herbal medicine specializes in curing hepatitis: contact the Chair of Nepal Ayurveda Association near the Bir Hospital in Kathmandu.

Most trekkers experience at least one bout of diarrhoea, but it usually goes away after a day or two or eating boiled rice and drinking tea.

The diet of most Nepali people consists mostly of *dal bhat,* which is lentils (fairly soupy) and rice. In humble restaurants in cities and on trekking routes, you will be served this meal automatically. Your plate will be refilled as many times as you like for the set fee of Rs5-Rs10. This simple meal, eaten twice a day by the locals, is very satisfying and surprisingly varied according to the spices used. Often there is an accompanying dish of curried vegetables. If you ever have the misfortune to be served the alternative staple of buckwheat steamed into a glutinous mass, you will come to appreciate *dal bhat.*

Tibetan restaurants offer a delicious steamed or fried equivalent of ravioli called *momos.* It is sometimes difficult to find the local Tibetan or Nepali restaurants in Kathmandu and Pokhara, since they may not be signposted in

English. Take a chance and step behind the curtain. In Kathmandu look out for the Welcome restaurant and the Ashta Mangal Restaurant.

Many travellers, especially those who have been on the road for a long time, patronize the pie shops of Kathmandu, where local cooks have learned to make Western specialities such as chocolate cake and lemon meringue pie. There are several Swiss-sponsored cheese factories in Nepal, restaurants which serve muesli and goulash, and several ice-cream parlours in Kathmandu for the truly homesick. Western style restaurants abound: the Rum Doodle is an institution in this category.

The most popular drink among the locals is *chang,* which is rice beer. The local spirit is *rakshi,* which takes a little getting used to. Unfortunately both are often served diluted with the local water so that they are not altogether safe. The German-style bottled beer is safe but very expensive, especially along trekking routes where it must be carried in by porters (Rs25-Rs30 per bottle). Tibetan beer, called *tomba,* is delicious and safe: it results as soon as boiling water is poured over fermented grain whereupon it is drunk through a straw. As the grain is repeatedly doused, the alcoholic content diminishes which is just as well.

Water is definitely not drinkable in either towns or villages, and great care must be taken while trekking. Take along a large supply of water purifiers (iodine, chlorine tablets, etc.) on a trek.

KATHMANDU

Kathmandu is the largest city and capital of Nepal with a population of 130,000. Records of the city go back to the 8th century and establish Kathmandu as an important centre of the fertile valley and on a major trade route between India and Tibet.

Until the 15th century Kathmandu was ruled by a series of feudal barons, but in 1482 it became the capital of King Ratna Malla, whose dynasty lasted for 285 years, and during whose rule most of the mediaeval buildings were erected. Until the 17th century, it was known as Kantipur, "City of Glory". The 19th century was also an era of development, with a large number of buildings erected in 18th and 19th century European styles. Most of these buildings are now used as foreign embassies or government offices.

Kathmandu still exudes a mediaeval atmosphere, with winding alleys converging on squares. The streets are full of people, cows, dogs and rickshaws. It is a great delight to sit on the steps of one of the temples and watch the world go by.

What to See

Hanuman Dhoka Palace — faces Durbar Square at the top of Freak Street. The palace is the former residence of the Malla kings and comprises several complexes and courtyards with temples and statues. The palace was built in the 16th century and enlarged in the 17th century, and is still guarded by a statue of the monkey god, Hanuman.

Jagannath Temple — has erotic carvings.

Swayambhu Nath — often called the Monkey Temple. 2000 year old Buddhist chaitya or stupa (holy mound). The hill on which this stupa and many other pagoda-like structures are located is 2 miles west of the city (about a 20-minute bike ride). The temple is crawling with belligerent monkeys who rummage through bags for sweets or chase small dogs.

Bodhnath — just west of Kathmandu. The largest chaitya after Swayambhu and a very important Buddhist shrine. The "all-seeing eyes of supreme Buddhahood" are painted on the tower on top of the dome.

Pashupatinath — the most popular pilgrimage place for Nepali Hindus, about 1½ miles from Kathmandu. Non-Hindus are not allowed inside the temple or enclosures, but may watch ritual bathing and cremations on the banks of the Bagmati River.

Accommodation

The two most popular areas for hotels in Kathmandu are Thamel in the north-west of town and "Freak Street" leading south from Durbar Square. The first six below are all in Thamel, which is somewhat upmarket and therefore more expensive than Freak Street. The latter has an element of sleaziness, but there are some bargains.

Kathmandu Guest House — P.O. Box 2769. Tel: 13628. Justly popular and often full, so booking advised. Clean, with pleasant garden. From $2 plus 12% government tax. Restaurant, bicycle hire, money changing, poste restante, travel counter, etc.
Star Hotel — next door to the Kathmandu Guest House. Rs30 double.
Tukchey Peak Lodge — Rs45 double.
Nepal Rest House — pleasant garden and good food. Rs60 double.
Eleve Lodge — cheaper than most in Thamel. Bicycle hire.
Mustang Lodge — far end of Freak Street. Rs20 single, Rs35 double.
Samiye Lodge — Freak Street. Cheap.
Annapurna Lodge — near Durbar Square. From Rs20 single.

Useful Addresses

Tourist Information — New Road near Durbar Square. Tel: 11293.
British Embassy — Lainchaur. Tel: 11588/9.
British Council Library — Kanti Path. Tel: 11305.
American Embassy — Pani Pohkari. Tel: 11199.
American Express & Thomas Cook — Yeti Travels Pvt. Ltd., Hotel Mayalu, Ground Floor, amal Tole, Durbar Marg. Tel: 13596/11234.
Royal Nepal Airlines — Kanti Path. Tel: 14511.

BHADGAON (Bhaktapur) and PATAN (Lalitpur)

Along with Kathmandu these are the three important towns of the Kathmandu Valley and only a few miles away from the capital. They have been less affected by 20th-century development and the mediaeval town plans are still evident. Both are full of Buddhist pagoda temples. Bhadgaon has the Lion Gate and the 16th-century Palace of the 55 Windows.

The best way of visiting these two towns in the Kathmandu Valley is by rented bicycle. Even on creaky crates, the ride is not very strenuous and very picturesque.

POKHARA

At 2160 ft. above sea level, Pokhara is nearly 2000 ft. lower than Kathmandu. The town is framed to the north by the snow-capped Annapurna Range which can be seen clearly on fine days. There is a large and interesting bazaar in the centre of town and a Tibetan refugee centre on the outskirts where carpets and handicrafts are made. There is also a wide choice of cheap accommodation mainly on the lake (Phewa Tal) which is a small distance from the centre of town. The lake is fed by glacial streams and rivers and is an emerald green in colour. There is a picturesque gorge just a 10-minute walk from the airport. Boats and canoes can be hired from the lake shore.

Pokhara is an ideal base for trekking, including the Jomsom trek described above. There are a number of trekking hire shops, though the equipment tends to be of inferior quality and more expensive than in Kathmandu.

Accommodation

Hotel Snowland — Tel: 384. Established lakeside hotel. Singles from Rs30 and doubles Rs40. Garden and rooftop restaurant.

Monal Hotel — one of the newer lakeside hotels. Rs30 single, Rs45 double. Cheerful atmosphere.

Superlodge Pardi — on the lakeside. Rs20 single, Rs30 double. Local trekking information and baggage storage.

Hotel Gaylord — Rs20 double. Nice people, excellent food.

Himalayan Tibetan Hotel — across from the airport. From Rs20 double plus 10% tax. Good food. Camping permitted. Can advise on buying Tibetan carpets and on trekking.

Ruby Hotel — on long road which links lake with bazaar, a little east of the bus station. Mainly patronized by Asian travellers.

Fish Tail Lodge — 4-star hotel with great mountain views and famous clientele. From $25 single.

CHITWAN

The huge Royal Chitwan National Park of Nepal, south-west of Kathmandu, presents a remarkable contrast with the mountainous north. It is the home of many jungle animals, including the rarely-seen Bengal tiger and increasing numbers of rhinos. The best season for seeing animals is spring, though autumn and winter are also possible with the exception of the first fortnight in January when local people are allowed into the park to cut the grass for building materials thereby frightening the animals deep into the jungle. The Park is closed during the monsoon.

The journey by road is less gruelling than it used to be before the road south from Mugling was completed. There are direct bus services from Kathmandu to Narayangarh where you can catch a mini-bus to Tadi Bazaar (the last place where you can exchange money). The last 4 mile stretch to the park entrance must be covered on foot, an enjoyable walk though you may have to ford the River Rapti.

There are several modest establishments for accommodation in addition to the fiendishly expensive luxury game lodges such as Tiger Tops. For instance try Wendy's which offers rough bunks and mosquito nets. Cleaner and more comfortable are the National Park Cottages nearby, also with a restaurant. They may allow you to camp if the cottages are full, but if you have a tent try to arrange to camp inside the park.

There is a steep admission of Rs100 to enter the park, so you should plan your forays carefully. It is possible to see wildlife, especially under the auspices of a local guide (ask at Wendy's Lodge) outside the park perimeter. Elephant rides (which take place inside the park are expensive but worthwhile, since rhinos do not flee in the presence of elephants. The best way of all to view the rhinos, wild boar, deer, birds and (perhaps) tigers is to sleep overnight at negligible cost in a *machan* or observation tower built on the edge of a jungle clearing. If a rhino charges while you're walking in the jungle, remember to run in an arc (since they charge in straight lines and their eyesight is bad) and to fling off items of clothing as you run which will distract and delay the angry beast.

Bibliography

Stephen Bezruchka, *A Guide to Trekking in Nepal* (Cordee, 1985), £8.95. By far the best trekking guide.

Prakash A. Raj, *Kathmandu & the Kingdom of Nepal* (Lonely Planet, 1985), £4.95.

John L Hayes, *Nepal Trail Guide No. 2; North of Pokhara* (Roger Lascelles, 1979).

Peter Matthiessen, *The Snow Leopard* (Chatto & Windus, 1979).

Stan Armington, *Trekking in the Himalayas* (Lonely Planet, 1985).

Roger Lascelles has several trekking maps of Nepal, all for £4.95.

Bangladesh

Capital: Dhaka **Government:** Republic (within the Commonwealth)

Henry Kissinger once labelled Bangladesh a "basket case" and this image persists in the Western imagination. The cyclone which ravaged the country in May 1985, affecting $2\frac{1}{2}$ million people, has yet again disappointed hopes that the country's economy was making some gains.

Relatively few travellers venture into Bangladesh, partly because of its uninviting reputation and also because of its inconvenient location. Although it is relatively easy to travel from Calcutta to Dhaka, Bangladesh is something of a cul-de-sac. If the border with Burma were ever to be opened, many more travellers would be tempted to pass through Bangladesh en route to South East Asia. However this is an unrealistic hope for the forseeable future.

Under British rule, Bangladesh was known as East Bengal. At the time of the British partition of India in 1947, the country widely supported the campaign for a Moslem national home, and as a result East Bengal was partitioned from India to form part of the newly created Islamic state of Pakistan. Aspirations for independence from West Pakistan reached boiling point in the late sixties, because Bengali interests were perpetually ignored in favour of Punjabi ones in the west. In 1971, with the last minute help of Indian troops and much international support, the separate state of Bangladesh was formed under the leadership of Sheikh Mujibur Rahman, who was slaughtered in a coup of 1975. After another presidential assassination in 1981, the country was placed under martial law and Lt-Gen Ershad assumed the title of Chief Martial Law Administrator, and later President. The government is always proclaiming its intention to hold free parliamentary elections, however the opposition is kept under tight reins and elections are postponed. Under the present government, the country has become more Islamic though it is still a more liberal society than that of Pakistan.

Climate

With an annual rainfall of over 100 inches in many places, Bangladesh is one of the wettest countries in the world. It is not uncommon for over 50% of the land area to be under flood waters during the monsoon which lasts from mid-June until October. It is also wise to avoid travelling in the hot season (March to May) during which the average daily temperature in Dhaka is often over 90°F. Unlike its neighbouring tropical countries, Bangladesh has no high mountains to which the heat-exhausted traveller can escape. The nearest Bangladesh has to a hill station is Sylhet in the north-east which is only 2,000 ft above sea level. Also it is one of the rainiest parts of the country, just a stone's throw from Cherrapunji in India which, with 40 feet of rain annually, is said to be the wettest place in the world.

The best time for travelling is between November and February, when the temperatures are not uncomfortably high, but still warmer than the British summer. Another advantage is that cyclones do not occur during these months. Cyclones do terrible damage to coastal areas; the one in June of 1985 killed 10,000 people and left a quarter of a million homeless.

Language

English is less widely spoken in Bangladesh than in India, partly because the level of literacy is even lower (25% instead of 36%). But among the population which has had some education, most speak a little English. The simple vocabulary for travellers (hello, please, etc.) is understood by almost everyone even in the villages. The native language is Bengali (sometimes called Bangla) which evolved originally from Sanskrit, just as Hindi, Gujarati and several other languages did. Much of the vocabulary overlaps with Hindi as you will see from the following list.

Useful Bengali Words

English	Bengali	Number
good-bye	— salam	1 — ek
thank you	— dhanayabad	2 — dui
yes	— haa	3 — tin
no	— naa	4 — char
yesterday	— gatokal	5 — paanch
today	— aaj (pronounced ahz)	6 — chhoy
tomorrow	— kal	7 — shaat
excuse me	— maf korben	8 — aat
how much is this?	— daam koto?	9 — noy
too much	— beshi	10 — dawsh
bus	— gari	20 — beesh
		100 — eksho

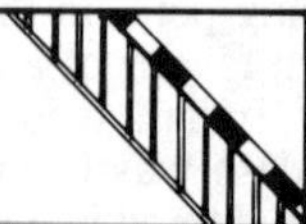

Visas

There is now a hefty £10 fee to British passport-holders for a tourist visa allowing a stay of up to three months. If you plan to enter Bangladesh more than once you will have to pay £20 for a multiple entry

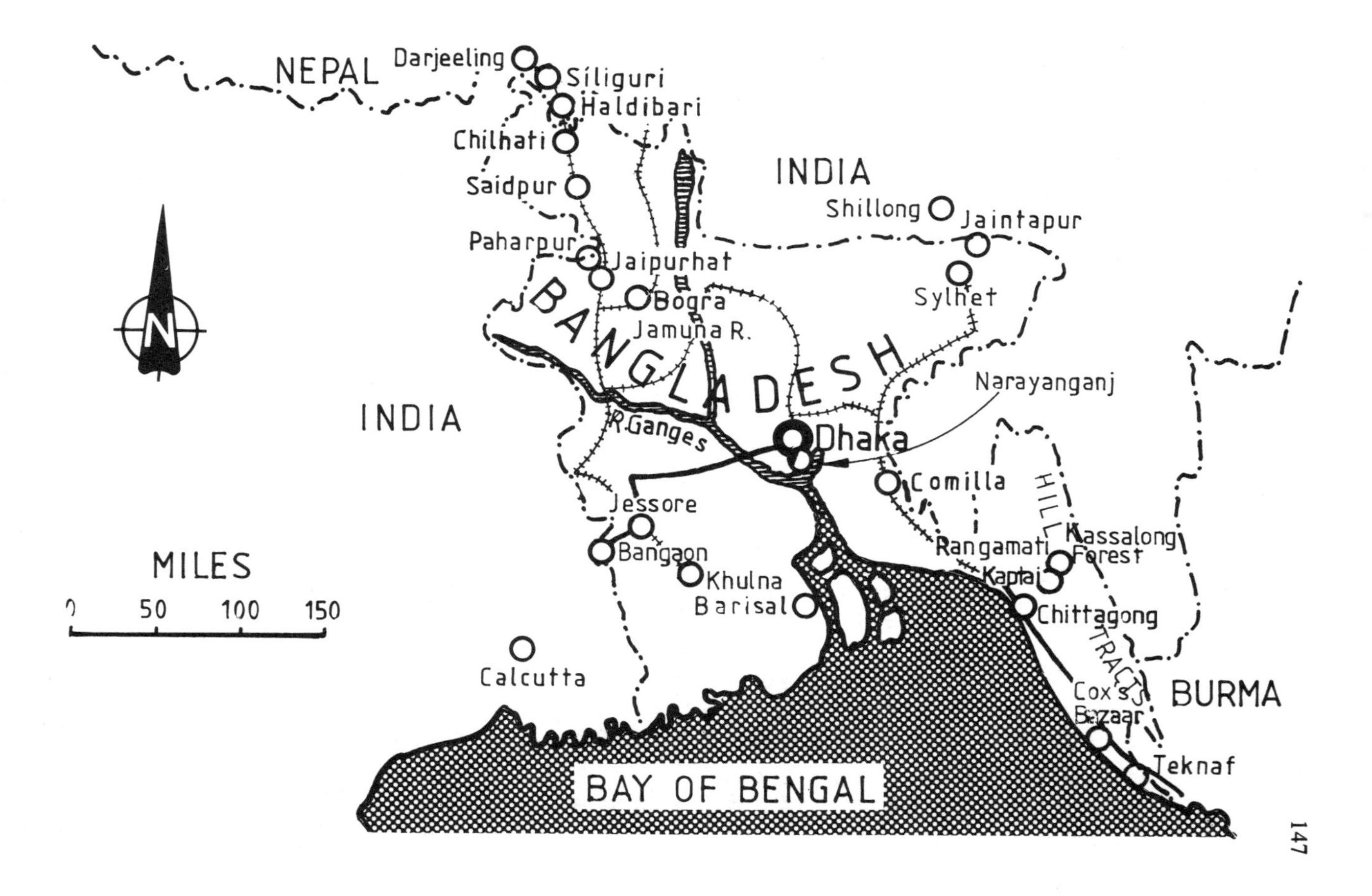
NEPAL
Darjeeling
Siliguri
Haldibari
Chilhati
Saidpur
Paharpur
Jaipurhat
Bogra
Jamuna R.
BANGLADESH
INDIA
Shillong
Jaintapur
Sylhet
Narayanganj
INDIA
R. Ganges
Dhaka
Comilla
HILL
TRACTS
Jessore
Bangaon
Khulna
Barisal
Rangamati
Kassalong
Forest
Kaptai
Chittagong
MILES
50
100
150
Calcutta
Cox's
Bazaar
BURMA
Teknaf
BAY OF BENGAL
N
W.S.

visa. The visa becomes invalid six months after the date of issue. Nationals of Australia, Canada and the U.S.A. who plan to stay less than seven days and who can show an onward ticket do not need a visa. You can be allowed into Bangladesh without a visa at the discretion of the border immigration official, but this seems an unnecessary risk to run when you can get a visa in Delhi or Calcutta. If you do not get in without a visa, you must register within 72 hours at the Foreigners' Registration desk at the Passport and Visa Office at Shantinagar in Dhaka, which is not very convenient to reach. You will have to go out there if you want to extend your visa or if you need an exit visa because you are leaving by road.

Customs
The standard international customs allowances apply for Bangladesh: you are allowed to import 200 cigarettes and two bottles of "spirituous beverages". Of course a reasonable quantity of personal effects may be imported, such as "medals bestowed by foreign countries", "one hair dryer for lady tourist only" and six sarees (whether you're male or female as of September 1985).

Currency Regulations
There is no maximum amount of foreign currency, cash or travellers' cheques which you may take into the country, though you may be asked to declare all currency on a form upon arrival. You may import and export up to 100 taka, though if you're crossing by land from India, it might be better to bring in more taka since it is difficult to change money outside the big centres.

Health Certificates
A vaccination certificate for cholera is required if you have been in a cholera zone within the previous five days. Yellow fever restrictions are enforced, even if you have only been in transit through an infected country, and you may be subjected to quarantine.

Motoring Documents
Motorists driving their own vehicles require third party insurance, an I.D.P. and a *carnet de passages*. No duty is charged provided the vehicle is re-exported within 6 months. Caravans may not be imported.

£1 = Tk36
$1 = Tk24

Tk10 = £0.27
Tk10 = $0.41

Currency: 100 poisha = 1 taka (Tk)

Notes
Tk1 (yellow and brown), Tk5 (brownish yellow), Tk10 (red), Tk50 (orange), Tk100 (grey, pink and yellow), Tk500 (multicoloured).

Changing Money
You may encounter great difficulty changing money outside the main towns, even at the main bank branches which indicate they have exchange facilities. The services of American Express are especially welcome in Bangladesh (see section on Dhaka for two offices and in Chittagong which also has two AmEx

branches). Prominent hotels are authorized to change money, even if you are not a resident.

There are no official exchange facilities at the frontier posts but you may be able to change money informally with the border officials. To avoid getting stranded buy taka in India; though this is strictly illegal, it is a common practice. Similarly you are not allowed to take any Indian rupees out of the country. And yet if you tell Bangladeshi customs that you have no Indian currency, you won't be believed.

There used to be a thriving black market around the area of the Central Mosque in Dhaka. This market existed because foreign currency which has been sent into the country by Bangladeshi workers abroad was auctioned daily at a more advantageous exchange rate than the rate fixed for tourists. Street dealers could then undercut the official rate and still make a profit. However a recent directive of the Bank of Bangladesh (late 1985) permits foreign tourists to change both travellers cheques and notes in sterling or U.S. dollars at the same rate as "wage earners" abroad.

When you leave Bangladesh, you may reconvert your taka into a hard currency at the airport. There is a Tk500 maximum or 25% of the foreign exchange previously converted into taka according to your currency declaration form.

Emergency Cash

Just as the black market in currency is dormant at present since American dollars are readily available, so the black market in goods is sluggish. Apparently foreign cigarettes are cheap and plentiful, so there are no large profits to be made. If you have any gadgets (such as cheap digital watches, Walkmen, cassette players or small stereos), approach the souvenir stall-holders opposite the Sheraton Hotel in Dhaka. If you do try to flog your duty-frees, beware of cheats who will damage the goods after sale, and then claim their money back. The way to avoid this is to get in a rickshaw after the sale and disappear.

Opening Hours

Because Bangladesh is an Islamic country, the working week is basically Sunday to Thursday. Some banks open on Friday mornings, others are closed all day Friday. Banking hours are normally 09.00-13.00. Government offices open 09.00-12.30 and 13.00-17.00, except during Ramazan when they open earlier and close about 14.30. According to a British government publication, shops in Bangladesh are open 10.00-12.30. However most Bengali shopkeepers are not quite so apathetic about business and the majority open 09.00-17.00 Sunday to Thursday.

Public Holidays

21st February	Martyrs' Day (or Shahid Day)
7th March	Anniversary of beginning of Independence Movement
26th March	Independence Day
14/15th April	Bengali New Year
1st May	May Day
23rd May (approx. date for 1986)	Buddhist Full Moon Day
June	Shab-e-Qadr
October	Hindu Durga Puja
7th November	Revolution Day

16th December Victory Day
25th December Christmas

For the dates of Moslem holidays such as Eid-e-Miladunna, Eid-ul-Fitr, Eid-ul-Azha and Muharram, see the Introduction. There are many other local and optional holidays in Bangladesh, but these are unlikely to affect travellers.

Arrival and Departure

Although Bangladesh depends heavily on its seaports (mainly Chittagong) for international trade, tourists arrive either by air to Dhaka or by land. Zia International Airport is 11 miles north of the city centre, which may be reached by taking the Tourist Corporation's bus to the Motijheel area or an autorickshaw which could cost about Tk40.

Bangladesh and India are not on friendly terms, and there is increasing resentment in the bordering states of West Bengal and Assam of illegal Bangladeshi immigrants. There is even a daft agreement to erect a barbed wire fence along the thousands of miles of border. There are just three border crossings available to foreigners: Benapol (on the Dhaka-Jessore-Calcutta route), Jaintapur (between Sylhet and Shillong in Meghalaya state for which you must get a permit in New Delhi, see page 98), and less commonly at Haldibari in the far north between Saidpur and Siliguri.

There are no through services on bus or train, and so normally you will have to walk or take a rickshaw between border posts. For example from Darjeeling and Siliguri, you can take a train as far as Haldibari where you should seek out Indian customs and immigration officials. If necessary sleep in the station (with permission). Then either walk, take a rickshaw or catch a bus to Hemkomari which is still 3 miles from Chilhati, the first village on the Bangladeshi side. Here there is a police check-post where you either will or will not be asked to show an entry road permit. If you haven't got one (either because you never applied or because the Bangladeshi mission which issued your visa claimed that it was not necessary), subtly offer some baksheesh, possibly in the guise of changing money (rupees or dollars) at a rate beneficial to the border guard. From Chilhati, you can catch a bus or train on to Saidpur and Bogra, where there are definitely exchange facilities.

The crossing at Bangaon/Benapol (about two hours from Calcutta by both rail and road) is more frequented and shouldn't cause any problems. It is necessary to take several rickshaw rides between the two towns. Be sure to negotiate with the drivers ahead of time.

In the extreme southeast of the country, Bangladesh borders on Burma. Although there is some local movement over the border (at Teknaf), the Burmese strictly prohibit land entry to all foreigners.

Flights

With an area just slightly larger than that of England, domestic flights in Bangladesh are not usually necessary, though they are so cheap that you might like to consider them. For example the 30 minute flight from Dhaka to Jessore (which is within easy reach of the Indian border) is Tk200 (£6). There is a departure tax on all domestic flights of Tk10.

In addition to Dhaka, there are airports at Cox's Bazar, Chittagong, Sylhet, Jessore, Ishurdi and Saidpur. Bangladesh Biman use Fokker Friendships which seat only 40 people.

Motoring

Both the Automobile Association and the Parjatan Corporation (Tourist Office) can advise on road conditions. The A.A. is at 3/B Outer Circular Road, Moghbazar, Dhaka 17 (tel: 243482). Neither Hertz nor Avis has representatives in Bangladesh, though it is possible to hire a car (with driver) from one of the international hotels. This will cost about Tk50 per hour plus Tk5 per mile.

Bus

The bus service connects all major cities and is well used. In Dhaka, it is possible to reserve tickets from the Bangladesh Road Transport Corporation, near the architecturally striking Kamalapur Railway Station. The main bus station is at Gulistan in central Dhaka. The Transport Authority fixes the prices of bus journeys. There is a charge of about 25-30 poisha per mile, with a surcharge for every ferry crossing, many of which last several hours. For example, the journey fron Dhaka to Chittagong which takes about 8 hours costs just Tk65. The distance between Dhaka and Sylhet is 215 miles and the cost is under Tk100. A journey of 50 miles can easily take 3 hours but will cost about Tk12.

There are also special air-conditioned buses along some routes which can be booked through the Parjatan Corporation. Prices are at least double, but may be worth it for long trips, especially in the hot season.

Train

The trains are just as crowded as those in India and slower. This is because the country is broken up by several major river systems which have to be crossed by ferry, for which there may be a surcharge. Also there is both broad and metre gauge track which means that you may have to transfer. There are four classes of train: air-conditioned, first, second and third. It is possible to reserve seats (which convert to berths on overnight journeys) in the first three classes up to 10 days in advance. Third class seats cannot be reserved. Mail and express trains are faster than ordinary (e.g. 9 hours between Dhaka and Chittagong rather than 15½) and cost very slightly more.

Student and tourist discounts of up to 50% may be obtained if you pre-book your ticket. In Dhaka the student concession office is near the Old Dhaka Railway Station. Ordinary fares are calculated approximately as follows:

1st class — 75 poisha per mile
2nd class — 22 poisha per mile
3rd class — 13 poisha per mile

This means that the second class fare is roughly equivalent to bus fares.

Like the railways of India, Bangladesh Railways offer a spectacular range of services involving dozens of bureaucratic procedures. One of the most impressive of these services is that you can order dinner from the conductor who then sends a "telegraphic intimation free of charge" and several stations later your curry will be brought to your compartment.

Boat

Bangladesh is the site of two enormous river deltas, the Ganges and the Brahmaputra. The extensive network of tributaries disrupts both rail and road communications. In addition to using ferries as part of a through train or bus journey (just as you do if you're travelling between London and Paris or Hamburg and Copenhagen), you can also choose to cover some distances entirely by boat in preference to land transport. The most heavily used routes are Dhaka to Khulna and Dhaka to Chittagong, both via Barisal. Many of the passenger services run by the Bangladesh Inland Water Transport Corporation (tel: 239779) are on authentic old paddle steamers, though these are being replaced by spanking new boats from Denmark (another water-oriented country). This unique mode of travel can be one of the highlights of travelling in Bangladesh.

The service between Dhaka and Khulna is called the Rocket. Tickets may be purchased from the B.I.W.T.C. office which is on the first floor of the building across from the Bangladesh Biman office in Motijheel. Several classes are available, with as wide a range of prices as on the railway. Boats leave Dhaka daily at 17.45 and arrive exactly 24 hours later. In the opposite direction, the boat leaves Khulna at 06.00, and you can ask if you can sleep on board the previous night, at no charge assuming you have booked a cabin. First class cabins cost about Tk450 and include a fan, a sink and a sybaritic atmosphere. Upper class accommodation is often booked up well in advance.

Unfortunately there is no direct service Dhaka to Chittagong, and an awkward connection in Barisal, i.e. a wait of about 16 hours if you arrive on a Tuesday or a Friday, and considerably more if you arrive on any other day of the week. It might be better to take the bus as far as Barisal (10½ hours, Tk55) and then catch the ferry. The 24 hour journey on to Chittagong costs Tk300 in first class, Tk190 second, Tk90 interclass (which means no seat or berth allocation) and Tk35 deck class. Travelling on the deck affords a wonderful opportunity for star-gazing but can be extremely crowded. No matter which class you choose, you will probably be the object of much curiosity, attention and generosity.

City Transport

As throughout the subcontinent, try to negotiate fares on both pedal and auto rickshaws in advance. You may find that a surprisingly large number of rickshaw drivers refuse to bargain, and will simply drive off. This is more likely due to their failure to understand than their willingness to take you for a lower price. The traffic jams in Dhaka, with a population of over 3 million, are as alarming as in any Asian city.

Post

There is a poste restante service at the G.P.O. in Dhaka, which is located just west of the Motijheel Commercial District next to the Baitulmukar Ram Mosque. They also undertake to forward mail for you to other post offices in Bangladesh. Use the blue post boxes for your letters abroad since the red ones are intended for surface mail.

Telephone

There are very few coin-operated telephones. You should make your calls either at the G.P.O. or at a major hotel. The cost of a call to the U.K. is Tk75 per minute with a minimum fee of Tk150. Local area codes are 02 for Dhaka, 031 for Chittagong, 0821 for Sylhet and 0341 for Cox's Bazar. Telegrams are fairly reliable and can be sent normal, fast or express.

Newspapers
There are 7 English language dailies in Bangladesh. The two best known are the *Daily News* and the *Bangladesh Times,* both published in Dhaka and widely circulated. The *New York Times* is on sale near the Dhaka Sheraton and British newspapers may be read at the Embassy.

Broadcasting
There are English news bulletins throughout the day on local radio. The final programme of the day is the "Slow Speed News" in English.

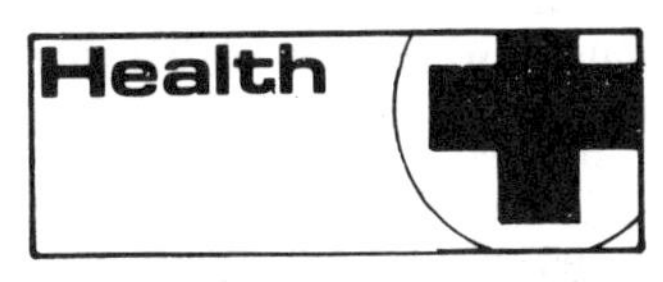

Malaria risk exists all year throughout the country except for central Dhaka. Resistance to chloroquine has been detected. So travellers should follow both the chloroquine and proguanil courses.

There are many government hospitals and clinics which provide free health care to foreign visitors. Among the best of these in Dhaka are the Post Graduate Medical and Research Hospital (PGMR) on Mymensingh Road (tel: 255194) and the Medical College Hospital on Diwan Bazar Road (tel: 254241).

Private treatment is available at the I.A.M.A.T. recommended Red Cross Holy Family Hospital on Eskaton Road (tel: 283115). This should not be very expensive, perhaps Tk200-300 per day including room and doctor's fee.

A large number of so-called Indian restaurants in Great Britain are in fact run by Bangladeshis so the food is likely to be familiar to you. Bengal curries often use meat (mutton or chicken especially) as a base. There is a wide choice of Chinese food also available. Especially recommended is the Beijing Restaurant near the Hotel Blue Nile in Dhaka. The Tourist Office (Parjatan Corporation) operates some reasonably priced air-conditioned restaurants, including a floating restaurant in Dhaka called the Mary Anderson.

Alcohol is easier to come by than in Pakistan but harder than in India. Almost all the profits which the Tourist Corporation makes come from the duty free shop at Zia International Airport. There are no off-licences, so you will have to buy your beer or whisky from a luxury hotel, but at least you don't need a special permit. Drinking is forbidden on Fridays. If you are willing to pay the price in fancy surroundings (e.g. Tk45 for a can of beer and Tk95 for whisky), you are free to drink. Soft drinks cost about Tk6, though there may be a surcharge for chilled (as opposed to "boiled") drinks.

DHAKA
The seat of Bangladesh's government is now spelled Dhaka rather than the old anglicized Dacca. The name possibly derives from "dhak", the Bengali word

for drum, an instrument which was put to enthusiastic use to welcome a Mogul governor. There is evidence of settlements in the area dating back to the 7th century, though the city wasn't officially established until 1608, soon after the Mogul victory. Under Mogul rule the city expanded, covering at one time well over 50 square miles on the Buriganga River. The city went into decline with the collapse of the Mogul empire and again under the British, who made Calcutta their headquarters, but has thrived since partition in 1947.

Under a succession of conquerors, a great number of mosques were built to display the grandeur of Islam. Today there may be as many as 1,300 mosques within the city.

There is a frequent steamer service to Narayanganj, where the largest jute mills in the world are worth visiting.

What to See

Lalbagh Fort — built by the Moguls in 1678 near the banks of the Buriganga River. The fort contains a mosque and the tomb of Pari Bibi, daughter of a former Mogul viceroy. There is a good view of the city's imposing river frontage from the fort.

National Museum — houses a collection of sculptures and paintings belonging to the Hindu and Moslem periods. Open from 09.00-16.30. Free admission. There is also a museum in the Balda Gardens which are themselves worthy of a visit for their botanical collection.

The Star Mosque — located in the old city (i.e. near the river) and one of the few mosques which retains its beautiful tiled interior. It has a pleasant and quiet pool.

Sadarghat — the bustling port area of Dhaka worth strolling around even if you aren't catching a ferry.

Accommodation

Y.M.C.A. — 96/97 New Eskaton Road. Tel: 401371. (Telegraphic address: Manhood Dhaka). Very central location. Tk120 double. Dorm beds for Tk50. Cheap cafeteria, but many restaurants nearby. If the Y is full, they should be able to recommend somewhere else.

Ambassador — 7 Airport Road. Tel: 310789. From Tk70.

Hotel Asha — Moonzu Mansion, 81/3 Paioniar Road, Kakrail. Tel: 413938. Tk20 single, Tk30 double.

Hotel Blue Nile — favourite among travellers. Friendly manager.

Tourist Hotel — 86 Kakrail Road (sometimes called Inner Circular Road). Both basic and more luxurious rooms with private bath, fan and mosquito nets for Tk100.

Useful Addresses

Tourist Corporation (called Parjatan) — Head Office, 233 Allenbari, Airport Road, Tejgaon. Also a tourist office inside the Hotel Intercontinental.

British High Commission — Abu Bakr House, Plot 7 Road 84, Gulshan (P.O. Box 6079). Tel: 300133/7.

British Council — Fuller Road, near Dhaka University; usually have copies of British newspapers. Tel: 500107-9.

American Express — 18/20 Motijheel Commercial Area. Tel: 238350-3.

American Express — Vantage International Ltd., Hotel Sonargaon, Kawran Bazar. Tel: 233183.

Thomas Cook — Olympic Travels Ltd., 49 Motijheel Commercial Area. Tel: 230212.

PAHARPUR

The most important historical site in Bangladesh is, ironically, Buddhist not Moslem. In fact Paharpur is the largest Buddhist *vihara* (monastic complex) in the subcontinent. It consists of a pyramid-shaped hill with a cruciform monastery on it, built in the eighth century. The walls are made of burned bricks and stand to a height of 70 feet.

There is a certain charm in overgrown and neglected sites as opposed to manicured and heavily marketed ones, however Paharpur has suffered excessively from long exposure both to the harsh elements (especially monsoonal rains) and to vandals and plunderers. So it is fortunate that U.N.E.S.C.O. has added the site to its world heritage list and is taking steps to restore it.

To get to Paharpur, take the train from Jessore north to Jamalganj (the station before Jaipurhat) and then walk the three miles to the site. There is an archaeological bungalow which serves meals, and there are plans to develop more tourist facilities.

CHITTAGONG

Chittagong, which is only 135 miles from the Burmese border, was a centre of Buddhist culture from the 6th century. It is now the chief port of Bangladesh, as well as an industrial centre for jute and cotton export. Because of its size (population 900,000) and its industrial importance, Chittagong is a very picturesque city. The docks are unprepossessing: mouldy and decaying. According to Paul Theroux, the people of Chittagong urge visitors who have just arrived to escape to Rangamati or Cox's Bazar.

Accommodation

Hotel Raj — 154 Kabi Nazral Islam Savah Sadarghat. Attentive service, good facilities. Tk80 single, Tk120 double.
Bahaddarhat Rest House — Tel: 86368. Basic accommodation from Tk15.

Useful Addresses

Tourist Information Centre — Yasmeen Palace, Jubilee Road. Tel: 89514.
British Council Library — Laldighi. Tel: 223632.
American Express — Nizan House, 31 Agrabad, Commercial Area.
American Express — 11 Ramjoy, Mohajon Lane, Khatunj.

CHITTAGONG HILL TRACTS

The Chittagong Hill Tracts cover 5,000 square miles and are still inhabited by colourful tribes, many of whom are Buddhist and resemble the tribesmen of Burma. Certain areas are forbidden to tourists, so make local enquiries before wandering off.

Rangamati

Rangamati is about 50 miles by sealed road from Chittagong, and is the headquarters of the Hill Tracts. The bus ride from Chittagong takes 3 hours and costs Tk12; the last bus returns to Chittagong about 17.00. The trip by river from Chittagong takes you through beautiful lush jungle. At the Raja's Palace there is a tribal museum, and not far from the G.P.O. is a Cottage Industry and Handicraft Centre. Crafts include homespun textiles, bamboo handbags and silver jewellery. The tourist information desk is situated inside the Tourist Cottage in Deer Park (tel: 366), along with a 32-bedroom motel, restaurant and bar. The government is investing heavily in tourist facilities here and soon there will be such amenities as a "jumping board on the lake". As one piece of literature describes it, it is a "good place for fishing, foing [?] . . . hiking or merely laxing in the dappled shade".

Kaptai

Forty miles east of Chittagong is the town of Kaptai, situated on a huge man-made lake and an impressive hydro-electric project. Water sport facilities are available. There is an air-conditioned government rest house, and a Buddhist temple nearby.

Kassalong Forest Reserve

Situated 50 miles to the north-east of Rangamati, this wildlife sanctuary extends over several ranges of hills along the Kassalong River. Forest bungalow accommodation is available: contact the tourist information office for details.

Sajek Valley

To the east of the Kassalong Reserve is the Sajek Valley, bordering Assam. The valley is inhabited by the Lushai tribe, who were at one time head hunters, but have now been converted to Christianity.

COX'S BAZAR

This popular, though rather down-at-heel, seaside resort close to the Burmese border is 96 miles south of Chittagong and linked by a surfaced road. Buses take 4-5 hours to make this picturesque journey. The town was founded by Captain Cox of the Madras Army, and it has one of the longest beaches in the world (70 miles). Swimming in the Bay of Bengal is safe and very pleasant, except during the cyclone season. The fish market is worth a visit, and the bazaar sells shell handicrafts. The tourist information office is located in the Upal Motel (tel: 246). The government is trying to develop tourist facilities in Cox's Bazar, and there are several government-run rest houses, motels and self-catering cottages near the beach.

SYLHET

Since it was amongst the earliest Moslem settlements in the area, the town has many mosques and tombs. The most famous is that of Shah Jalal who, with his Arab followers, came from Turkestan in 1303 A.D. But tribal traditions including music and dance are maintained.

Sylhet is in the hilly eastern part of Bangladesh which is well-suited to tea-growing. There is a guest house at the Tea Research Institute in nearby Srimangal, as well as a tourist rest house.

Sri Lanka

Capital: Colombo **Government:** Republic (within the Commonwealth)

Despite the Moslem belief that Sri Lanka is the place to which Adam and Eve fled after being expelled from the Garden of Eden, many people consider the island to be a paradise on earth. The lush scenery, beautiful beaches and smiling people do often combine to create an impression of paradise. Travellers to the subcontinent often fail to include Sri Lanka on their itinerary, especially now that the cheap ferry connection with South India has been discontinued, and thereby miss an interesting contrast. The sarongs worn by the men, the Buddhist temples, the coconut, rubber and tea plantations and the jungle evoke comparisons with Burma and Malaysia as much as with India. And since you can spend much longer exploring Sri Lanka than you can Burma (where all visits are limited to seven days) and since it is a much more manageable size than India (smaller than Scotland), it seems a very desirable destination for travellers to the East. In many ways it is an easy country in which to travel and a good introduction to Asia for the apprehensive traveller.

The earliest inhabitants of Sri Lanka were aboriginal, living off the abundant fruit and game of the jungle. Today only a handful of Veddah settlements survive, consisting of stilt houses designed to keep out roaming wildlife.

The Sinhalese, who now comprise 74% of the population, are thought to have come from northern India in about the sixth century B.C. The country's history prior to European colonization is one of invasion and counter-invasion of and by South India. The principal warriors were the Tamils who, in about the thirteenth century, took over the northern part of the country, spreading Hinduism and persecuting Sinhalese Buddhists. The situation is of course now reversed, so that the Tamils (18% of a total population of 15.3 million) are discriminated against by the Sinhalese majority.

The first European power to colonize Sri Lanka were the Portuguese in 1505, though most of their activity was confined to the coast. A number of Sri Lankans today have Portuguese names, which were given to their families during this period, and 7% of the population is Christian (principally Roman Catholic). The Portuguese were eventually displaced by the Dutch in 1651, and then the British took effective control of the island in 1796. Independence was peacefully granted in 1948.

The riots of 1983 and 1985 are not a new phenomenon, since there have been outbreaks of communal violence between Tamils and Sinhalese for decades, over language, religion and status. However the situation does seem to be worsening, and sometimes it seems as insoluble as that of Northern Ireland. There is extreme press censorship (e.g. the *Times* correspondent is banned) and so it is difficult to assess the conflict accurately. Jaffna, in the extreme north, is a Tamil stronghold to which many southern Tamils have fled to escape persecution. It is certainly off-limits for tourists as was much of the east coast (with the exception of Trincomalee) at the time of writing. Public transport to potentially dangerous areas is searched by the police or army and foreigners will be turned back. Of course the situation changes constantly. For example Anuradhapura, the ancient capital of Ceylon situated in the North Central Province, was considered to be a safe zone for tourists in April 1985. In May, a group of Tamil terrorists (known as Tigers) hijacked a bus, drove to the site of the 2,200 year old bo-tree sacred to Buddhists, opened fire and killed 147 civilians, including a Buddhist monk and some school children. This was in retaliation for many similar acts of violence committed against Tamils.

Naturally this problem has seriously damaged the tourist industry which was flourishing and expanding through the late 70s and early 80s. Travellers undaunted by newspaper reports of riots and violence will therefore not find it difficult to avoid tourist crowds, and will be able to negotiate very favourable rates at the numerous empty hotels throughout the country. Since the atmosphere in many areas is still serene, it seems that Sri Lanka is a good country to visit at present.

Climate

The climate is tropical, though it is always possible to escape the heat and humidity by going to the hills which rise to 8,000 ft. The best time of year to visit is between October and February, since in March the temperatures on the coast begin to rise and hover around 30°C (86°F) and stay there for many months. The southern coastal areas, Colombo and the interior massif are affected by the south-west monsoon which (unreliably) starts in early or mid-May and continues into July. The east coast is subject to a winter monsoon (November to February) though in the present political climate, it is unlikely that this area will be of interest to many travellers.

Language

Part of the present trouble in Sri Lanka is due to the government's decison in 1956 to make Sinhalese the only official language, although a later amendment

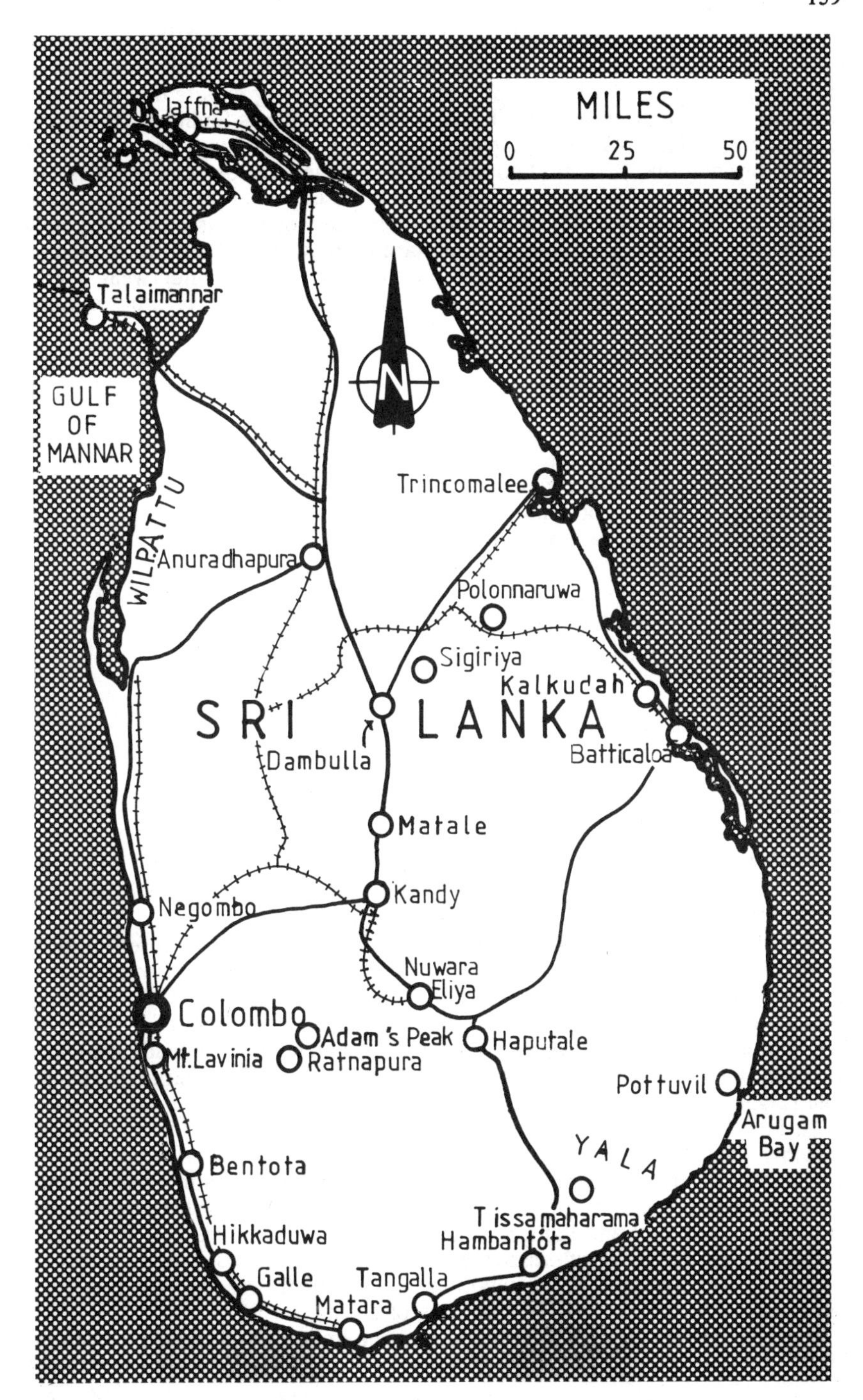
MILES
0
25
50
Jaffna
Talaimannar
GULF
OF
MANNAR
WILPATTU
Trincomalee
Anuradhapura
Polonnaruwa
Sigiriya
Kalkudah
SRI LANKA
Dambulla
Batticaloa
Matale
Kandy
Negombo
Nuwara
Eliya
Colombo
Adam's Peak
Haputale
Mt.Lavinia
Ratnapura
Pottuvil
Arugam
Bay
YALA
Bentota
Tissamaharama
Hikkaduwa
Hambantota
Galle
Tangalla
Matara

has deemed both Sinhalese and Tamil "national" languages. With more and more Tamils fleeing to the north, you may not hear much Tamil, though it is spoken by nearly a fifth of the population. It is interesting to note that although there are only a quarter as many Tamil-speaking people as Sinhalese, there are just as many Tamil-language newspapers (with a minimum circulation of 10,000) proving that the Tamil population is relatively literate. English was the official language until 30 years ago, so most older educated people speak some English. In fact you probably won't encounter many occasions on which you'll have to struggle with Sinhalese, but here are a few words. Watch for amusing subcontinental errors in English such as "nuderwear" for "underwear". The script, with over 50 letters, will remain impenetrable on signs, etc., but a large number of shopfronts are labelled in English, e.g. "Grammar Gardens: Stationers, Duplicators, Grocers".

Useful Sinhalese Words

yes	— ou	1	— eke
no	— naha	2	— deke
please	— karunakara	3	— tuna
thank you	— bohoma istuti	4	— hatere
hello/good-bye	— ayabowan	5	— paha
beach	— walla	6	— haya
good	— hondai	7	— hate
bad	— narakai	8	— atta
water	— wathure	9	— namaya
left	— vametha	10	— dahaya
right	— dakuna		
Jaya wewa!	— cheers!		

Visas

British, Canadian, Australian, U.S. and Irish passport holders do not require a visa for stays of up to 30 days as tourists. You may be asked to show an onward ticket and/or sufficient funds before you're admitted for 30 days. Visas may be extended by applying to the Controller of Immigration and Emigration, Galle Buck, Colombo 1, Unit 6 (tel: 29851/21509). For this you should be able to show an onward ticket and the equivalent of US$15 per day. Nationals of non-Commonwealth countries who intend to extend their visas must register with the Aliens' Bureau, 4th Floor, New Secretariat Building, Colombo 1.

Customs

A customs declaration must be made on the Immigration Landing Card and stamped by the customs official upon arrival. You should keep this card throughout your stay and hand it in as you leave the country. You are meant to declare all your currency (see below) and all valuable items. You are allowed to bring in 200 cigarettes or 50 cigars or 375 grams of tobacco, plus two 70cl bottles of wine, and one and a half litres of spirits.

When leaving the country, you are permitted to take away 3 kilos of tea before duty is payable, though it is very rare for departing travellers to be searched.

Currency Regulations
The import and export of Indian or Pakistani rupees is prohibited. You are allowed to bring in a maximum of Rs250. Otherwise there are no restrictions on the movement of foreign currency and travellers' cheques. You should keep all receipts of exchange transactions, which will also be noted on your Currency Declaration Form.

If you change more money into rupees than you need, you may reconvert the rupees into a hard currency (usually American dollars) only after producing receipts of exchange. This can be done fairly painlessly at Colombo Airport. No more than Rs300 may be reconverted into a foreign currency.

Health Certificates
Yellow fever inoculations are required only if coming from an infected area (i.e. most of Africa and Latin America). Immunization against cholera and typhoid is recommended but not required.

Drugs
The penalties for drug offences range from a fine to a prison sentence of up to 10 years.

Motoring Documents
If you are driving your own vehicle to Sri Lanka, then you will require a *carnet de passages,* which allows the vehicle to remain in Sri Lanka for up to 6 months without payment of duty. If you arrive with no *carnet* then duty must be paid in full, but will be refunded provided the vehicle is re-exported within a year. Third party insurance is obligatory and can be obtained in Colombo from the Insurance Corporation of Sri Lanka, Amir Building, Sir Baron Jayatilleke Mawatha. Although an International Driving Permit is not required, it is highly recommended and should be endorsed by the A.A. of Sri Lanka (Box 338, Colombo). The national driving licences of many countries are acceptable for 90 days if endorsed by the Commissioner of Motor Traffic, Narahenpita, Colombo 5.

£1 = Rs36
$1 = Rs27

Rs10 = £0.28
Rs10 = $0.37

Currency: 100 cents=1 rupee (R)

Coins
1, 2, 5, 10, 25 and 50 cents; Rs1, Rs2 and Rs5. The 5 rupee coin is silver and seldom found in general circulation.

Notes
Rs2 (brown and iridescent); Rs5 (red and iridescent; red and green reverse); Rs10 (green, mauve and iridescent), Rs20 (green and mauve); Rs50 (blue and iridescent); Rs100 (purple and iridescent), Rs1,000 (violet, grey and iridescent). All notes are issued by the Central Bank of Ceylon. Many prices are written in the form Rs50/- or Rs2/50. For an explanation of lakhs and crores, see page 97.

Emergency Cash

The price of a bottle of duty free Johnny Walker on sale to arriving passengers in Colombo Airport, is virtually the same as in the Heathrow duty-free shop. There is not the obvious demand for whisky in Sri Lanka that there is in India, since potential profits are small. Unlike India, Sri Lanka imports all sorts of Western gadgets which are readily available in the shops. There is also a duty-free shop on the Galle Road where you can shop if you show your passport and pay the Rs25 admission fee. Purchases such as cameras and electrical goods are noted in your passport, so you can't sell them. Saris bought in India can sometimes be sold for a small profit in Sri Lanka, though you will be competing with shrewd and experienced businessmen. The black market for foreign currency is barely worthwhile.

Opening Hours

The working week is Monday to Friday. Banks normally open 09.00 to 13.30, though they close half an hour early on Mondays. Offices are open from 08.00 or 09.00 to 16.15 or 17.00. Many offices close for an hour over lunch. Shops are open from 08.00 to 17.00 although some stay open until 20.00 or 21.00.

There is a *bureau de change* at the Intercontinental Hotel in Colombo open every day of the week from 08.00 to 20.00. The Overseas Trust Bank next to the Colombo YMCA seems to offer favourable rates. Avoid the Bank of Ceylon on York Street which subtracts a large service charge.

Public Holidays

The Poya is a Buddhist festival which occurs at each full moon. In 1986 the dates will be approximately: 26th January, 24th February, 26th March, 24th April, 23rd May, 22nd June, 21st July, 19th August, 18th September, 17th October, 16th November and 16th December. During the Poya, all places of entertainment are closed, no alcohol is served, and often there are festivals.

The Moslem, Hindu, Christian and Buddhist holidays reflect the diversity of religion in Sri Lanka. Dates are given for 1986.

14th January	Thaipongal
4th February	Independence Day
February/March	Maha Siva Rathri
28th March	Good Friday
Mid-April	Sinhalese and Tamil New Year
1st May	May Day
22nd May	National Heroes' Day
9th June	Id ul Fitr (end of Ramazan)
16th August	Hajj Festival Day
1st November	Deepavali
13th November	Mulid al-Nabi (Prophet's Birthday)
25th December	Christmas

Arrival and Departure

There used to be two methods of approach to Sri Lanka, by ferry from India (which was very cheap — less than £5) and by plane to Colombo. Each winter the ferry service was suspended during the severest part of the northern monsoon (November/December). Due to the political instability in the Tamil-dominated north, the service was not resumed in 1985, since the 25 mile stretch of water is constantly patrolled by the Sri Lankan army in search of Tamil terrorists travelling to and from India.

The only approach is now by air to Colombo International Airport (Katunayake) which is 22 miles north of the city centre. Aeroflot probably offer the cheapest return fare from London, or you can arrange a stopover in Sri Lanka on PIA if you are flying with them to Singapore or Kuala Lumpur or on Air Lanka if you are continuing to Bangkok or Hong Kong. Alternatively you may be arriving from India: cheapest flight is Colombo-Trivandrum at the southernmost tip of India, which is about Rs2000 return for the 45 minute flight. Other frequent destinations are Tiruchirapalli (known as Trichy) in central Tamil Nadu and Madras. If you want to book an outgoing flight while in Colombo, visit George Travel (68 Bristol Street, opposite the YMCA), Sri Lanka's modest answer to London's bucket shops.

Colombo Airport is a well organized and pleasant place. You can change money at the exchange counter (where no commission is charged), buy stamps at the 24 hour post office (but don't buy the ludicrously overpriced post cards at the adjoining shop), pick up some literature at the tourist counter and proceed into town. Turn right when you leave the terminal and board a city bus or a mini-bus bound for the Fort area (central Colombo). This trip should cost Rs5, though they may try to charge you double for a large piece of luggage.

When leaving the country, you can get an airport bus from the Central Bus Station in the Pettah area or the Negombo bus station (Rs2.50) which is much nearer the airport. Buses do not run very late from either station, so if you have an awkwardly timed flight, you may have to spend a few hours in the airport. There is a departure tax of Rs100.

An alternative way of leaving the island is by crewing on one of the many private yachts that call in at Colombo and Galle. Ask around at the visitors' yacht basins. The man in charge of Galle Harbour is Don Simpson, who might be able to advise.

Motoring

Sri Lanka has an extensive network of metalled roads connecting all the major towns, which are in varying states of repair. Up-to-date information on road conditions can be obtained from the A.A. of Ceylon, 40 Macan Markar Mawatha, Galle Face, Colombo; tel: 21528. There are A.A. outstations in Kandy, Ratnapura and 6 other towns. The roads are often badly pot-holed, and care must be taken whenever a pedestrian or cyclist heaves into sight. Local driving techniques are not completely safe, possibly because driving instruction is not quite up to BSM standards. Apparently several learner drivers are taken out together on practice runs. When it comes time to change drivers, they don't bother to stop the vehicle but, as if in a relay race, the fellow in the back simply clambers over the back seat and takes over the wheel.

Vehicle Hire

Avis has an office in Colombo at 11-A York Street; tel: 29888. Hertz is represented in Colombo by Quickshaws Ltd., 3 Kalinga Place; tel: 583133. Europcar's office is at 498 Galle Road, Colombo 3; tel: 573778. The cost of car hire will be about $18 per day, among the cheapest in Asia. The minimum age for hiring is usually 25.

Motorcycles can be hired in most major towns. The bikes are mainly Japanese and engine sizes vary from 50 c.c. to 500 c.c. Prices are usually about Rs175-Rs200 per day. You may have to bargain, especially if you are hiring one in a resort like Hikkaduwa. In small private rental outlets, you may not even be asked to show a licence, though it is not a good idea to start learning to drive any vehicle on the roads of Sri Lanka. From a multinational company like Avis, you will not only have to show a licence, but also be aged over 23. Petrol costs Rs65 per gallon, which should take you about 90 miles if you hire a big bike.

Bus

Buses provide the simplest and cheapest way of moving around the island, costing approximately 15 cents per kilometre or 24 cents per mile. The government-run SLTB (Sri Lanka Transport Board) buses are marginally cheaper than private minibuses, and are often less crowded and therefore more comfortable. Minibuses vary in degree of luxury, but the average procedure is to pack an astonishing number of bodies into a small space — say 42 people (not counting babes-in-arms) into a 16 seater. You often have to have your wits about you since, if your concentration slips, you may be catapulted out of an open door or sear your flesh on the platform over the engine. Unless it's during the monsoon, try to avoid sitting near the back, since the back windows are often permanently closed. People with long legs can sometimes persuade the conductor to let them have a front seat, possibly after paying an extra couple of rupees.

Some sample prices:

Colombo — Galle	Rs18
Galle — Matara	Rs8
Kandy — Dambulla	Rs15
Dambulla — Anuradhapura	Rs8.50

Train

Buying a train ticket in Sri Lanka is more like doing business with Swiss Railways than with Indian Railways. Compared to Indian stations, Sri Lankan stations are like fur coat showrooms in a heatwave. It is rarely necessary to reserve a seat in advance. Trains are not nearly as versatile as buses, neither as frequent nor as wide-ranging. They also tend to be very slow, often averaging no more than 15mph.

The principal train routes are Colombo to Matara along the southwest coast, Colombo to Kandy and Badulla, Colombo to Anuradhapura and beyond, with branch lines east to Batticaloa via Polonnaruwa and to Trincomalee. There are three classes — first, second and third. Because the trains are not generally overcrowded and distances are small, third class is adequate and even sometimes comfortable. Many trains have no first class facilities whatsoever, for example of the six daily trains Colombo to Kandy, none has first class coaches.

There are several InterCity expresses, including two daily between Kandy and Colombo and Galle, which reduces the $3\frac{1}{2}$ hour journey Colombo-Kandy by an hour for example. The train ride to Kandy and through the hill country is very beautiful, and it is worth catching one of the trains which has an observation car (though there will be an extra charge for the ticket). There are sleeper carriages on some longer routes, e.g. Colombo to Badulla and Colombo to Batticaloa, which cost Rs30-Rs50 extra. There are also three InterCity services per week to Jaffna which visitors are unlikely to be taking. Prices and departure times are clearly posted in stations, including the central Colombo station called Fort. For further information contact the Railway Tourist Office (tel: 35838).

City Transport

In addition to the city buses in Colombo, there are hundreds of private minibuses clamouring for your one or two rupee fares. Unlike the municipal buses, most urban minibuses are at least numbered and sometimes also labelled in the Roman alphabet (e.g. "Pettah", "Dehiwala"). If you want to travel south from the Fort along the Galle Road (to Kollupitiya, Bambalapitiya, Dehiwala, Mount Lavinia), stand on Chatham Street and hail the minibus showing an appropriate destination. Locals will help you both to flag down a vehicle and to recognize your destination (which can be all but impossible when the hordes of bodies block your view out of the window). It is very easy to reach any destination along the Galle Road — though traffic is frantic, especially at midday — but much trickier to get to an address inland, for example in the diplomatic quarter known as Cinnamon Gardens. Unfortunately, auto-rickshaws are not nearly as widely used as in India; they charge about Rs2 per mile.

Outside Colombo and Kandy, it is normally possible to get round town on foot. Taxis are usually Morris 1000s with yellow roofs and red on white licence plates. Most will use a meter; threaten to report any who do not to the Tourist Police (tel: 26941).

Post

Poste restante services are of course available from the General Post Office, Janadhipathi Mawatha, Colombo 1, opposite the Presidential House. To save you a trek into Colombo, the phone number for poste restante service is 26203. You will need your passport or student card when collecting mail. There is a night counter at which you can buy stamps 24 hours a day. Aerogrammes cost Rs5 (a bargain), and post cards cost Rs6 to send. Telegrams cost Rs3.45 per word. American Express operate a very efficient postal counter and will reliably forward mail if you pay the fee of US$3 or rupee equivalent.

Telephone

The minimum charge for a local call is Re1. International telephone and telegraph services are available 24 hours a day at the Central Telegraph Office, Duke Street, Fort Colombo; tel: 24340. There are also many private telephone companies with direct dial facilities (assuming the lines are working). The "Salaka" agency near the railway station seems reliable and there are several along Galle Road. A 3-minute conversation with Britain will cost about Rs300. The fee will be less if you are prepared to wait around at the Central Telegraph Office.

Newspapers

There are five daily English newspapers, demonstrating the degree to which English is still an important force in Sri Lanka. The country boasts 84% literacy, among the highest in Asia. *The Daily News,* one of the most widely circulated, has the best cinema coverage. *The Island* is a few shades more independent, and the *Sunday Observer* has a good magazine section. Watch for a paper called *The Terrorist Review* (Rs1.50), a pro-government and frankly propagandistic and anti-Tamil paper. If you wish to read British papers, go to the British Council where the papers are on display.

Broadcasting

Apart from locally produced educational programmes in English, the Sri Lanka Broadcasting Corporation transmits some programmes in English. For BBC World Service frequencies, see the Introduction.

Voice of America also has a transmitter in Colombo, which broadcasts in English on the short wave band only from 01.00-03.30 and from 13.00-18.00.

There are television broadcasts every evening, though reception is restricted to certain parts of the country. Most programmes are British or American.

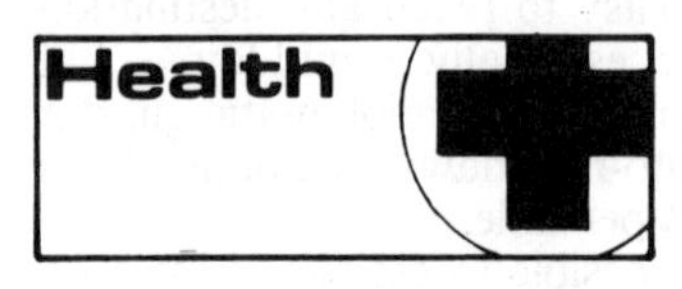

There is a malaria risk throughout the year in all parts of the country except central Colombo, and areas like Nuwara Eliya which are above 800 metres (2,625ft). The dangerous falciparum malaria is very rare, and an ordinary regimen of chloroquine should be fine for Sri Lanka. The recommended locally available brand of repellent is called "Flypel" (Rs30).

There are many good doctors throughout Sri Lanka, though facilities are best in Colombo. Medical treatment is free, but the service is very over-subscribed, so it might be worthwhile paying for any treatment which is urgent.

Colombo General Hospital: Regent Street, Colombo 8. Tel: 91111.
Lakeside Medical Centre: Kandy. Tel: 3466.
Government Ayurvedic Hospital: Cotta Road, Borella, Colombo 8. Tel: 595855.

Because of the prevailing Buddhism, meals are almost always vegetarian, and rice is the staple. Moslem establishments serve meat curries but are not always easy to locate. Coconut plays a large part in the diet and is mixed with chillis to make a delicious *sambal* or side dish. Most dinners include *mellung,* a dish of shredded boiled greens flavoured with coconut and spices. A full meal with bananas for dessert will cost about Rs25. The local food is even hotter than South Indian food, and Sri Lankans think that a meal without chillis is like a day without sunshine. For breakfast they eat rice cakes with a fiery chilli sauce. Vendors even sprinkle chilli powder on slices of fresh pineapple. The mildest curry is *kiri,* medium is *badun* and the fieriest is *rathu.*

The quality and variety of tropical fruit is excellent. Seafood is not as easily obtainable as the tourist literature indicates: fish curries are often made with tinned rather than fresh fish. A delicious variety of sweets, some of which are versions of coconut fudge, are made for festivals.

The local brew is called toddy, which is made and consumed daily from various kinds of palm tree. Kitul toddy is reputed to be the best. When fresh, it is delicious, tasting a little like dry cider. The only shop authorized to dispense it on the south coast is the toddy shop in the town of Hambantota. Otherwise ask your hotel to arrange with the locals. The spirit is called arrack distilled from coconut sap (not related to the Middle Eastern aniseed-flavoured drink of the same name). It can be bought in a wide range of quality and hence price; an average half bottle costs less than Rs40 from liquor ships. Sri Lankan brewed beer (a pilsener-style lager) is quite passable. There is even a "real ale" outlet called De Silva's near the Victory Hotel in Kandy.

Tea in Sri Lanka, unlike in India, is usually served without milk but with plenty of sugar, and called "plain tea". The best of Sri Lankan tea is exported, and the tea consumed at home is generally weak and not very exciting. It is interesting to have a tour of one of the many tea gardens and factories in the Hill Country. A few offer bungalow accommodation from about Rs100 per night.

lamprais — rice cooked in stock with curry flavourings, then baked in an oven, eaten at festivals

hoppers — spongy pancake with a crisp edge, and served with a fried egg curry and/or sambal

string hoppers — similar to the above but the pancake is replaced by a nest of noodles

jaggery — a sort of treacle fudge, very sweet

thambili — the milk of the young coconut, which is not very full of flavour and very difficult to drink from the shell without dribbling down the chin, but refreshing

COLOMBO

Colombo is a name derived from the Sinhalese word for "Haven from the Sea", which is somewhat more picturesque than its other title, "the Charing Cross of the East". The city covers more than 15 square miles with a population of one and a quarter million. It is neither as chaotic nor as impoverished as many Indian cities, and in many ways the atmosphere is more like that of Athens than of Calcutta. The Fort area has some fine old colonial buildings and contains the G.P.O., railway station, travel agencies and government handicraft shop. It is easily negotiable by foot and also easy to walk inland along Olcott Mawatha past the bus station and explore the Pettah (from a Tamil word meaning "outside the fort") which is the colourful bazaar district.

What to See

Sea Street, Pettah — several Hindu temples which local idlers will show you round (for a consideration). The Pettah is predominantly Tamil, as you will see from the number of signs advertising coach trips to Jaffna.

National Museum — south of Viharamadevi Park in Cinnamon Gardens, the diplomatic quarter. There are some fine early bronzes, masks, ola leaf manuscripts and the crown and throne of the last King of Kandy. Rs20 admission.

Dehiwala Zoo — 15 minute walk from Galle Road. Interesting variety of birds and reptiles as well as mammals. A well-maintained zoo, so heed the sign:

> If you with litter will disgrace
> And spoil the beauty of this place
> May indigestion rack your chest
> And ants invade your pants and vest.

A circus-type dancing elephant performance takes place every day at 5.15 p.m. Zoo admission Rs30.

Accommodation

The suburb of Dehiwala, six miles and a Rs2.5 bus ride south of the Fort, is a pleasant place to stay. Get off the bus when you see the large St. Mary's Church on your left, cross the road and go down one of the lanes leading to the beach. Most of these have houses offering accommodation. Try 34 or 47 Albert Place, 2 or 37 Campbell Place or 9 Second Lane. Don't be put off by the absence of signs.

Adhihetty Family — 26 Muhandiram Lane, Dehiwala. Pleasant family home 3 minutes from beach. Rs35 single. No meals but near Concord Restaurant on Galle Road.

Y.W.C.A. — 393 Union Place (bus 138 from Fort Station). Upmarket and quiet with good food served in a rather gloomy dining room (a relief after a day in the glaring sun). Singles from Rs125 bed and breakfast. Dinner Rs40.

Y.M.C.A. — 39 Bristol Street in central Fort. Usually full because of prime location.

Ex-Servicemen's Institute — next door to the Y.

Youth Hostel — 50 Haig Road, Bambalapitiya.

Haniya Beach Hostel — 28 Charlemont Road (near Savoy Theatre), Wellawatte. Rs25 per bed.

Travel Inn — 61 Alexandra Place in Colombo's posh Cinnamon Gardens. Basic single Rs100, luxury rooms Rs270. Air conditioning available for extra $4.

There are many private homes offering paying guest arrangements starting from about Rs100, but most closer to Rs200. An accommodation guide to the whole country, updated every six months, is available from tourist offices, but doesn't include many budget places.

Useful Addresses

Tourist Information — 41 Glen Aber Place, Colombo 1. Tel: 589585. Also an information counter in the large government building off Lower Chatham Street.

Tourist Police — New Secretariat Building, Fort. Tel: 26941.

British High Commission — 190 Galle Road, Kollupitiya. Tel: 27611.

British Council — 47 Alfred House Gardens, Colombo 3. Tel: 580723.

American Express — MacKinnons Building (corner of York Street and Leydian Bastian Road). Tel: 22641.

Thomas Cook — Lloyds Building, 15 Sir Baron Jayatilake Mawatha. Tel: 22511.

U.S. Embassy — 44 Galle Road. Tel: 21271.

NEGOMBO

Negombo is a pleasant beach resort north of Colombo Airport, full of Catholic churches and tourist hotels and shops. The local fishermen still use their traditional canoes and sell their catch on the beach and in the market. It is easy to hire a bicycle to explore the town itself, the long beach road called Lewis Place and villages beyond. If you're using Negombo as a jumping-off place for the airport, make sure you don't miss the last airport-bound bus (around 21.00).

Accommodation

Rodrigo Family — 8 Ramlyn Mawatha, opposite the Sun Flower Beach Hotel (bus 905 from Negombo bus station or a half hour's walk). Lovely clean rooms, friendly family, excellent food. Singles Rs40-Rs50.

HIKKADUWA

In addition to being an ultra-developed tourist resort, Hikkaduwa has a sort of exiled Australians' surfing camp located in the south of the town. The bathing and snorkelling are very good. Snorkels and flippers, surfboards and windsurfers can be hired from the local shops. Serious surfers might prefer the more remote Arugam Bay on the east coast. Serious travellers may wish to seek out beaches not quite so thronged with foreigners.

Accommodation

There is plenty of accommodation ranging from Rs15, and also several places for camping.

The Coral Front Inn — 279 Main Road. Tel: (09) 3304. Member of Youth Hostels. Economy singles from Rs15 and doubles Rs20; luxury rooms from Rs35. Bicycles for hire.

Sam's Surfers Rest Guest House — all facilities including late night restaurant. Rs60 double, Rs75 with breakfast.

Prince Monty — Brother's Spot, Narigama.

Hotel Francis — 389 Galle Road. Tel: (09) 2019. Bed and breakfast Rs125 double, Rs100 single.

Pink House — Rs100 double bed and breakfast, Rs75 single.

Poseidon Diving Station — Galle Road. Tel: (09) 3294. Expensive rooms. Also run diving courses including loan of equipment.

Dreem Village — Dodanduwa (2 miles south of Hikkaduwa).

GALLE

The picturesque Fort area of Galle, situated on a peninsula of land, contains some perfectly preserved eighteenth century Dutch buildings, including churches, traders' houses, towers and gates. It is pleasant to walk around the grass-covered ramparts. The Fort is remarkably peaceful, and if you stay for more than a day or two, the local gem and lace hawkers will give up pestering you. If you are interested in purchasing local handicrafts, visit the government-run handicraft workshop and store (73A Kandewatte Road) which is outside the Fort, about a 15 minute walk from the station along a Dutch-built canal.

Unfortunately the splendid beach of Unawatuna just a few miles along the coast, has developed a "scene". In addition to glamorous European sun-worshippers, transparent insects which behave like Mexican jumping beans also infest Unawatuna beach in some seasons.

Accommodation

There are plenty of guest houses in the Fort. Try along Lighthouse Street, which bisects the peninsula and (predictably) leads to the lighthouse, for instance numbers 61, 65, 71 or 79. Just east of the lighthouse is a gracious old Dutch building now appropriately named the Sea View Hotel, with spacious verandahs. When tourism is at a low ebb, you can bargain and get a room for Rs40. If you are looking for a room outside the Fort, try Lucky Cottage, 86 S. H. Dahanayake Mawatha, three streets west of the station.

There is a youth hostel at Ahangama about 10 miles further along the coast, a Y.W.C.A. on Church Street and a Y.M.C.A. on Pedlar Street which has accommodation only for longer term residents.

MATARA

Matara is the railway terminus of the coastal line 100 miles south of Colombo. There is a Buddhist hermitage called Chula Lanka situated on an islet which is connected to the mainland by a causeway. A short excursion from Matara takes you to the Weherehena Temple which looks like a multi-storey car park and boasts one of the largest Buddhas in Asia. Off the track leading to Weherehena is a dagoba abandoned to the jungle. Locals will offer to guide you.

Accommodation

Government Rest House — splendidly situated near the beach. Rs100 singles, Rs150 doubles. Tel: (041) 2299.
Jez-Look Batiks — 12 Yehiya Mawatha.

TANGALLA

This fishing town, 30 miles west of Matara, has empty beaches and relatively few tourists. Turtles come onto the beaches in early summer to lay their eggs.

Accommodation

The Magic Circle — Matara Road, 1½ miles from the centre of town. Modest facilities but proprietor, Titus the Magician, is a fascinating character. He will entertain you with his reminiscences, if not with his magic tricks, which include "Beheading Human Beings" and "Mid-air Sleeping". Rs30 double; Rs10 dorm bed. If coming by road from Matara, ask to be dropped as soon as you see the sign on your left (which also has the advantage of bypassing any touts in the bus station).
Peace Haven Beach Hotel — ancestral home in coconut plantation with individual cabins close to the beach. Popular among Sri Lankan families on holiday. Quite expensive.
Beach Inn — Beach Road, run by Mrs. Gothami Fernando.

ADAM'S PEAK

Although at 7,300 ft, not the highest mountain in Sri Lanka, Adam's Peak is the most famous. Thousands of pilgrims, most of them Buddhists, congregate in the village of Dalhousie where the ascent to see Buddha's footprint at the summit begins. Travellers are welcome to join the throng. Most pilgrims set off at 02.00 to avoid the daytime heat and to enjoy the surpassing beauty of the sunrise, together with the otherworldly shadow which the peak casts on the cloud to the west a few minutes after sunrise. The tiring climb takes about three hours, though there are plenty of opportunities for refreshments and rests en route.

Vehicles bound for Adam's Peak are usually adorned with a sheaf of grain. You can easily get to Dalhousie from Colombo via Hatton and Maskeliye (for about Rs32) and from Nuwara Eliya (for Rs17). There are direct buses during the season which lasts approximately from December to May (the view is obscured during the monsoon). There is not much choice of cheap accommodation in Dalhousie, but you may think it is worth having spent Rs35 for a cell in the Wijitha Hotel when you return exhausted about 08.00.

NUWARA ELIYA

The hill country of Sri Lanka is sometimes known as "Little England" because of its lush and neatly manicured landscape. The area is cool and forested with tea plantations. Like the hill stations of India, Nuwara Eliya is full of visitors escaping from the hot humid lowlands, especially around the Sinhalese New

Year (mid-April). It used to be the summer retreat of the British planters, with a golf course and racetrack which are both still functioning. Some have compared the town to Tunbridge Wells or Reigate. In winter it is cool enough at nights to have a frost, so warm clothes will be needed.

There are pleasant municipal gardens called Victoria Park (entrance Rs5), but the real highlight is the Hakgala Botanical Garden (entrance Rs15), 6 miles from town (Rs3 bus ride). The gardens are stunningly situated in the lee of Hakgala rock (meaning jaw rock). This is a good opportunity to identify common tropical plants such as blue jacaranda, hibiscus, frangipani, jasmine, pepper trees, etc. Don't bother with the "Scented Garden" which has not much more than a straggling mint plant. The gardeners may offer to show you around, which is very worthwhile.

The other attraction of Nuwara Eliya is the Hill Club (located beyond the golf course) which is highly evocative of the colonial era. If you decide to splash out and eat a formal meal (from Rs130), you will have to dress up; men can hire a tie.

Accommodation

Molesworth Youth Hostel — Glenfall Road (near the Grand Hotel). Tel: 581. Dorm beds from Rs20. Ask about bicycle hire.

Service Centre — small youth hostel.

Hemamala Guest House — Old Bazaar Street behind the main street. A little gloomy. Singles from Rs60.

Touts are a problem at the bus station, so dismiss unwelcome attendants if possible.

KANDY

Although only 1,600 feet above sea level, Kandy's climate is much preferable to Colombo's. It is built on the banks of a picturesque lake which itself was constructed by the last Kandyan King in the early nineteenth century. There are many beautiful temples in the vicinity of Kandy.

What to See

The Dalada Maligawa or Temple of the Tooth — located near Kandy Lake. The Buddha's tooth is reputed to have been smuggled into Ceylon in the 4th century A.D. in the hair of a princess. Annually in July/August, a 10 day festival called Esala Perahera takes place, culminating in a huge and colourful perahera (parade) which features 60 ornamented elephants. There are two ceremonies daily (09.30 and 18.30) when the temple drummers drum and good Buddhists queue up to file past the casket containing the sacred tooth. Try to prevent a guide from tagging along with you; elderly monks (most of whom are, ironically, toothless) will happily show you around in exchange for a small donation to the temple. Rs6 admission.

Museum — beyond the temple. Interesting collection of Sinhalese kitchen utensils, miniature medical books written on ola (palm) leaves, weapons, furniture, etc. Rs25 admission.

Peradeniya Botanical Gardens — many buses (Rs2) to what were formerly royal gardens 4 miles from town. Highlights include an orchid house, a collection of spice trees, splendid palm-lined avenues and nesting flying foxes. Entrance Rs15.

Kandyan Dancing — performances held each night at 19.30 at Keppettipola Hall. As with Balinese dance shows in Ubud, Bali, these are solely for tourists, but interesting nevertheless. Rs100 admission.

Uduwattekelle Bird Sanctuary — up the hill behind the museum. Apparently during the shooting here of a Steven Spielberg movie, the staged explosions destroyed the radar of the large local bat population which could be seen circling aimlessly for months afterwards.

Accommodation

"Lucktissme" — 125 Pitakanda Road, Mahayaya. Tel: (08) 22725. Delightful guest house 1½ miles from town near Katugastota elephant baths. If you phone from the station or post office, someone will collect you. Rs75 single, Rs150 double. Good meals, very helpful proprietress and staff and pleasant "crispy modern bedrooms" (sic).

Woodstock — 7/5 Anagarika Dharmapala Mawatha (first left after museum). Good views of lake and surrounding hills. Doubles Rs50-Rs150, single Rs35 and dorm beds Rs20.

Burmese Guest House — D.S. Senanayake Vidiya (past Trinity School). Run by gentle Burmese monks. Residents' kitchen freely available. Very inexpensive.

Olde Empire — centrally located. Large verandahs, faded splendour. From Rs100.

Shanti Youth Hostel — 36 Sangamitta Mawatha.

Y.W.C.A. — Piachaud Gardens.

Y.M.C.A. — 88A Kotugodella Vidiya. Reasonable rates. Men only.

Useful Addresses

Tourist Information — Kandyan Arts Association, Building 72, Sangarana Mawatha (lakeside road).

British Council — 170 Senanayake Vidiya.

Cindy's Bookshop — Torrington Lane near bus station. Decent choice of English books and also post cards.

Thomas Cook — Maurice Travels, 331 Perideniya Road. Tel: (08) 4120.

SIGIRIYA

After killing his father in 500 A.D., King Kasyapa built his palace on top of a striking, flat-topped rock overlooking the flat central forest. From his throne (which can still be seen) he kept watch for his avenging half-brother. Although little of the palace remains; the ruins are impressive, and the view of the plains amazing. Steps have been carved into the rock, and pass by the famous frescoes of the king's courtesans. The entrance fee is Rs75.

Accommodation

Since the Sigiriya Rest House is expensive and the archaeological bungalow difficult to reserve, you might prefer to stay in nearby Dambulla (13 miles) where there is not only a wealth of cheap accommodation stretched along the main Kandy Road (ask to be put down before you go to the town centre), but some interesting cave temples as well (admission Rs50).

Oasis Welfare Centre — traditional Sinhalese house run by an interesting and helpful Sinhalese character known as Sikura. He may share a bottle of

arrack with you, and tell you local tales of elephant encounters and ayurvedic (herbal) medicine. Rs15 single. Excellent dinners for Rs25.
The Cottage — near the Rest House. Pleasant rooms for Rs30 single.
Traveller's Inn — directly across from cave temples.

ANURADHAPURA

Anuradhapura is a huge ruined city, founded in 377 B.C., which reached the height of its importance at the beginning of the Christian era. The city was ruled by a succession of kings, but was finally deserted in the 9th century due to Tamil invasions. There is much to see, such as the oldest dagoba in the country (dagobas are bell-shaped constructions built over Buddhist relics) and the 2,000 year old Bo-Tree, sacred to Buddhists, which was fortunately not harmed by the Tamil attack near it in May 1985. There are many other ruins and dagobas, the largest of which is allegedly made from enough bricks to build a 10-foot wall from London to Edinburgh.

Accommodation

King's Dale — Mihintale Road, about 1½ miles from station. Clean and pleasant rooms from Rs25 single. Interesting food including Sri Lankan breakfast of rice cakes and chilli sambal if desired. Bicycle hire for Rs15.
Traveller's Halt — 15 Jaffna Junction. Dormitory and singles from Rs25. Left luggage facilities, laundry, cycle hire, restaurant.
Sarvodaya District Centre Youth Hostel — New Town. Tel: (025) 2738.

POLONNARUWA

This replaced Anuradhapura as the capital in the eighth century A.D. though the extensive ruins date mostly from the twelfth century. There is a magnificent palace, audience hall, elephant pavilion and a number of tanks, dagobas and statues of Buddha. The ruins cover a large area, and like Anuradhapura, can best be explored by bicycle.

THE EAST COAST

At the time of writing Trincomalee was the only east coast town accessible to travellers. Because of its fine harbour, it is a major centre for fishing, and the catch is trucked daily to Colombo and elsewhere. Since the local fishermen are predominantly Tamil, "Trinco" may also become out-of-bound. Good beaches stretch to the north.

The town of Batticaloa is situated on an island in the middle of a salt water lake, separated from the sea by a sandy belt planted with coconut groves. "Batti" is famous for its singing fish, which make a high-pitched hum similar to a person rubbing a glass. There is also a Dutch fort in good condition.

If you are able to get to Passekudah, Kalkudah, Nilaveli or any of the beach towns, you will probably find hotel owners very grateful for your custom and willing to negotiate good prices.

WILDLIFE PARKS

Along with the exotic flora which can be enjoyed at the botanical gardens, Sri Lanka's fauna is worth pursuing. You may already have encountered scorpions in your hotel room or ravenous monkeys who loiter around peanut salesmen, but you will probably have to go to a wildlife park to see crocodiles, elephants or the elusive leopard. Dawn and dusk are the most rewarding times to spot wildlife. Unfortunately Sri Lanka doesn't seem to offer accommodation in observation towers as at Chitwan in Nepal or Periyar in South India. You can hire a jungle bungalow through the Department of Wildlife Conservation whose offices are in the Dehiwala Zoo in Colombo.

Yala in the southeast corner of the country is best known for its colony of elephants. The favourite access point is Tissamaharama, where there are many guides and jeep drivers competing for business. You may go in on a safari bus, which is cheaper though not as versatile as a jeep. Although it is officially forbidden, you may be able to persuade a guide to take you in on foot (for, say, Rs200) which is the best way to see the game. But the guides are understandably reluctant in view of the number of people killed by charging elephants every year.

A few miles past Hambantota, there is a bird sanctuary called Udamalala, consisting of flat shimmering parkland and sand dunes by the sea, where great flocks of parrots, pelicans and flamingos can be seen. The land is intersected by streams which are infested with crocodiles. If you want to be accompanied by a sharp-eyed guide, ask for Mohammad Razik at the Sunshine Guest House behind the Hambantota bus station (also a pleasant place to stay).

Wilpattu National Park is another sanctuary, famous for its leopards. Again you must enter either by jeep or minibus. There is a charge of at least Rs500 for jeep rental in addition to the Rs50 park entrance fee. This can be arranged in Anuradhapura, 22 miles away.

South East Asia

DJANGGER, NORTH SUMATRA

While you are travelling in India or Nepal etc., you are bound to meet Australians, Germans and Brits raving about Bali and Thailand. If you happen to be en route to Australia or New Zealand you will certainly be tempted by the idea of a stop-over in Bangkok or Singapore. Enquire among travel agents in Calcutta or Colombo for cheap flights to South-East Asia. (Unfortunately you cannot go by land transport since the borders of Burma are closed). Once you get past Burma, it is easy to travel around the Malay Peninsula (Thailand, Malaysia, Singapore) by bus or train. Further east, Indonesia comprising 13,000 islands presents its own problems of getting around. For a more detailed guide to these countries see *South-East Asia on a Shoestring* published in 1985 by Tony Wheeler and distributed in Britain by Roger Lascelles.

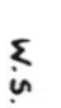
W.S.

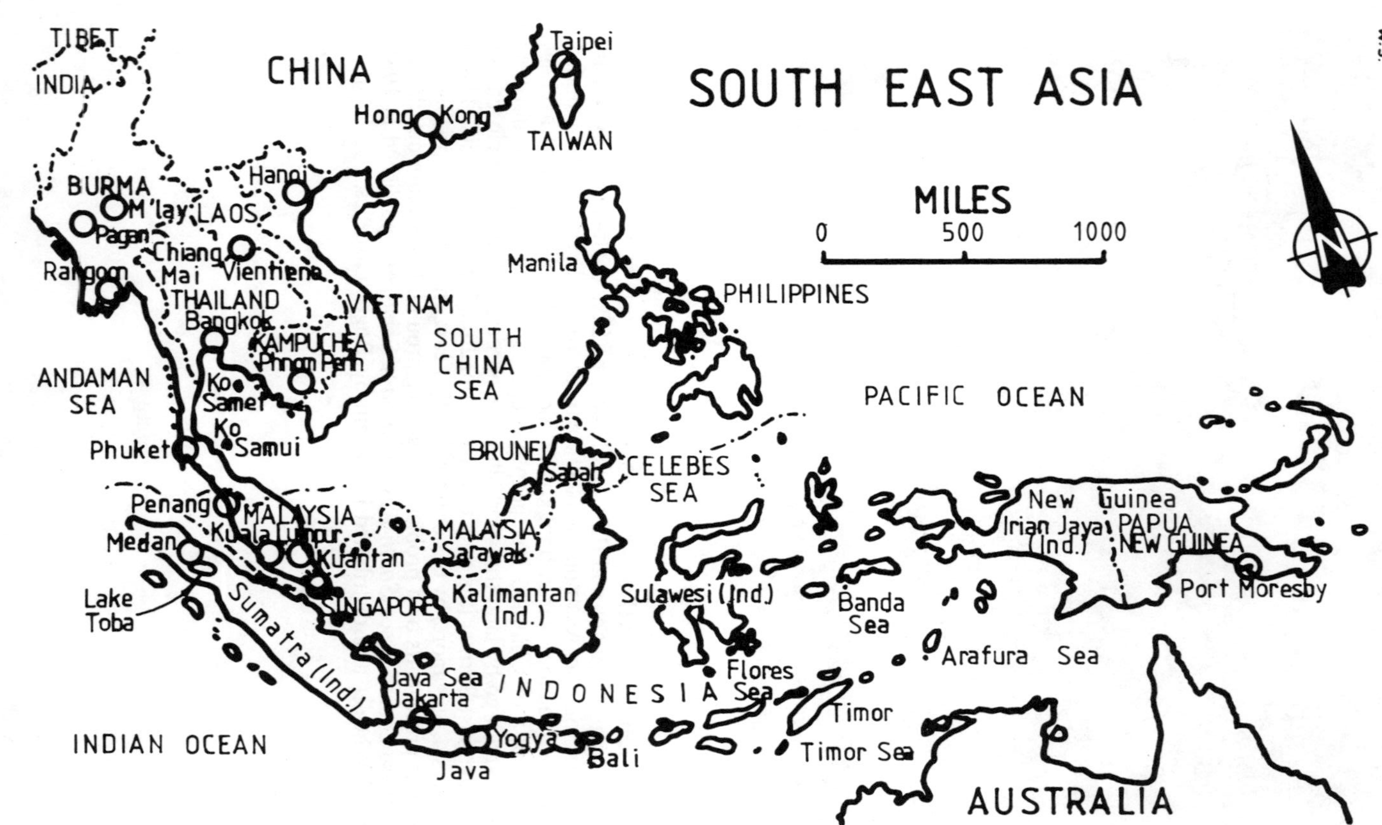
SOUTH EAST ASIA
MILES
0
500
1000
TIBET
INDIA
CHINA
Hong Kong
Taipei
TAIWAN
BURMA
M'lay
LAOS
Hanoi
Pagan
Chiang Mai
Vientiane
Rangoon
THAILAND
VIETNAM
Bangkok
KAMPUCHEA
Phnom Penh
SOUTH CHINA SEA
Manila
PHILIPPINES
ANDAMAN SEA
Ko Samet
Ko Samui
Phuket
BRUNEI
Sabah
CELEBES SEA
PACIFIC OCEAN
Penang
MALAYSIA
Kuala Lumpur
Kuantan
MALAYSIA
Sarawak
Medan
Lake Toba
SINGAPORE
Kalimantan (Ind.)
Sulawesi (Ind.)
New Guinea
Irian Jaya (Ind.)
PAPUA NEW GUINEA
Port Moresby
Banda Sea
Arafura Sea
Sumatra (Ind.)
Java Sea
Jakarta
INDONESIA
Flores Sea
Timor
Timor Sea
INDIAN OCEAN
Yogya
Bali
Java
AUSTRALIA

Burma

Capital: Rangoon **Government:** Socialist Republic

The cities of Burma retain a large measure of British colonial architecture and atmosphere. However much of the countryside is populated with rebellious tribes similar to those who inhabit the Chittagong Hill Tracts of Bangladesh. The combination of familiar English scenes and jungle tribes is interesting.

The economy is very backward partly because of the nationalization of all industry in 1962. Although the socialist government attempts to curb the wanderings of visitors, it does so fairly leniently. You are supposed to pay for train tickets, hotels and other tourist expenses at Tourist Burma offices, partly so that they can keep an eye on your itinerary and partly to make sure you convert your hard currency at the official exchange rate. But despite these sometimes irksome restrictions, the remarkable friendliness of the people leaves the more lasting impression. Because of the isolation of their country, they are always eager to hear reports of the "outside world".

Climate

Even in winter the temperature is seldom less than sweltering: the average January high in Rangoon is 89°F, though evenings bring a 20° drop. In summer there is less respite, though the monsoon rains which fall from May to October do moderate the temperatures slightly.

The humidity and rainfall are worse in Rangoon than in Mandalay. The hottest month in both Rangoon and Mandalay is April, when the temperatures regularly soar over 100°F. Since you have only seven days to see the country, you may find that you resent having to spend the mid-day hours under your hotel fan. November to February is the favoured season, which means that there is a higher concentration of travellers competing for space in hotels, airplanes and trains.

Language

Burmese is the national language along with some of the dominant tribal languages such as Chin, Shan and Karen. Because Burma was so heavily anglicized after 1885 when it was annexed to the British Empire, many people know some English. Relatively few signs are shown in English and you will have great difficulty making any sense of the Burmese alphabet.

Useful Burmese Words

hello	— hey	yes	— hoke ket
good morning	— min ga la baa	no	— mah hoke boo
good-bye	— pyan dor mai	festival	— pwe
please	— chay-zu pyu pah	Mr.	— U (pronounced "oo")
thank you	— chay-zu tin baa dai	Mrs/Miss	— Dah
how much?	— bah loud chat the le?	market	— zay

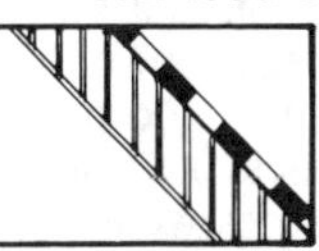

Visas

Visas are granted quite readily but they are strictly limited to 7 days. If you overstay your visa by even a day there are stiff penalties. Visas are available from the Embassy in London (19A Charles Street,

W.1.; tel: 01-499 8841) after submitting 2 forms, 3 photos, a flight ticket in and out of Rangoon or a letter from a travel agent giving flight details and the fee of £3. The procedure may not be so complicated if you apply for a visa in Bangkok, Calcutta or Kathmandu. In the latter place you can get one in less than half an hour even if you haven't yet purchased your air ticket.

Rangoon is also a good place to collect other visas such as Thai, Indian and Nepalese, since these embassies realize that in Burma haste is essential.

Customs
You may take in duty-free 1 quart of alcohol and 200 cigarettes. You should carry in your full quota even if you're a non-smoking teetotaller since you can sell them at great profit. All jewellery (even wedding rings) should be declared on arrival if worth over £25.

Currency Regulations
You may take in as much foreign currency as you like, but must declare it upon arrival. This is no mere formality since you will have to show the exchange document again when you leave and bank transactions should account for the difference between the total brought in and the total taken out. It is of course impossible for the authorities to verify the accuracy of your original declaration. See section below on changing money for the relevance of this. It is illegal to carry Burmese kyats over the border, though people do buy them on the black market in Northern Thailand.

£1 = K11 K10 = £0.90
$1 = K8 K10 = $1.25

Currency: 100 pyas=1 kyat (K) pronounced "chat"

Changing Money
The Burmese government fixes the kyat at an artificially high rate against the dollar, so there is a thriving black market offering about twice as much as the banks. Unfortunately any major expenditures such as flights or hotels should be registered on your currency exchange document. You will soon learn from fellow travellers which hotels are willing to risk accepting unofficially exchanged kyats. Some travellers get away without a single official transaction. Changing money with taxi drivers and hotel staff is very common and stories of rip-offs are surprisingly rare. There are, however, stories in circulation of counterfeit dollars being palmed off on tourists.

Emergency Cash
There is a big demand for cigarettes and whisky (especially 555 and Johnny Walker Red Label). Unlike exchanging money on the black market, selling these items is legal. You can make between 2 and 3 times what you paid in a duty-free shop. Don't necessarily accept the first offer; this is a seller's market. You can also make a profit by selling cigarettes purchased in one of the 3 "Diplomatic Shops" in Rangoon, which are open only to tourists and privileged Burmese.

Other goods, such as Western clothing, cosmetics, pens, etc., can be sold or bartered for local handicrafts. Since all the industries were nationalized and a policy of strict economic isolationism was introduced, very few western gadgets are available except if tourists and sailors bring them in.

Opening Hours
The working week consists of Monday to Friday. Banks are open 10.00-14.30. Government offices keep longer hours: 09.30-16.30.

Public Holidays

4th January	Independence Day
12th February	Union Day
2nd March	Peasants' Day
27th March	Resistance Day
1st April	Bank Holiday
13th-15th April	Burmese New Year (called Thingyan)
1st May	May Day
19th July	Martyrs' Day
1st October	Bank Holiday
25th December	Christmas

Because 85% of the population is Buddhist, the full moon days are also celebrated (see chapter on Sri Lanka).

Arrival and Departure
The airlines which fly into Rangoon's Mingaladon Airport are:

Thai International	— daily from Bangkok
Bangladesh Biman	— weekly between Bangkok and Dhaka/Calcutta
Burma Airways Corporation	— daily from Bangkok, twice weekly from Singapore, thrice weekly from Kathmandu and Calcutta
Royal Nepal Airlines	— weekly from Kathmandu

If for some reason one of the weekly or twice-weekly flights out of Rangoon is cancelled, you may be allowed to extend your visa. There is a departure tax at the airport of K15.

The airport is 13 miles from the city centre and is predictably full of clamouring taxi drivers who charge K35-K40 for the trip into Rangoon. It is a 2-mile walk to the main road from which you can catch a cheap bus into town. The Burma Airways Corporation provides a bus from the Strand Hotel and other pick-up points to the airport but not vice versa. The cost is K5.

Flights
With such limited time, flying is an attractive option. Tourist Burma operates several chartered flights just for foreign tourists between Rangoon, Pagan and Mandalay. Unfortunately they charge more for these than the regular BAC flights, which can be booked through the airline offices. The single fare Rangoon-Pagan is a very modest K120 and Mandalay-Heho (about half an hour) costs K45. Unfortunately package tourists take up many of the seats, so you should try to book up as soon as you arrive. It is not advisable to buy internal flights from a travel agent outside Burma since BAC have been known not to honour these.

Motoring
You can hire a private car with driver from the main hotels in Rangoon (e.g.

the Strand and the Inya Lake) for a minimum of K150. More common is for a group of people (up to 8) to hire a jeep or converted pick-up truck which allows great flexibility, since you don't have to arrange much through Tourist Burma (including getting official receipts for your currency conversion). The rumour is that the price which jeep-drivers are charging must cover the unofficial fees paid to the police en route. The price of jeep hire starts at about US$200 including petrol for 6 days. There can be delays due to petrol rationing (2 gallons per vehicle per day). A good place to find drivers is the YMCA cafeteria in Rangoon. Before committing yourself to this, it is wise to spend some time with your prospective guide/driver. Many know English well and will be able to answer your questions about the country, but others are reckless drivers and uninformative guides.

Bus

Burmese buses are supplemented by converted Japanese trucks left over from the war. Although prices are low, the slowness of progress is a distinct disadvantage. For example the daily trip Mandalay to Pagan takes 10 hours to cover 125 miles and costs K16.50. The advantage is that tickets and routes are not as thoroughly under the watchful eye of Tourist Burma as on trains and airplanes. Whereas you are usually forced to buy your rail tickets at the tourist office, this is not necessarily the case with bus tickets. Some travellers think they are being clever when they ask a local to buy a ticket for them to an unapproved destination, but this can get the Burmese person in serious legal difficulties.

You may want to take the tourist minibus from difficult-to-reach Pagan to the train station at Thazi, since public transport is difficult on this route with several awkward connections.

Train

The tricky part about travelling up-country is that you have to be back in Rangoon in time for your flight and before your 7-day visa expires. This involves careful planning and much discussion with the tourist officers and locals. You must book all rail journeys through Tourist Burma who are very helpful when you want to travel along the standard routes but who may cause problems if you want to book shorter legs or to more out-of-the-way places. If the tourist office won't cooperate or claims that all the seats are gone, it can be worth asking the station-master for one of their VIP tickets.

As with flights, Tourist Burma operate several express trains Rangoon to Mandalay specifically for tourists. The four daily services range in duration from 14 to 17 hours: the two fastest are the overnight departure at 18.15 and the all day trip which departs at 06.00. There are first and second class (called upper and lower) on most trains and upper class berths on the tourist expresses. The cost of an upper class ticket is about K100, only K35 less than the flight. It is wise to carry your own water and food on long trips.

Boat

It is possible to take a boat from Mandalay to Pagan. There are daily early morning departures which arrive at Nyaungu near Pagan nearly 24 hours later. You should board the boat the previous afternoon to be sure of a place on the deck. The trip costs about K30.

It is also possible to take the riverboat up the Irrawaddy River from Rangoon to Mandalay, à la Rudyard Kipling. However the trip can take as long as 10 days and the brevity of your visa makes this impossible. For a very short but enjoyable boat ride go to the ferry port opposite the Strand Hotel in Rangoon, and go for a tour of the Rangoon waterfront for about 5 pence.

City Transport
The taxis of Rangoon are remarkable for their advanced age and hence unreliability; the charge is K25/K30 per hour. The 3-wheeled vehicles, which are seldom metered, are much cheaper, about 75 pyas per mile. Buses run within cities and are very cheap. However you will have to push and shove to get on.

The risk of malaria exists throughout the country except in the urban areas of Rangoon, Mandalay/Sagaing, Magwe and Pegu. Although January to March is a lower risk period it is advisable even then to take both chloroquine and Paludrine. Mosquitoes abound, and are a particular nuisance on river journeys.

If you become ill, go to the Ideal Nursing Home in Rangoon (tel: 11200). If you are so ill that you cannot travel before your visa expires, get a government doctor to certify this in writing.

Curries are the most popular dish, often served with soup. Indian and Chinese food is more readily available in restaurants than Burmese food. For good Burmese food try the Burma Kitchen at 141 Shwegondaing Road or the more downmarket Narawath Restaurant at 84 30th Street, both in Rangoon.

Beer is brewed in Mandalay and is quite reasonable. They also make rum in Mandalay which is cheap and good.

RANGOON
The capital of the country is a delightful, decaying Victorian city. About 2 miles from the city centre there is a large Buddhist temple called the Schwee Dagon Pagoda, lavishly embellished with gold and precious jewels. There are many other temples strewn around the city.

Women might like to stay at the Y.W.C.A. at 119 Bogalay Zay Street (tel: 72108). The cost of a single room with bath is K25. The Y.M.C.A. accepts women as well as men and is located at 263 Maha Bandoola Street (tel: 72110), where the cost is about the same. This is a good place to collect information for your travels up-country. One main advantage of the Y is that it is one of the few places where you can pay on the spot without having to pre-pay at Tourist Burma (next to the Sule Pagoda in the heart of Rangoon). Officially all lodgings must be paid for in advance, though not all hotels bother about this.

PAGAN

This was an important centre of Buddhism from 1050 to 1300 A.D. when the 5,000 temples were built. Of course many of them are very ruined but there is the same feeling of lost grandeur as there is at Fatehpur Sikri near Agra. The best way to visit the temples is by horse-cart which costs about K16 per hour or by bicycle which costs the same for a complete day.

MANDALAY

Mandalay was once the royal seat of Burma, and the watch-tower and moat of the old palace remain. There is a monastery nearby (called Shwe Nandaw) which has delicately carved walls.

If the heat becomes unbearable you can visit the former colonial hill station of Maymyo which is over 3,000 feet higher than Mandalay. There is a Y.M.C.A. hostel which accepts both men and women.

Thailand

Capital: Bangkok **Government:** Constitutional Monarchy

This country, formerly called Siam, prides itself on being the only Asian nation to have resisted European colonization. In the entire history of the Thai people they have never been under foreign domination. This fact has not prevented a huge influx of American and Japanese money, consumer durables and commercial development, though Bangkok has not been rebuilt to the extent that Singapore has. Under the aegis of the much revered Royal Family, there is an active conservation movement to preserve old buildings and neighbourhoods.

Of the 50 million inhabitants, over a tenth live in and around Bangkok, which rivals other Asian cities for having the worst traffic problems. Outside Bangkok, the distances to be covered to see the interesting places in the south and north are great; the area of the country is the same as France's.

The two mainstays of Thai culture are the Monarchy and Buddhism, and one should show respect to both at all times. In addition to their smiling friendliness, one of the distinguishing characteristics of Thai people is their politeness. Their greeting is not a handshake but a *wai,* the gesture of placing your hands together as if for the Indian "Namaste". Avoid touching anyone's head and do not point your foot at anyone. On the other hand Thais are also extremely tolerant and are unlikely to take offence when none is intended.

Climate

The temperatures throughout Thailand are uniformly tropical, almost always over 30°C (86°F) during the day and usually very humid. There is very little seasonal difference. Seasons are distinguished not by whether they are cold or hot, but by whether they are rainy or dry. The rainy season lasts from the end of May till mid-November and is more extreme in the south. Flooding in Bangkok is commonplace.

Language

Thai is spoken in most places. English is taught in the schools, and is often spoken in the main centres, especially in government and commercial circles. However, in rural areas, you can travel for days without meeting any English speakers. It is more important to learn a few words of Thai than of Hindi, Sinhalese or Urdu when travelling in India, Sri Lanka and Pakistan, for example.

Useful Thai Words

hello/good-bye	— sawadee	1 — neung
please	— dai proad	2 — sorng
thank you	— khapkoon	3 — sahm
yes	— chai (or kha-khrap)	4 — see
no	— mai (or plow)	5 — ha
excuse me	— kaw thot	6 — hok
how much?	— raka tao-rai?	7 — chet
yesterday	— meu-a wan nee	8 — pat
today	— wan nee	9 — kow
tomorrow	— proong nee	10 — sip
very good	— dee maak	20 — yee-sip
no good	— mai dee	100 — neung-roi

The words *Krab* and *Ka* are polite expressions for "Sir" and "Madam", or the all-purpose *Khun* can be used for anyone.

Red Tape

Visas
Visas are not necessary if you are staying less than 15 days and have a confirmed onward air ticket. If there is even a faint chance you will want to stay longer than 15 days, you should apply for a tourist visa (validity 60 days) before you get to the border since it is impossible to extend the 15-day limit. If you enter by land and don't have an air ticket out of Thailand, you should have a visa. The cost from the Royal Thai Embassy in London is £5 (30 Queen's Gate, S.W.7; tel: 01-589 0173).

Customs
The duty-free limit is 200 cigarettes or 250 grams of tobacco and 1 litre of wine or 1 litre of spirits. Pornographic magazines are prohibited.

Currency Regulations
Visitors are not allowed to import more than 2000 Baht or export more than 500 Baht. There is no limit to the amount of foreign currency which can be brought into the country, though you are supposed to declare it if over $2000.

Health Certificates
No vaccinations are required unless you are coming from yellow fever or epidemic-affected areas; however cholera and typhoid shots are highly recommended.

£1 = 37 Baht — 10 Baht = £0.27
$1 = 27 Baht — 10 Baht = $0.37

Currency: 100 satang = 1 Baht (฿)

Opening Hours
Banks are open Monday to Friday 08.30-15.30. Offices stay open until 16.30 but close for an hour at lunch. Shops open at varying hours; but some stay open until 21.00.

Public Holidays

31st December/1st January	New Year's
6th April	Chakri Day (honouring King Rama 1, founder of the present dynasty)
13th April	Songkran (traditional Thai New Year)
5th May	Coronation Day
12th August	Queen Sirikit's Birthday
23rd October	Chulalongkorn Day (commemorates death of present king's grandfather)
5th December	King Bhumibol's Birthday
10th December	Constitution Day

About 95% of the population is Buddhist, so there are many Buddhist holidays and festivals throughout the year. Many of these are tied to full moon days.

early March	Makha Bucha (first preaching of Buddha)
early June	Visakha Bucha
end of July	Asalaha Bucha
mid-August	Khao Phansa (Buddhist Lent)

Getting Around

Arrival and Departure

With the Thai-Burmese border closed, most people arrive at Don Muang International Airport, 15 miles north of Bangkok. Entry procedures are usually painless, and there is a hotel booking desk inside the airport. There is an 80 Baht air-conditioned bus service to downtown operated by Thai Airways International. There are also public buses which travel along the road outside the airport gate which cost 15 Baht in air-conditioned and 3 Baht in ordinary. It's only about a 10-minute walk to the surburban station of Don Muang on the direct train line to Hualamphong Station in the city centre.

There are also direct rail and bus services from Bangkok to Butterworth, Kuala Lumpur and Singapore. Be prepared for long delays for customs and immigration at the border.

Motoring

Most roads are now surfaced. Traffic circulates on the left. International Driving Permits are required. The Royal Automobile Association of Thailand has offices on 151 Ratchadaphisaek Road, Bangkaen, Bangkok 10900; tel: 511-2230.

Car Hire

Avis hires cars from its offices at 981 Silom Road, Bangkok, for 650 Baht per day plus a kilometre charge of 2.5 Baht. Unusually Hertz's smallest car is available for slightly less than this.

Bus

There are three bus terminals in Bangkok: Northern, Eastern and Southern. Your destination determines the terminal you will use. The Northern terminal is located on the airport road (Paholyothin Road), tel: 279-6221. The Eastern station is on the Sukhumvit Road. The Southern one is across the river on Charan Sanit Wong Road, tel: 411-4978/411-0112.

Buses are a good means of transport, often faster than trains and about the same price as third class rail fare (unless air-conditioned). For example buses leave the Southern Bus Terminal for Phuket at least eight times a day. The journey takes 18 hours and the fare is 165 Baht. Buses leave from the northern terminal for Chiang Mai eight times a day. This trip takes 8 hours and costs 160 Baht. The mark-up on air-conditioned buses is substantial: between 100 Baht and 150 Baht.

Train

All trains depart from Hualamphong Station, and most have three classes. All tickets may be booked in advance at the main station in Bangkok between 08.30 and 18.00 or on Saturday and Sunday mornings up to 30 days in advance. First class fares are more than triple third class. There are five trains a day from Bangkok to Chiang Mai. The direct journey takes 12½ hours and the cost is 116 Baht in third class and 243 Baht in second class. Sleepers are available on most long distance trains for a surcharge of about 100 Baht for a lower berth in second class. There are no student discounts. If you are phoning for information, ring 223-7010. The Tourist Office (even in London) distributes useful little timetables.

Hitch-hiking
Hitch-hiking is reported to be good especially with trucks.

City Transport
No taxis use meters and the fare must be agreed before the journey. Journeys in Bangkok are usually around 50 Baht. There is an extensive network of city buses within Bangkok, though the traffic is among the worst in Asia. The cost of a single journey is 2 Baht. There are some air-conditioned buses on the city routes also which are more expensive and less crowded. Other forms of city transport include *tuk-tuks* (like auto-rickshaws but noisier), *samlors* (bicycle rickshaws) and *songthaew,* small pick-ups or mini-buses.

Malaria is a very serious risk throughout the country, but especially in rural, forested and hilly areas. Resistance to chloroquine has been extensively reported, so you should take both chloroquine and paludrine. On the south-eastern border with Kampuchea, the most dangerous strain of malaria (falciparum) may be resistant to both.

There are a number of I.A.M.A.T. recommended hospitals in Thailand, including the Bangkok Adventist Hospital (tel: 281-1422) and the Medi-Clinic, 968 Rama IV Road (tel: 233-2533). There is also the British Hospital near the Post Office on Oriental Avenue.

Water
Although the tapwater in Bangkok is chemically treated, visitors should purify their own water. This is essential in the rest of the country.

Thai food can be hotter than most Westerners can enjoy, though some restaurants *(ran-ahan)* will hold back on the chillis *(prik)* for foreigners. A pleasant way to cool the heat is to drink coconut milk or eat bananas, both more effective than water.

It is possible to find "jungle food" in the more expensive establishments, e.g. fried, spiced python, crocodile or lizard. Street snacks may have similar exotic overtones, though some caution is called for: in late 1985 a Bangkok construction worker died of insecticide poisoning after eating four bags of locusts. Seafood should be cheaper and fresher than it is, considering the nearby sources of fish. There are lots of exotic fruits, such as guavas, durian, noinar (custard apples) and mangoes.

There are three locally produced beers, the strongest of which is Thai Amarit, and the most traditional of which is Singha. The local spirit is Mehkong whisky, potent but palatable when drunk with chilled soda water; a quarter bottle will cost about 26 Baht. Rice wine is called *lao argoon.*

BANGKOK

Bangkok is highly Americanized, with lots of prosperity and pollution. It sprawls over miles and the traffic is appalling. The seedy/glamorous night life found in the Patpong district appeals to some. There are many Buddhist temples and monasteries, some beautiful, some garish, e.g. the Emerald Buddha, the Golden Buddha, the Reclining Buddha, etc. Some charge a slight admission, and a neat appearance is essential. An interesting spectacle takes place between February and April: kite flying and kite fighting at the Royal Ground in front of the Grand Palace.

What to See

Weekend Market — at Chatoochak Park, Paholyothin Road (near the Northern Bus Terminal). Held every Saturday and Sunday. Foods, household goods, souvenirs, cloth and all sorts of plants and flowers, from sophisticated hybrids to deepest jungle plants.

The Grand Palace and Wat Phra Kaeo — the Emerald Buddha is housed here in the private chapel of the King and Queen. The Thai word *wat* means monastery/temple. Open 08.30-12.00 and 13.00-1600 (admission 10 Baht).

Snake Farm — Pasteur Institute on Rama IV Road. Visitors may watch reptiles being fed and having venom extracted. Open daily (admission 10 Baht).

National Museum — houses objects to show the economic, religious and cultural development of the Thai Kingdom. Enquire about lectures in English on Buddhist history and art. Open Tuesday-Thursday 09.00-12.00 and 13.00-16.00 (admission 5 Baht) and Saturday-Sunday (admission free).

Accommodation

VIP Guest House — Khao San Road. Dorm beds 40 Baht, single 60 Baht. There are other reasonable hotels along this road (e.g. the Bonny Guest House, the Tum Guest House, and the New Sri Phranakhon Hotel). This area of Banglamphu (conveniently close to the Museum) is generally good for accommodation.

Swan Hotel — 31 Customs House Lane (beside the New Champagne Room). 240 Baht double. Swimming pool.

Malaysia Hotel — 54 Soi Ngam Duplee. Popular and trendy, with a large notice board for travellers, which isn't as useful as it once was. Dormitory beds available for 100 Baht, but most rooms are air-conditioned and expensive.

Sri Hualamphong Hotel — next to station. Clean rooms for 80 Baht.

Y.W.C.A. — 13 Sathorn Tai Road. Not central.

Y.M.C.A. — 27 Sathorn Tai Road. US$16.

Useful Addresses

Tourism Authority (TAT) — 4 Ratchadamnoen Nok Avenue. Tel: 282-1143.

Tourist Police — same address. Emergency tel: 281-5051/281-0372.

British Embassy — Wireless Road (corner of Ploenchit Road). Tel: 252-7161.

British Council Library — 428 Rama I Road, Siam Square. Tel: 252-6136.

American Embassy — 95 Wireless Road. Tel: 252-5040.

American Express — S.E.A. Tours, Room 414, Siam Center, 965 Rama I Road. Tel: 251-4862.

PHUKET

At one time a Portuguese trading post in the Andaman Sea, this island is now a favourite stop-over with budget travellers. The Sarasin Bridge connects Phuket Island to the mainland, but there are plenty of small islands scattered about, accessible by boat or by swimming. Some of the beaches are lovely and good for snorkelling. Tourist development has concentrated on the coast west of Phuket town (Patong, Karon and Kata). Bungalows may be rented (especially in September/October) for a mere 1500 Baht per month. In any area bearing a heavy burden of tourism, it is wise to guard your belongings with care.

There are other less frequented island resorts off the east coast such as Ko Samui and Ko Samet.

CHIANG MAI

Although fairly touristy, this city in Northern Thailand is interesting for its temples and ruins and because it is a centre for hill tribes. It is possible to arrange short or long treks into this rough but friendly country, though some travellers have begun to complain that the area is over-visited. Many handicrafts are available in Chiang Mai as well as cheap fakes and there is a museum of tribal culture.

For jungle scenery and tribal people, you might prefer to vist Kanchanaburi, due west of Bangkok, where *The Deerhunter* was filmed.

Malaysia

Capital: Kuala Lumpur

Government: Constitutional Monarchy (within the Commonwealth)

The modern state of Malaysia comprises the southern part of the Malay Peninsula between Singapore at the tip and Thailand to the north, plus the two distant provinces of Sabah and Sarawak which occupy the northern third of the island of Borneo. The country gained its independence from Britain in 1957 and dropped the name Malaya, which is still sometimes used by visitors and is resented by natives. Because of its huge rubber and tin exports (over a third of the world's output of both commodities) it has the highest per capita income in South-East Asia after Singapore.

Peninsular Malaysia is the part most often visited by tourists, mostly because the majority fly into Kuala Lumpur (often abbreviated to KL). A mountain range, with peaks of up to 7,000 ft, forms a central spine and provides some hill resorts where you can escape the heat. Vast sections of the country are still covered by tropical forest. Compared to Indonesia and Thailand, Malaysia is a relatively progressive country, which makes travelling around fairly easy.

Climate

There is very little variation in the tropical temperatures throughout the year. Hot and humid days are followed by slightly cooler nights. If you wish to escape the 35°C (95°F) temperatures, go to the central highlands where the nighttime temperature often drops to 10°C (50°F).

The wettest months are between October and February, though in the tropics it rains all through the year. The average annual rainfall is between 100 and 120 inches, more on the coasts than in the interior, and heavier on the east than on the west coast.

Language

Many languages are spoken: Malay (the official language, sometimes called Bahasa Malaysia), Chinese and Tamil are the most important. English is widely spoken.

Some Useful Malay Words

hello — selamat pagi
good-bye — selamat jalan
please — silakan
thank you — terimah kaseh
how much is this? — berapa harga?
yes — ya or ada
no — tidak
good — baik
post office — tampat kirim surat

Visas
Visas are not required by Commonwealth passport holders. Americans need a visa if they intend to stay longer than 3 months. If you wish to stay for a longer period than was originally granted by the immigration officer upon entry, you must apply for an extension at Immigration Headquarters, Bangunan Bukota, Jalan Pantai Bahru, Kuala Lumpur or in any of the 13 state capitals. Just look up *Jabatan Imigeresen* in the telephone directory. As in neighbouring Singapore your way at immigration will be smoothed by a respectable appearance.

Customs
The allowance is 1 litre of wine, spirits or beer and 200 cigarettes or 50 cigars or 225gr tobacco. The authorities are strict about "hippies" and you will be treated better if you look reasonably clean-cut. To illustrate the high moral tone adopted by Malaysian officialdom, all video tapes brought into the country must be submitted to the censor.

Currency Regulations
The are no currency restrictions.

Health Certificates
No certificates are required except yellow fever if relevant. Cholera shots are recommended.

Drugs
The Malaysian government shares Singapore's horror of drugs. A law was passed in the summer of 1985 which made the death penalty compulsory for possessing 15gr or more of heroin or morphine. Many of the loiterers and drivers in Penang's tourist area (Chulia Street) are police informers.

Motoring Documents
A British driving licence will suffice for 3 months from the date of arrival.

£1 = M$3.47 M$1 = £0.29
$1 = M$2.49 M$1 = $0.40

Currency: 100 sen=1 Malaysian Ringgit (RGT) or Malaysian dollar (M$). Both terms are in use, though the dollar sign predominates.

Changing Money
Whereas the exchange counter is open 24 hours a day at Kuala Lumpur's Subang Airport, you may have difficulty at smaller international gateways such as Kota Kinabalu on Sabah. It is wise to bring in some Malaysian currency to cover this contingency.

Opening Hours
Although Malaysia is a Moslem country, most banks and offices observe the Monday to Friday week. Some regions close on Fridays for example the north-east coast of the peninsula. However banks in most of Peninsular Malaysia and

in Sarawak are open 10.00-15.00 Monday to Friday, and 09.30-11.30 on Saturday. Banks in Sabah are open 08.00-15.00 Monday to Friday but close for lunch 12.00-14.00, and again on Saturday mornings 09.00-11.00. Offices are normally open throughout Malaysia from 08.00-16.00 with variable lunch-time closings.

Public Holidays
Holidays vary greatly from state to state. For example Good Friday is a holiday in Sabah and Sarawak but not on the mainland. Holidays are celebrated for the state governor or sultan's birthday or coronation. The following are country-wide unless otherwise stated.

1st January	New Year's (in most states)
1st February	Federal Day (mainly celebrated in Kuala Lumpur)
10th February (1986)	Chinese New Year
1st May	Labour Day
23rd May (1986)	Wesak Day (full moon in May)
4th June	Birthday of King Yang di-Pertuan Agong
31st August	National Day
1st November	Deepavali
25th December	Christmas

Also all Moslem festivals are important; e.g. the Prophet's birthday, Muharram, etc. The end of Ramazan is called Hari Raya Puasa and Id-ul-Adha is called Hari Raya Haji (for dates see Introduction). The Hindu festival of Thaipussam (during which devotees pierce their flesh with needles) is celebrated in January mainly in Penang, Selangor and Perak; the 1986 date is 26th January.

Arrival and Departure
Although newer than Singapore's Changi Airport, Kuala Lumpur's Subang is not quite as shiny and efficient. A taxi ride into town (12 miles away) will cost M$18. There is a cheap and frequent bus service, but it takes a long time as it calls on all the hotels en route. There is an international departure tax of M$15 except for departures to Singapore which cost only M$5.

There is a twice monthly overnight boat service between Penang and Belawan (near Medan) on Sumatra, Indonesia. The one way fare is M$67 (compared to M$100 by plane).

Flights
Because the Straits Steamship Company no longer run a passenger service between Peninsular Malaysia and Sarawak or Sabah, domestic flights are crucial. It is cheaper to fly with MAS (Malaysian Airline System) from Johor Baharu (about an hour north of Singapore) than from Singapore. The main airport in Sarawak is at Kuching, and Sabah's main town connected by air is Kota Kinabalu. There is a M$3 airport tax on all domestic flights.

Motoring
The A.A. of Malaysia, which is federated with the A.A. of Great Britain, will advise on current motoring regulations. Their address in Kuala Lumpur is: 30 Jalan Datuk Sulaiman, Taman Tun Dr., Ismail. If you are involved in an accident

in remote areas, it is better to go to the nearest police station as promptly as possible, rather than try to sort it out with the local people who may be hostile. Traffic moves on the left and petrol costs about M$5.50 per gallon.

Car Hire
All the international care hire firms have one or more outlets in Malaysia. Of the big chains, Godfrey Davis (in the Hotel Equatorial, KL) offer the most advantageous rate: M$37 per day plus 37c per kilometre or M$95 unlimited mileage per day. This is considerably cheaper than in Singapore.

Bus
The long distance buses of Malaysia are efficient and comfortable, as well as picturesquely decorated. Whereas the main train lines run north/south, it is possible to go cross-country by bus, for example Butterworth (jumping off place for Penang) to Kota Baharu and Kuala Lumpur to Kuantan. Prices are comparable to third class railway fares, with a premium for the (ultra) air-conditioned buses. For example the two journeys mentioned above cost M$17 and M$11 respectively for distances of 220 and 160 miles.

Train
In addition to the main Singapore-Kuala Lumpur-Butterworth line (which continues into Thailand) there is a more rugged jungle line which bisects the peninsula and is highly recommended for its scenery. There is usually no problem booking a seat or a berth in the class of your choice, except around festival times when everyone travels.

A 10-day rail pass (which includes Singapore) is sold to foreigners for M$70 and a 30-day pass for M$150, valid on any class. Since the first class fare Butterworth to Singapore is well over M$70, this could be worthwhile. Travellers who enjoy third class trains (which in Malaysia are quite acceptable) probably won't be tempted by the rail pass.

Boat
A proposed new service will travel between Kuantan on the coast east of KL and Kuching in Sarawak at sporadic intervals. Since the Straits Steamship Company stopped sailing to East Malaysia, there has been no ferry service.

The 12-minute crossing from Butterworth to Penang Island is very frequent. The service is free from Butterworth but costs 40 sen from Penang.

Hitch-hiking
Hitching is easy, especially for travellers who are dressed respectably.

City Transport
Most taxis in KL and other peninsular cities not only have meters but use them. Fares in Sabah are about 80 sen per mile, and half that in Sarawak; meters are not used in either state. It is also worth enquiring about shared taxi rides, which can be very reasonable even over long distances.

Ask the tourist office for a pamphlet called *This Month in KL and Penang* which lists the city bus routes. There are also Chinese tri-shaws in some cities such as Georgetown, which are propelled by a cyclist/driver at the rear.

Malaria mosquitoes are active in a few areas of Malaysia, especially deep in the hinterland. Kuala Lumpur, Penang Island, other big cities and coastal areas are reported to be free. But if you are going inland, you should take both chloroquine and something to combat chloroquine-resistant malaria. Danger is confined to altitudes of under 5,500ft. There is a risk throughout the year on Sabah.

The following hospitals are recommended by I.A.M.A.T.:

Goh Clinic (Kelinik Goh) — Sungei Wang Plaza, Jalan Sultan Ismail, Kuala Lumpur. Tel: 423773.
Penang Adventist Hospital — Georgetown, Penang. Tel: 24134.
Wong Clinic — 80 Newcome Road, Malacca. Tel: 2919.
Sabah Clinic — Kota Kinabalu. Tel: 33355.

Water
Although some city water is chlorinated, you should not drink it before purifying it yourself.

Malaysian food overlaps with Indonesian food at many points, mainly *satay* (grilled meat with coconut or peanut sauce), *gado gado* (salad with peanut dressing), *nasi goreng* (rice fried with vegetables), *ketupat* (rice dumplings) and many other delights. A tasty meal from a street stall will cost M$2-M$4. There are also lots of restaurants specializing in seafood or in Malay, Chinese, Thai or Indian food. The British colonizers realized that strawberries could flourish on the uplands, and now strawberries and cream are a speciality of the Cameron Highlands.

Tea *(teh)* is grown extensively and is the most popular drink. Hotels often serve complimentary tea to their guests. The strong-of-stomach may want to try the local Mekong whisky. Tiger is the name of the well-known beer which is brewed by a local brewery set up by Heineken in the 1920s, but it is unfortunately expensive (about M$3 a bottle).

The great attraction of Malaysia is its varied tropical scenery, from the coral islands and beaches on the east coast of the peninsula to the jungles of Sabah and Sarawak in East Malaysia. Malaysia also has its hill stations, which can make ideal centres for hill and jungle walking, especially Tanah Rata, the travellers' centre of the Cameron Highlands, which rise nearly 6,000ft above sea level (nearest railway station Tapeh Road). Only 60 miles from Kuala Lumpur, Fraser's Hill is less frequented and also pleasant. The town of Malacca (or Melaka) is a picturesque coastal settlement with a 16th century Portuguese church and a 17th century Dutch town hall.

Many beaches in Malaysia are magnificent, especially along the less developed east coast. Although Penang (in the north west) is famous as a beach resort — especially Batu Feringgi located 20 minutes from the main town of Penang Island — there are hordes of tourists and hawkers, and even sewage on the beach. Despite this, many travellers congregate in Georgetown (Penang's town) to arrange onward travel (either by air or private yacht), to eat fast food and to participate in the "travellers' scene", as well as to visit the unique snake temple (full of live snakes) and Kek Lok Si, reputed to be the largest Buddhist temple in South-East Asia.

KUALA LUMPUR

Kuala Lumpur is not a great city for sightseeing. The National Museum is in a pleasant lakeside situation, and the National Museum of Art, near the railway station, contains some interesting exhibits. Most of KL's architecture is very modern, including the Masjid Negara (National Mosque).

Accommodation

Coliseum Hotel — 100 Jalan Tuanka Abdul Rahman. Clean and central. M$18-M$23. This is a good area for hotels.

Y.M.C.A. — Tan Chi Kiong, 95 Jalan Kandang Kerbau. Tel: 441439. From US$5 per person.

Youth Hostel — 9 Jalan Vethavanam (off Jalan Ipoh) 5 miles from city centre. Tel: 660872. M$4-M$5.

Useful Addresses

British High Commission — 186 Jalan Ampang. Tel: 487122.

British Council Library — Jalan Bukit Aman. Tel: 987555.

American Embassy — A.I.A. Building, Jalan Ampang. Tel: 326321.

American Express — Mayflower Acme Tours, 18 Jalan Segambut Pusat. Tel: 486739.

Thomas Cook — 71 Wisma Boustead, Jalan Raja Chulan. Tel: 419044.

Tourist Information Centre — Bukit Nanas Complex, Jalan Raja Chulan.

Singapore

Capital: Singapore **Government:** Republic

The name Singapore comes from the Sanskrit for "Lion City". It was not an important place until Sir Stamford Raffles established a trading post there. Its excellent natural harbour and its proximity to the wealth of the Malay Peninsula rapidly increased its importance. Even now it is the biggest harbour in the world after Rotterdam.

Although it is just 225 square miles (just over half the area of Hong Kong), it is a sovereign nation. This area includes 54 small islands as well as Singapore Island itself. Because of its commercial success and its small population ($2\frac{1}{2}$ million), it is one of the wealthiest countries of Asia. You may find its obtrusive prosperity hard to take after the rest of Asia. On the other hand you may feel relief to be back in "civilization" again.

Eating and shopping seem to be the two chief pastimes. You can buy anything from bootleg tapes (five for S$3.75) to exotic silks, not in a typical Eastern bazaar (noisy, smelly, colourful, chaotic) but in antiseptic shopping complexes, such as those along Orchard Road. Fortunately the government has stopped levelling old and dilapidated neighbourhoods, and is now engaging in expensive renovation schemes. All laws and policies seem to be geared to beautifying Singapore for the benefit of tourists; for example there are large fines (S$500) for littering or smoking in post offices.

Climate

Because it is so close to the equator, the sun shines throughout the year. The average daily high for 12 months is a remarkably consistent 88°F (31°C). It drops only about 10°F at night. Although the sea has a moderating influence the heat is sometimes unbearable due to tropical humidity.

Heavy though brief rains fall from November to January.

Language

Malay is the national language though English is the language of business and government. Many Chinese dialects are spoken as well as Tamil and other Indian languages. 76% of the people are of Chinese descent.

Visas

Commonwealth citizens do not require visas if they intend to stay less than three months. Whether you are allowed in and for what length of time is completely at the discretion of the immigration officers, who are not known for their liberality. They had a long-lasting reputation for turning away male visitors who sported hair over their collars. You are quite likely to be asked to show a return ticket and a decent amount of money. If you are short of cash, tell them you have arranged to have money sent and show them a letter from your family, if possible, which promises funds.

Customs

You are permitted to bring in the usual tobacco allowance (200 cigarettes or 50 cigars or ½ lb tobacco) plus 1 quart of alcohol. The duty-free shop at Changi Airport is open to arriving passengers. Singapore customs are notorious for their toughness, especially if you do not look completely respectable. They are also rather puritanical about the reading matter they allow in; for a while *Cosmopolitan* magazine was prohibited.

Currency

There is no restriction on the amount of foreign or local currency you can take in or out of Singapore.

Health Certificates

No more than a yellow fever certificate is required if travelling from an infected area. Singapore is a very healthy place.

Drugs

The penalties for transgressing are very stiff. Trafficking can be punished by death, and the definition of trafficking is not as different from possession as one might have expected.

£1 = S$3.025   S$1 = £0.33
$1 = S$2.23   S$1 = $0.49

Currency, 100 cents=1 Singapore dollar (S$)

Changing Money

The Chartered Bank charges a sizeable commission for travellers' cheque transactions — about US$2.50. American Express is preferable (address under Useful Addresses). The authorized money-changers along North Bridge Road give a favourable rate. Singapore is one South Asian country where credit cards can be very useful.

Opening Hours

Banks are open 10.00-15.00 weekdays and 09.30-11.30 on Saturdays. There is almost no limit to the hours of shops; there is an itinerant market called *Pasar Malam* (Night Bazaar) which is held Wednesday, Friday and Saturday evenings next to Tudor Court (where the Tourist Office is).

Public Holidays

The cosmopolitan population of Singapore means that several calendars are in use and many Moslem and Hindu holidays are celebrated in addition to the 1986 dates given below:

1st January — New Year's Day
9th-10th February — Chinese New Year
28th March — Good Friday
1st May — Labour Day
23rd May — Wesak Day
9th June — Hari Raya Puasa (end of Ramadan)

9th August	National Day
16th August	Hari Raya Haji
1st November	Deepavali
25th December	Christmas

Arrival and Departure

Singapore is a stopover for many airlines flying between Europe and Australasia. The modern and efficient Changi Airport is located about 12 miles east of downtown. The taxi ride into town costs about S$25. There are also frequent buses which take 30-45 minutes to reach the centre of town. Look for bus number 390. There is a departure tax of S$6 for flights to Malaysia and Brunei, and S$12 for departures to any other countries.

Several daily train services run between Singapore and Kuala Lumpur, capital of Malaysia. The Rakyat Ekspres takes about 6½ hours to do the 250 mile trip. Customs and immigration formalities are conducted at the station rather than at the frontier, so if you are leaving by train, be sure to allow enough time at the station.

There are many long distance buses heading into Malaysia and on to Thailand, most of which have air-conditioning, TV, stereos and hostesses. For about S$20 (£7), you can travel 300 miles.

Although Singapore is such an important harbour, there is very little passenger shipping. Ferries leave from various piers (e.g. Clifford Pier) to cross to Sentosa Island and other less visited islands such as Pulau Tekong which can be explored by bicycle.

Motoring

There is an excellent and well sign-posted network of roads and the traffic is very well-behaved. Driving is on the left. Tourists may import cars with a *carnet*. The A.A. of Singapore is at 336 River Valley Road.

There are many car rental agencies from which to choose. An I.D.P. is not required but you must be over 23 to hire a car. Prices begin at $60 a day plus mileage from Godfrey Davis; local rental agencies may be slightly cheaper. Public transport is so convenient, it hardly seems worth considering car hire.

City Transport

Since the government raised the price of fuel by six times, taxis are no longer a bargain. The official rate is $32 for the first 2 km plus 10¢ per 375 metres thereafter. There are surcharges for having more than two passengers, for luggage, for rides into the central business district during the rush hour and for rides at night. Most taxi drivers now switch on their meters without being prompted. The Tourist Office is very strict with drivers who cheat tourists so do not hesitate to report any irregularities.

A hyper-modern Mass Rapid Transit (M.R.T.) underground system is under construction and should be opened within the next few years. It will be many years however before it reaches the airport.

There are remnants of old-fashioned modes of transport like tri-shaws and bicycle rickshaws (especially in Chinatown).

Singapore is free of malaria and most other unpleasant diseases bred in unsanitary conditions. If you do become ill, contact the Youngberg Memorial Adventist Hospital (tel: 889 271). Singapore General Hospital is good for emergency cases (tel: 772 141).

Water
Singapore is the only country covered in this book in which the tap water is safe to drink.

Because Singapore is such a cosmopolitan city, all of the world's cuisines are represented, especially Chinese, Indian, Malay and Indonesian. One of the highlights is Rasa Singapura, the collection of eating stalls, in the Singapore Handicraft Centre. Although it was originally set up to cater to tourists, many locals eat there, and the quality is good. On a similar principle there is a wonderful variety of savoury and spicy snacks available from the stalls in the "hawker centres" (e.g. Bugis Street). Try Malay *satay* (small pieces of skewered spiced meat) and Indonesian *sambals*. In Chinatown (Temple Street and Smith Street) try *claypot rice,* bowls of rice and vegetables with fish or chicken. Little India is located around Serangoon Road and Arab Street. Because Singapore is so prosperous, dining out is not very cheap and there are many gourmet establishments, some of which may serve such dishes as monkey brains or python soup. Drinking is not cheap either: a bottle of beer will cost about S$4. Many people believe that tea at the Raffles Hotel is a worthwhile investment for the ambience which really is very grand and impressive. But their Singapore slings (the drink that was invented at the hotel) are now made in industrial vats to satisfy the voracious tourists willing to pay S$8, and should probably be avoided.

Outside the restaurants and shopping centres, there is not a great deal to do or see in Singapore. You may want to browse in the Singapore Handicraft Centre on the Tanglin Road, though most goods are pricey and will involve you in some serious bargaining. Even the National Museum is not very exciting, though it has a good collection of jade. Jurong Bird Park in the western end of Singapore island has a good aviary, and the Botanic Gardens near the Tourist Office are worth visiting, especially on Sunday afternoons when music is performed. Another way to pass the time in Singapore is to wander around Chinatown or Little India, watch the bustling harbour, or take a ride on one of the public ferries.

Accommodation
There are many small hotels in the area of Beach Road and Middle Road. Also Bencoolen Road specializes in cheap accommodation.
Bencoolen Dormitory and Room Service Centre — Hong Guan Building,

173-B 2nd floor, Bencoolen Street. Tel: 336 5874. S$10 for space on the floor, S$12 for a dorm bed.
Airmaster Travel Centre — 36G Princep Street.
Sandy's Place — 355 Balestier Road, Goodwill Mansions. Tel: 01 361.
New Handy Place — 3A Angullia Park (near Orchard Road). S$8-S$10 in dorm.
"Sim's" — 114A Mackenzie Road near Albert Street. Tel: 336 1957. S$8 for a mattress on the floor.
Friendly Hostel — 175 Serangoon Road. Cheap.
Y.M.C.A. — 60 Stevens Road. Tel: 737 7755. US$25 per person.
Y.M.C.A. — International Centre, 70 Palmer Road. Tel: 222 4666. US$12 per person.
Y.W.C.A. — Fort Canning Centre, 6-8 Fort Canning Road. Tel: 336 1212.

Useful Addresses
British High Commission — Tanglin Road. Tel: 639333.
British Council Library — Singapore Rubber House, Collyer Quay. Tel: 5337644.
American Embassy — 30 Hill Street. Tel: 6530251.
American Express — Holiday Inn Building, 4th Floor, Scotts Road. Tel: 7375988.
Thomas Cook — Phoenix Building, 1-12 Palmer/Mistri Road. Tel: 2210222.
Singapore Tourist Board — 131 Tudor Court, Tanglin Road. Tel: 2356611.

The *Singapore Weekly Guide,* distributed free, is a standard tourist promotion board product, but may contain something of use to you.

Indonesia

Capital: Jakarta **Government:** Republic

The "Spice Islands" attracted early explorers and merchants who colonized the islands. The Dutch soon became pre-eminent and controlled much of the area from the mid-17th century until independence in 1949. Because of the important role played by maritime activities throughout its history, many other external cultural and ethnic influences have been absorbed. An important intrusion into the indigenous culture took place after 1500 when Islam came to Java. Today 90% of the Indonesian population is Moslem though the fundamentalist movement is not very strong. The most important foreign influence at the moment is Western and Japanese capitalism which prompts occasional demonstrations against economic imperialism.

The country is made up primarily of Java (where three-fifths of the population live), Sumatra (still largely covered by jungle and wilderness), Sulawesi (Celebes), Kalimantan (Borneo) and Irian Jaya (Western New Guinea). Java is by far the most highly developed island and Bali is the most popular for tourists. There are over 13,000 other islands (half of them inhabited) with many different tribes and cultures which make it difficult to keep the country unified and harmonious.

Climate

The temperatures, along with the humidity, are consistently high. The average high in Jakarta, for example, throughout the year varies only from 29°C-31°C (84°F-88°F). The hilly interior is a little cooler; the Puncak area between Bandung and Bogor is a popular weekend retreat.

There is some rainfall throughout the year however the skies are clearest between May and September.

Language

Bahasa Indonesia, which is almost identical to Malay, was invented after independence, in order to provide a national language and unify the country. There is a new *Indonesia Phrasebook* published by Lonely Planet (£1.95). The standard greeting is "Salamat pagi" for "good morning". Most high school graduates have studied some English.

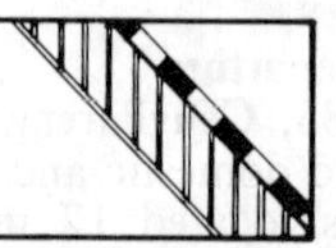

Visas

Tourist visas are no longer required for stays of less than 2 months. However you may have to prove to the immigration officials that you have an onward ticket and substantial funds. Extensions are rarely given, so you will have to leave Indonesia and then re-enter if you wish to travel for more than two months.

Customs

Two litres of liquor and 600 cigarettes are permitted duty-free if you intend to stay more than a fortnight. Any expensive items such as a camera or radio should be entered in your passport upon entry, though they are not usually very strict about this.

Currency Regulations
You can import and export up to Rp50,000.

Health Certificates
As usual, a yellow fever certificate is required by people coming from the infected areas of Africa and South America. Typhoid and cholera shots are recommended.

Internal Travel Restrictions
You must have a special permit to visit the interior of Irian Jaya, which shares the island with Papua New Guinea. Go to the police station in Jayapura and ask for a permit *(surat jalan)*. A small fee will be required as well as four photos.

£1 = Rp1,600 Rp1,000 = £0.62
$1 = Rp1,100 Rp1,000 = $0.91

Changing Money
The rate of exchange varies from place to place; Jakarta banks generally offer the most favourable rates. In remote areas you may have great difficulty changing travellers' cheques so always have a reserve of cash when venturing away from the cities.

Opening Hours
Banks are open 08.30-16.00 on weekdays and 08.30-11.00 on Saturdays.

Public Holidays

1st January	New Year's Day
28th March (1986)	Good Friday
March	Nyepi (Hindu New Year)
23rd May (1986)	Waisak
17th August	Independence Day
25th December	Christmas

Moslem holidays are also celebrated (with varying degrees of enthusiasm,) e.g. Mohammed's Birthday, Ascension of the Prophet, Id-ul-Fitr, and so on. The month of Ramadan is called Puasa in Indonesia.

Arrival and Departure
Opened in 1985, Cengkareng Airport has replaced the old domestic and international terminals. It is located 12 miles west of Jakarta. The taxi fare into town should be about Rp6,000; insist that the driver use his meter.

There is also an international airport at Denpasar on Bali, and Garuda flights to Australia allow free stopovers. Walk out to the airport gate to get a bemo (see the section on Buses below); the fare to nearby Kuta is only Rp200. Many bemo drivers will try to lure you into a vehicle and then charge you 10 or 20 times the going rate, claiming that you have "chartered" it.

There is an international departure tax of Rp4,000 and domestic air tax of Rp2,500.

Flights

Because of large distances and bodies of water separating the islands, flying is a popular option. Garuda (the name of a mythical Hindu bird) is the national carrier, and not nearly as risky as many travellers (especially Australians) seem to believe.

In addition to Garuda there are several domestic lines, all of which try to avoid competition with Garuda by flying to different destinations. Schedules to these out-of-the-way places can be somewhat erratic. If there is duplication on a route, do some comparison shopping, since fares are not standard.

Motoring

If you are determined to hire a car in Indonesia, you should do your research more carefully than usual because there is an enormous discrepancy between prices. For example Hertz offers only chauffeur-driven cars at $100 a day. Avis lets you drive yourself for $80 per day, unlimited mileage, (compared to $36 in Malaysia, $30 in Sri Lanka). One of the best prices is offered by Europcar in Jakarta of $50 a day unlimited mileage, but prices are $20 higher in Bali.

Motorcycles may be hired in a few locations, especially Bali, where a 100cc bike might cost about Rp3,000 per day plus the same amount for a tankful of petrol. It is not recommended that beginners learn on Indonesian roads. Generally, the rule that motorcyclists need a proper licence is ignored, though you will be taking a chance if you ignore it. It's safer to hire a bicycle, though of course it will be more difficult to reach the out-of-the-way corners.

Bus

On the main islands, there is a very extensive bus service. Javanese buses are faster and more efficient than Sumatran ones but more expensive. Bemos are small trucks which act as buses or can be chartered as taxis.

Train

Trains are more popular than buses and can be comparable in price. There are three classes (first class is usually twice as expensive as third). The major towns on the island of Java are served by trains, and there are a few lines on Sumatra. There are four or five services each day between Jakarta and Yogyakarta, a trip which takes about 12 hours and costs Rp4,500 in third class.

Boat

It is possible to sail between Jakarta and Sumatran ports. The ships are run by Pelni, the government shipping company located at Jalan Wahid Hasyim 1A, Jakarta (tel: 43737). There are less regular sailings to islands other than Sumatra. There is also a regular ferry from Gilamanuk on Bali to Banyawangi on Java (cost Rp500). Among the remote islands, you will have to use government launches, cargo boats and missionary boats as available. It is a fairly expensive business to go island-hopping but very interesting.

Hitch-hiking

Public transport is so cheap and hitching so unfamiliar, that there is little point in trying to travel by thumb.

City Transport

Apart from big city taxis there are *beceks* (pedalled 3-wheelers) and *dokars* (carts drawn by ponies) in many cities. The upmarket version of the *becek* is the motorized *helicak*. You can rent bicycles in many places, including Yogyakarta. Be very careful on crowded city buses in Jakarta not to be pickpocketed.

Malaria risk exists all year below 4,000 feet, with the exception of the cities of Jakarta and Surabaya. Resistance to chloroquine has been reported throughout the country, so you should take both kinds of prophylactic.

If you become seriously ill on one of the outer islands, try to get back to Java to one of the following hospitals which conform to international standards of medical practice:

I.A.M.A.T. Center — Jalan Singamangaraja 51, Jakarta. Tel: 771445.
Bethesda Hospital (Rumah Sakit Bethesda) — Yogyakarta. Tel: 2281.
Kediri Baptist Hospital — Kediri. Tel: 21170.
I.A.M.A.T. Center — 100 Jalan Dinoyo, Surabaya. Tel: 67722.

Water

The water throughout Indonesia is unsafe. If you are drinking tea, make sure it is steaming not tepid.

Indonesian cuisine is delicious, though some travellers object to an over-emphasis on chillis. It overlaps with the dishes mentioned in the relevant section of the Malaysia chapter (e.g. *nasi goreng, gado gado,* sea food, *satay,* etc). The Dutch word *rijstafel* (literally rice table) is better value in Holland than Indonesia, where the large selection of meat, fish, egg and vegetable dishes are served primarily at fancy hotels. A lot of the fish is smoked to preserve it in the heat.

The spirit is called arak; rice wine is not as potent. Indonesian beer is fine, though expensive at Rp1,200 per bottle.

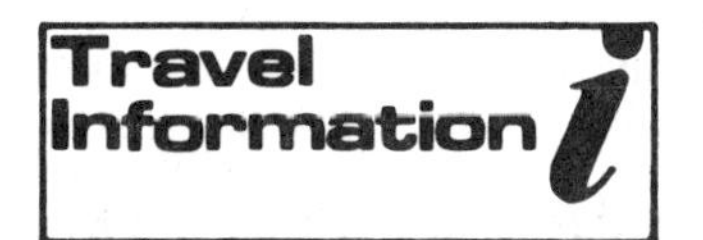

There is a great wealth of interest in these 3,000 miles of archipelago. There are orang-utan reserves in North Sumatra, steam trains in West Java, stone age tribes in Irian Jaya and surf beaches in Bali. However tourism is making rapid changes in the most heavily visited places such as Bali. For a remarkably detailed guide to Indonesia, get a copy of Bill Dalton's *Indonesia Handbook* (Moon Publications).

JAKARTA

Jakarta is even less representative of Indonesia than most other Asian cities are of their countries. It is noisy, chaotic and rumoured to be rife with thieves and pickpockets.

The National Museum — on the western side of Medan Merdeka (Freedom Park). Contains artefacts from Indonesia's various historical periods and provides a good introduction to the civilizations whose remains you may visit later in your trip.

Pasar Baru — the main market and very colourful.

Accommodation

Lodgings are more expensive in Jakarta than elsewhere in the country. Try the Wim Hostel at 1 Jalan Kebon Sirih Barat Dalam. It has a family atmosphere and is in an area with a choice of other reasonable guest houses, e.g. the Borneo Hostel at No. 35. There is a youth hostel at 5 Jalan Jacksa which has doubles at Rp4,000 and cheaper dorm beds.

Useful Addresses

Visitors' Information Centre — Jalan Thamrin.
British Embassy — Jalan Thamrin 75. Tel: 330904.
British Council Library — S. Widjojo Centre, 57 Jalan Jenderal Sudirman. Tel: 587411.
American Embassy — 5 Medan Merdeka Selatan. Tel: 340001.
American Express — P. T. Pacto Ltd., 24 Jalan Cikini Raya. Tel: 320309.

YOGYAKARTA

The historic and cultural centre of Java is interesting in itself (e.g. for the Sultan's Palace and the wonderful markets) and within easy access of some spectacular sites. Borobudur is an 8th century Buddhist stupa, which is being heavily restored by U.N.E.S.C.O., and is just 25 miles from Yogya.

Again, if you wish to escape the heat, go to the village of Kaliarung, located on an active volcano which it is possible to climb.

There is plenty of cheap travellers' accommodation *(losmen)* in Yogya, either near the station or grouped in the south of the town.

BALI

Whereas not long ago Balinese people were famous for their sincere hospitality, many have now been spoiled by the huge influx of both affluent Australian package tourists and impecunious surf-bums. One sociologist has described the native behaviour situation in Bali as "staged authenticity". However this is mainly confined to Kuta Beach and the new artificial resort of Candi Dasa on the eastern shore of Bali.

When the heat and beer-swilling crowds become irritating go inland to the lovely inland lake of Bratan near which are the temple at Bedugal (one of 20,000 on the island) and the flower market at Candikuning. Ubud, a popular tourist centre, is famous for its theatre and music, as well as its monkey temple and tropical ambience. Although tourism can be blamed for many evils, it also has its benefits. Without tourists to support the arts, the gamelan players, dancers and artists would not be as active as they are.

INDEX

Topics which are dealt with in each of the country chapters under their own headings, such as visa requirements, medical facilities, etc. are not included below. The main entry for place names has been indicated by a page reference in bold type.